Buddhist Care
for the Dying and Bereaved

DISCARD

BUDDHIST CARE *for the* DYING AND BEREAVED

EDITED BY
Jonathan S. Watts
and Yoshiharu Tomatsu

WISDOM PUBLICATIONS · BOSTON
in collaboration with
THE JODO SHU RESEARCH INSTITUTE (JSRI)

Wisdom Publications
199 Elm Street
Somerville MA 02144 USA
www.wisdompubs.org

Library of Congress Cataloging-in-Publication Data

Buddhist care for the dying and bereaved : edited by Jonathan S. Watts and Yoshi-haru Tomatsu.
   pages cm
Includes bibliographical references and index.
ISBN 1-61429-052-0 (pbk. : alk. paper)
   1. Terminal care—Religious aspects—Buddhism. 2. Bereavement—Religious aspects—Buddhism. I. Watts, Jonathan S., 1966– II. Tomatsu, Yoshiharu, 1953– .
R726.8.B83 2012
616.02'9—dc23

                              2012025779

ISBN 9781614290520
eBook ISBN 9781614290636

16 15 14 13 12
5 4 3 2 1

Cover design by Phil Pascuzzo. Interior design by Gopa & Ted2, Inc. Set in ITC Galliard Pro 10.5/15.

Table of Contents

Introduction

Jonathan S. Watts

BUDDHIST CARE FOR THE DYING AND BEREAVED: PAST AND PRESENT

Buddhist understandings of death and of practices developed for dying and the specific moment of death have been hallmarks of the tradition since its beginning in India twenty-five hundred years ago. Over the last forty years, they have been an important part of the global revival of Buddhism, especially in the West—from the popularization of the *Tibetan Book of the Dead*, to Zen poetry about death, to Theravadan meditation on the decaying body, to belief in the welcome of Amida Buddha on one's deathbed. Today there is a plethora of new titles by various authors on how to use Buddhist teachings and practices to face death and the dying of loved ones—a quick search for "Buddhism" and "death" on amazon.com pulls up 543 entries. These entries by and large focus on how an individual or family member can face and prepare for death, either as an inner journey or as a journey with intimate relations.

Relatively little is known, however, about the number of Buddhist-based initiatives for caring for the dying and bereaved that focus on the development of trained professionals and the building of facilities, though these facilities have mushroomed since the late 1980s. While a number of these initiatives have been created by high-profile Buddhist teachers, like Sogyal Rinpoche and Joan Halifax, who have written heart-moving books on death, their initiatives and others are not as highly publicized in the mass media. In fact, when one even speaks of "hospice"[1] one is drawn back to its Christian origins in eleventh-century Europe—the Irish nun Mother Mary Aikenhead (1787–1858) and the Religious Sisters of Charity, who created the modern hospice archetype; and Dame Cicely Saunders, the Anglican nurse who founded the first modern hospice, St. Christopher's Hospice, in London in 1967. As we will see in this volume, Saunders has had an especially major impact on the Buddhist hospice movement around the world.

The modern-day Buddhist hospice movement is, however, one with a long historical precedent. The Vihara Movement in Japan has consciously named itself using the traditional and ancient Buddhist term for "temple," *vihara*. Like the term "hospice," *vihara* has also had the meaning of a place for travelers to take rest in addition to a place that might offer social welfare and medical care for the poor. Rev. Yozo Taniyama explains in his chapter how the famous Jetavana Vihara established by the historical Buddha himself eventually developed into such a comprehensive center for spiritual, economic, and medical care. The great Indian monarch, Ashoka (r. 270–232 BCE), who is credited with first unifying the Indian subcontinent under one rule, was also known to have promoted the development of herbal medicine and dispensaries through Buddhist temples. This tradition of social service by Buddhist temples, first established in India, eventually spread throughout the Buddhist world. Japan, the last frontier of the ancient spread of Buddhism, inherited this tradition from the beginning with the establishment of Shitenno-ji temple in present-day Osaka in 593. Shitenno-ji was not only the first officially administered Buddhist temple in Japan but also included a hospital, a poor house, and a pharmacy that grew and cultivated medicinal plants. In this way, there is a long-standing template for Buddhist institutions serving as centers of care for the ill and dying.

The historical Buddha himself offers an original template for the role of the Buddhist caregiver. One of the Buddha's epithets is the "Great Physician"—which refers to his core teaching of the Four Noble Truths examining the nature of suffering as dis-ease, its causes, its cure, and the course of cure. There are also numerous examples of the Buddha and his close disciples guiding both ordained persons and laypersons through painful physical illnesses to illumination on their death beds; these stories serve as the primary Buddhist template for dying with a monk as a deathbed counselor (in Sanskrit, *kalyanamitra*). However, two striking examples show the Buddha as much more than a deathbed counselor. The first is the story of the monk Putigatta Tissa, who had become gravely ill and had festering sores that emitted smells so foul that all his fellow monks abandoned him. The Buddha, upon finding out about his situation, not only admonished the other monks to care for him but also was the first to go clean his body, his robes, and his room and establish a plan for his further care. The second story, which is detailed in Rev. Julie Hanada's chapter, is about the laywoman Kisa Gotami whom the Buddha supported in her grieving over her dead child; by asking her to find a house that had not experienced death, the Buddha not only led her to a realization of the impermanence of life and the reality of death but also initiated her into a support community with all those others who had faced death.

Buddhism has many other ancient and contemporary examples of dedicated practitioners working to support both the dying and those who live on afterward in grief. The important point to make here is that many Buddhists today are drawing upon this long and deep tradition to find their own models for developing forms of Buddhist engagement that not only confront but also transform the many problems facing people dying in the world today. In this volume, we have culled some of the best and most inspired examples of Buddhist care for the dying and bereaved from all over the world, covering the entire Buddhist spectrum with essays from the Theravada tradition in Thailand and Cambodia; the Tibetan tradition in the Rigpa Spiritual Care Programme, which functions primarily in Europe and the United States; the East Asian Mahayana tradition in Taiwan; and the Lotus Sutra, Pure Land, and Zen traditions in both Japan and the United States.

Essential Themes in Buddhist Care for the Dying and Bereaved

While the founders and members of the initiatives presented in this volume have some mutual knowledge of and influence on each other, many have developed their work quite independently. For example, most of the authors from Japan have no knowledge of the initiatives going on outside of Japan. While the Tibetan Rigpa initiatives and the American Zen–based initiatives are knowledgeable of each other, they have both developed their own unique programs without direct collaboration. The initiative in Cambodia has had some direct influence from the Thai one, yet these two have distinctively different styles and have developed largely on their own. Finally, the initiatives in Taiwan, while being influenced by the modern British hospice model, have developed in total isolation from other Buddhist initiatives around the world. In this section, however, we will introduce many of the common and overlapping themes that emerge in the variety of essays in this volume. On the one hand, the diversity and cultural appropriateness of each initiative is an important part of their successes—as well as a warning to those who wish to replicate them in their own contexts. On the other hand, the points of congruency show an underlying, common wisdom implicit in the work that not only validates it empirically but also provides key elements for the adaptation of the work in a variety of social and cultural contexts.

Buddhist Spirituality for the Dying

As mentioned at the beginning of this introduction, Buddhism has a long and deep tradition of practices surrounding the time of death. The goal of all of the initiatives in this volume has been to revitalize and apply them to the modern world, specifically to modern medical contexts. For example, there is the original Buddhist emphasis on the importance of a calm and meditative mental state at the time of death. This is felt to be important not only in terms of the soteriological import of the future transmigration of the consciousness but also more simply in terms of a "good death": one that is filled with peace rather than struggle and angst. The Theravadan and Zen perspectives emphasize this point the most. On the other hand, the East Asian Buddhist tradition, specifically the Pure Land tradition, has developed the practice of chanting Amida Buddha's name both by the dying and the bereaved in support of the dying to ensure a "good death" and the soteriological goal of rebirth in Amida Buddha's Pure Land. Tibetan practice contains both these meditative and faith-oriented practices while adding further elements, such as the *tonglen* practice of voluntarily taking on the suffering of others as one's own and seeing one's illness as the fulfillment of this bodhisattva vow.

Across these basic Buddhist traditions, certain tensions exist concerning the dying process. One the one hand, there is a common, shared belief that the state of the mind at death is paramountly important, and thus open mourning and the disturbing or moving of the corpse for a period after death should not be done. Traditions that particularly emphasize this idea prescribe strict, disciplined, and formalized forms of dying where a religious professional, usually a monk or nun, is employed to support the dying as a guide and the achievement of a peaceful, "good death" is critical. In terms of the modern initiatives in this volume, this orientation expresses itself in the emphasis on highly trained religious professionals called chaplains who understand how to properly handle the issues that arise not only for the dying but for their families and caregivers as well. In this way, the modern-day Buddhist chaplain is akin to the traditional Buddhist deathbed counselor (*kalyanamitra*). This orientation may also express itself in more specifically Buddhist facilities, such as the special room for one's last moments with a large painting of Amida Buddha and his Pure Land and the special morgue for chanting and keeping the body undisturbed at the National Taiwan University Hospital, or the construction of a care center alongside a retreat community of practitioners in the Rigpa Spiritual Care Programme in Ireland. This belief has also led certain Buddhists, especially in Japan, to shun organ donation as a violation of the dying person's consciousness and subsequent transmigration.

On the other hand, the Buddhism views intention as the fulcrum for karmic action and the eventual transmigration of the consciousness. This belief has led certain Buddhists, in contrast to those mentioned above, to promote organ donation as an act of bodhisattvic compassion; they understand that an enlightened intention would override any disturbances to the consciousness of the deceased. This is an orientation that is strongly emphasized in the initiatives in modern Taiwanese Buddhism, even while they otherwise seek to maintain traditional Buddhist death practices. In terms of care for the dying and bereaved, this emphasis of intention over form dovetails with the modern hospice movement's focus on presence and compassionate listening by the caregiver, including not imposing the caregiver's religious vision on the patient but rather acting as a facilitator for the patient to discover his or her own spirituality. This orientation is perhaps best expressed by Issan Dorsey, the Soto Zen priest who founded Maitri Hospice in San Francisco in the late 1980s: "You need to meet people where there are and not where you want them to be." This orientation also does not attach to the concept of a "good death," although it may still hope for it. In practical terms, initiatives that emphasize this belief eschew the use of chaplains and instead rely on volunteers of varying levels of training. This model is prominent in the hospices of the large Tzu Chi denomination in Taiwan as well as the Maitri Hospice and the Zen Hospice Program in San Francisco.

This less formalistic orientation, as Rev. Mari Sengoku writes in her chapter, sees that "people die as they have lived" and that in most cases it is not possible and often counterproductive to try to teach new spiritual orientations or practices, especially meditation, to people who are dying. This has been a common experience for many groups in the volume, such as the Brahmavihara/Cambodia AIDS Project and the Kosei Vihara in Tokyo. On the other hand, many of the authors in this volume concur that those who have developed spiritual orientations before becoming ill seem to have better deaths. These experiences have led to a very significant movement by Buddhists within the scientific and medical communities to empirically verify the importance of spiritual care as part of a more comprehensive form of holistic care for the ill and dying. Jon Kabat-Zinn's work in mindfulness therapy at the University of Massachusetts Medical School, Joan Halifax's initiatives with the Dalai Lama and western scientists through the Mind and Life Institute, and Dr. Gian Borasio's research team at the Interdisciplinary Center for Palliative Medicine (IZP) at Munich University Hospital are important such examples found in this volume.

These two tensions coexist among the initiatives in this volume; there is a sentiment that the patient should not be evangelized yet should still be offered spiritual pathways for actively moving into death and what lies beyond. In this way, one of the more surprising results of studying these initiatives is that we find an emphasis on developing a strong and committed Buddhist practice more for the caregiver than for the patient. That is, while these initiatives have varying levels of agreement on how much a patient should be offered Buddhist teachings and practices, they are in much more common agreement that Buddhist teachings and practices offer essential competencies for caregivers, whether they are actually Buddhist or not. From Zen volunteers in San Francisco who meditate together, to German and American medical professionals with Christian or secular orientations who learn Buddhist self-care methods from the Rigpa and Upaya programs, to ordained Buddhist chaplains in Taiwan and the United States who must internalize their seminary educations through practice as interns, a common perspective and point of emphasis is the need to properly train in spiritual competencies to sustainably carry on the intense work of "being with dying."

Informed Consent and Truth Telling

"Informed consent" and "truth telling" are curious, specialist terms developed by the modern medical system. The former refers to the process of medical professionals, usually the head doctor, informing a patient of the particulars of their medical situation—in short, their diagnosis. The latter refers to the process of the doctor informing the

patient of the outlook for their improvement or perhaps the inevi-
tably of their death—their prognosis. One wonders what these two
processes looked like in the premodern era when people did not rely
on hospitalization and usually died in their own homes. Probably it
was a mix of the medical or care professional dealing directly with the
patient and also working in consultation with his or her family. In the
present era, a bias has developed that Asian societies, especially conservative Buddhist ones in East Asia that deeply value collectively, do
not agree with these two concepts and feel that they reflect Western
notions of individual autonomy. This claim is perhaps understandable
from an East Asian cultural standpoint, but not so much from a Buddhist one. In fact, Buddhism has often been criticized for focusing
on individual salvation or enlightenment as well as for placing greater
emphasis on individual endeavor rather than divine intervention.

What the variety of chapters in this volume expose is that the kind
of denial of death that has lead to tragic forms of silence concerning
the informing of patients of their condition and impending death,
especially in Japan, appears to be more of the result of the culture of
modernism than an inherent predisposition in Asian culture to collec-
tivity and silence. Caroline Brazier shows in her chapter that a culture
of silence around death developed in Britain from the trauma of mass
death during the two world wars, the development of modern psychology based on Freud's admonition to "forget the dead," and the
scientific materialism prevalent in modern medicine that sees death
as defeat. Various medical professionals in the chapter on Germany
attest to how they also had a culture of silence around death until
very recently and that it persists in their Eastern European immigrant
community. In his chapter, Carl Becker has not only pointed out how
the Japanese in a short period of fifty years have gone from a culture
comfortable with death to one in fear of it, but has also shown how
the Buddhist culture of venerating ancestors through regular and frequent grave visits and memorial services kept death as a common
presence in the lives of traditional Japanese.

Most modern societies struggle with facing death, and, ironically,
modern physicians may struggle the most. In terms of the achieve-

ment of a good death and doing many of the meaningful Buddhist practices surrounding death as outlined above, the path toward this direction is completely shut off if the fundamental step of acknowledging death is not taken by caregivers, families, or patients. However, this is a very difficult and nuanced issue that precludes the simple conclusion that patients must simply be told point blank what is their diagnosis and prognosis without the interference of their families. Both Rev. Yoshiharu Tomatsu and Rev. Mari Sengoku, proponents of truth telling, have stated in their chapters that if patients are told of their terminal prognosis but then are left to cope by themselves without a supportive family or caregiver structure, then such "truth telling" can be devastating. Unfortunately, in many modern societies, where the dying are left in abandoned corners of hospitals with infrequent family visits and little team care from the institution, this could well be the result of the standardization of truth telling. In this way, many of the initiatives in this volume show how to build communities of care around patients and their families, whether it be a comprehensive team-care system of professionals in a hospital, a community of volunteers and fellow patients in a hospice, or a religious or local community in support of a patient dying at home or in a temple. Further, in the final chapters of the volume, we see the development of ethics committees in hospitals in the United States that are sensitive to the cultural differences of patients and the best way to handle the important work of informed consent and truth telling.

Communication Skills in Medical and Religious Professionals

These above issues of communication between caregivers and patients and their families lead directly into another common critical issue: the communication skills of both medical and religious professionals in the work of being with dying. Besides cultural issues, one of the causes of the lack of informed consent and especially truth telling is the fact that modern medical doctors are poorly trained in interpersonal communication skills. Rev. Yoshiharu Tomatsu's chapter gives us an inside look into the way Japanese doctors are trained and his attempts to support their development as compassionate communicators. In many of the chapters, the authors note how modern medical education drums out of students many of their initial idealistic motivations for becoming doctors, such as the desire to serve and to heal. In response, both the Upaya Being with Dying Program and the Rigpa Spiritual Care Programme have specific teaching components for developing the interpersonal communication skills of medical care professionals.

On the other hand, we find a perhaps more shocking revelation throughout the chapters of the equally poor communication skills of religious professionals. Indeed, the core motivation of Congregationalist minister Rev. Anton T. Boisen to create the first Clinical Pastoral Education (CPE) programs for developing chaplains in the United States in the 1920s was due to his own experience as a patient with a priest who could only spout back religious doctrine and not meet him as a person. Similar issues appear throughout the Buddhist world, most notably in the chapters on Japan where many priests reluctantly succeed their fathers into a vocation they view more as a business than a calling. In general, monastic education across the Buddhist world often makes monks into preachers more than listeners and compassionate companions—the root meaning of the term *kalyanamitra*.

Buddhist Chaplains and the Team-Care System

The cultivation of the Buddhist chaplain is thus an important theme running through many of the chapters in this volume. While we have seen that there are varying emphases on the need for certified religious professionals—that is, ordained monks and nuns as opposed to volunteers—the development of chaplain training is a significant response to the marginalized role of religious professionals in many modern societies and the need to find ways to reengage with society. Rev. Julie Hanada points out in her article that ideally there would be no need for chaplains if the typical monk or nun would receive the proper type of training in his or her seminary to engage with common people in a variety of environments, not just within the temple environment. However, in so many Buddhist countries, monastic education has become confined to the rote memorization of texts, sectarian interpretations of doctrine, the study of ritual minutiae, and the management of the religious institution—in many ways not very different from the style of education for medical doctors.

Clinical Pastoral Education (CPE), as Rev. Thomas Kilts, a Tibetan Buddhist CPE supervisor in the United States, notes, is "about dealing with relationships and crises and not just a temple congregation. One has to learn that in being out in the world with people in crisis, not just in a temple, when to use Buddhism and when to not." This is one of the first important competencies of chaplaincy. As part of the emphasis on deep listening and presence over preaching, chaplains must learn how to speak in a variety of ways so that, as Issan Dorsey said, they can meet people where they actually are. Many of the authors in this volume note the great challenges experienced by chaplains in such training: first, in terms of adapting to the intense demands of medical environments, and second, in terms of learning how to bring their intellectual knowledge of spirituality into the heart as a practical and engaged way of relating to people. In this way, Clinical Pastoral Education (CPE) in the United States has a mandatory emphasis on ecumenical and nondenominational competencies; that is, chaplains must be able to work equally well with patients from other faiths as with ones from their own denominations. This is one of the greatest challenges in the cultivation of chaplains, because, as we will see in certain chapters, when religious denominations train and remunerate their own chaplains, there may be a reluctance to cultivate them fully in an ecumenical manner. The key in the US system is that chaplains are remunerated by the hospitals and are considered a part of the medical team, and so they must practice with a professional nonbias toward patients.

This is one significant difference from the chaplaincy model over the volunteer model. Chaplains work as paid professionals in medical institutions that are often publicly funded. In this way, they have a wider range of skilled responsibilities, such as ethics work as part of a team of professional clinicians in the hospital, work with the community, and nurturing the spiritual health of the medical organization itself. This first aspect of being part of an interdisciplinary care team is a critical new development in modern medical systems around the world. Modern medical care has been structured exclusively around the control of medical care professionals—that is, doctors—with little to no decision-making roles for nurses, social workers, psychiatrists (often reduced to pharmacologists), various types of therapists, and chaplains. However, over the past twenty to thirty years, considerable developments in the understanding of holistic care, led by pioneers like Jon Kabat-Zinn, have helped create a mandate for spiritual care. These developments have not only shown the efficacy of spiritual care but also how it can save expenses for medical institutions and governments through preventative medicine as well as hastened healing. Rev. Julie Hanada sums up the role of the chaplain in this way: "Chaplains can help shorten length of stay in the hospital, communicate with the medical team, and help patients and families feel heard—all of which can reduce complaints and lawsuits, and facilitate end-of-life and medical ethical discussions."

Another key aspect of this mandate for chaplains is not only working with patients and families but also with the other caregivers and professionals in the medical institution. Rev. Julie Hanada has remarked that in her experience chaplains may spend up to 50 percent of their time working with the care team itself, dealing with a whole host of issues that plague medical professionals in their demanding work—as explained in detail by Rev. Joan Halifax in her chapter. On this level, the chaplain becomes much more than a compassionate companion to a dying individual or consoler to a grieving family. As a number of authors have noted, the role of a chaplain also involves overseeing and nurturing the spiritual culture of the entire professional care team and in some places the entire medical institution in which they work. This is indeed a huge and complex type of work that includes special skills and competencies. The Upaya Being with Dying Program established and run by Rev. Joan Halifax is perhaps the most compelling example in this volume of a cultivation system for chaplains that offers such knowledge and skills in this area of community and institutional transformation—most of it amazingly based on adaptations and interpretations of core Buddhist teachings.

Institutions: Hospitals vs. Hospices vs. Home Care

These above points lead us into one of the final major issues of the volume, which is two pronged: the reform of existing medical institutions and the development of holistic medical care environments in which spiritual care is integral. As seen throughout the volume, the first front is incredibly difficult and challenging work since modern medical institutions are built around cultural concepts of denial of death, death as defeat, and scientific materialism, which are the antithesis of the values in the holistic care movement to which Buddhist care belongs. While we have seen a number of different initiatives to try to influence this culture, specifically the work to scientifically prove the efficacy of spiritual care, the personal power of a sympathetic chief doctor or medical administrator has often been the key for driving change. In the chapters on Taiwan and Germany, it was high-level doctors with strong Buddhist leanings who paved the way for progressive holistic care to be introduced in their hospitals. Ironically, Japan, a supposedly predominantly Buddhist country, seems to have the greatest lack of such medical professionals and government bureaucrats sympathetic to Buddhist or other forms of spiritual care. Yet the existence in Japan of Buddhist priests who are also medical doctors, almost always working incognito, may serve as a ray of hope that social attitudes toward Buddhism and religion can start to change.

On the other front, we can see in the volume numerous groundbreaking and radical initiatives for Buddhist-based care beginning as grassroots activities, particularly with the marginalized. In Thailand, Cambodia, and the United States, Buddhist-based care for the dying and bereaved began in the AIDS communities, with Maitri Hospice and the Zen Hospice Project in San Francisco, the Dhammarak Niwet Hospice on the grounds of Phrabat Nampu Temple in Thailand, and the Brahmavihara/Cambodia AIDS project. These projects are deeply meaningful for their realization of the true religious ideals of compassionate caring. As Caroline Brazier sums up in her chapter, "The quality and character of a culture is reflected in its care and concern for its weakest members." While these initiatives have faced huge obstacles in serving a community in which the patients have so few of their own resources—such as family, money, and a sense of personal self-worth—they also have benefitted from the creativity afforded in serving a constituency that no one else took an interest in. Unlike hospitals and medical systems that have entrenched power systems and vested interests, working with marginalized communities can offer a certain freedom of creativity to develop programs in line with the ideals and values of these Buddhist practitioners.

In this way, much of the hospice movement, both Eastern and Western, Christian and Buddhist, has developed from home hospice care by volunteer groups. It is at this level that perhaps the most radical visions in this volume are presented. The reform of modern medical institutions through the development of holistic care teams, which include chaplains, is certainly a heartening development. However, when looking at the economic difficulties behind maintaining massive, centralized medical systems, as seen in Carl Becker's chapter, one wonders whether there is any future in such systems and whether we would be better served with more localized, community-based holistic care. This is the vision of a number of the authors from Japan. Rev. Yozo Taniyama in his chapter envisions the Vihara Movement as expanding the scope of its work beyond caring for the dying and into community social welfare. Both he and Rev. Tomatsu see the meaningful care for the dying and bereaved and its extension into greater community participation as keys for reviving Japan's "Funeral Buddhism"—a pejorative term denoting the narrow focus of priests and temples on performing funeral and memorial rituals for financial remuneration. Perhaps the closest manifestation of this ideal is the work of the Maitri Hospice embedded in and nurtured by the community it serves in San Francisco. There is also the developing vision of the Rigpa Spiritual Care Programme, which is building religious communities and spiritual care centers side by side.

They seek to go beyond simply caring for people to building a community or society where encountering the Buddha's first noble truth of suffering—in birth, aging, sickness, and death—is part of the very fabric of daily life.

Grieving

The common issue that we have left for last to discuss is what happens after death. This is an area where many of the initiatives discussed in this book are actually somewhat undeveloped. Perhaps this is the natural outcome of working within the compartmentalized field of death and dying in the modern world. Rev. Tomatsu in his chapter speaks at length about the separation between premortem and postmortem worlds in Japan; that is, the medical world of dying and the religious world of death. Many of the chapters discuss how the culture of death as defeat leads to the abandonment of the dying within medical institutions, pushed off into the back of wards. The holistic health and chaplain movements have sought to bring the dying back out of exile and to care for them as an integral part of hospital work. Still, the work of grieving that comes after death is not something that hospitals or palliative care wards are mandated to do, so the wall persists between pre- and postmortem worlds with grieving families moving on to try to find new communities to support them in the postmortem process.

Many of the initiatives in this volume attempt to support these grieving persons, but most grief-care programs are not highly developed, perhaps due to these initiatives' heavy emphasis on dying and offering a specific alternative to the functions of a hospital. The Rigpa Spiritual Programme's wider vision of a religious community embedded in birth, aging, sickness, and death shows the potential for a community that can support people through the pre- and postmortem worlds and link them together as one total process. This is where Japanese Buddhism in particular has critical potential for the ongoing Buddhist hospice movement. As many of the Japanese authors discuss, the Japanese Buddhist practice of regular memorial services for the dead has served for hundreds of years as a highly developed grief care system uniting spiritual values with the regular practice of remembrance, all connected to a community of support. The ironic point is that the power of these Eastern practices is being shown to the world in a roundabout fashion—by Western researchers, such as renowned suicidologist and thanatologist Edwin S. Shneidman and his concept of "postvention" and Dennis Klass and his notion of "continuing bonds." This is one major area of endeavor that many of the Buddhist hospice movements could further develop and which makes potential Japanese Buddhist contributions to this field highly significant. The spirit of holistic care that runs throughout the hospice movement could invite the extension of hospice care into regular grief care work, thus building a bridge to not only a more holistic culture of living with death but also the subsequent birth of institutions and communities that reflect this culture.

CONCLUSION

This volume is the second major publication of the Jodo Shu Research Institute's (JSRI) project "*Ojo* and Death: Its Meaning for Pure Land Buddhism, Japanese Buddhism, and Contemporary Society." The project was initiated in 2006 by the chief of the JSRI International Relations Section, Rev. Yoshiharu Tomatsu, who had been active in the Institute's bio-ethics study group, grappling with Buddhist positions on brain death, organ transplants, stem cell research, and so forth. The *Ojo* and Death Project has sought to confront a variety of practical issues that directly impact the average Japanese: Japan's rapidly aging society, coupled with its low birth rate, and the subsequent financial crisis in the ability to take care of the elderly and dying; and the Japanese medical establishment's outdated approach to patient care. The project has also, of course, tried to confront the crisis of the growing irrelevancy of Buddhist priests and temples in the lives of their lay followers. It has also sought to bridge various divides in Japan, such as (1) the gap between parochial academic teachings and practical medical approaches to bio-ethics; (2) the gap between a medical system that neglects the spiritual needs of the dying and a ritualistic Buddhist temple system that neglects the spiritual needs of the living; and (3) the gap between classical Buddhist ritual practices and their application to modern living and dying. In this way, the project has sought to bring together care professionals across the spectrum from within Japan to cooperate on bringing comprehensive transformation to the way the critically ill, dying, and bereaved are cared for.

By 2011, the project had held two international roundtable discussion conferences, four special seminars with foreign and domestic specialists in the field, four complete panels as parts of international academic symposia, and one large public symposium and workshop, while conducting research trips to Taiwan, Southeast Asia, the United States, and Europe, and completing our first major publication, *Never Die Alone: Death as Birth in Pure Land Buddhism* (Jodo Shu Press, 2008). To address these critical issues within Japan, the project has studied the growing number of Buddhist-based hospice, spiritual care, and bereavement care activities around the world as well as within Japan. The wide variety of encounters we have had through this research is presented in this volume with grateful appreciation to the authors whose work we have come to know. We would also like to extend a final thanks to those in the Jodo Shu Research Institute who provided special support to this work: Rev. Zenno Ishigami, the director of the institute, for his ongoing interest and support; Rev. Tatsuyu Imaoka, senior fellow at the institute, for his interest in this work from the beginning and promotion of it to an independent project within the institute; Rev. Jin Sakai, for his help with translation; Rev. Ryodo Kudo, Ms. Akiko Ominami, and Rev. Yasuhiro Shima for their unending logistical support; and the rest of the members of the *Ojo* and Death Project team for their ongoing dedication to the work.

JAPAN
Challenges of Caring for the Aging and Dying

Carl B. Becker

A TERMINAL SOCIETY

Why should a reader care about terminal care in Japan? First, no country in the world has ever been as old or as crowded as Japan is today. As of 2011, more than 30 percent of Japanese are over the age of sixty; in another decade, more than 30 percent of Japanese are expected to be over age seventy. Seventy years is the average lifespan of the human species, but before long, a third of Japan's population will exceed that average lifespan. Furthermore, in the next forty to fifty years, roughly 80 million Japanese people will die due to natural causes. Never in the history of humankind have 127 million people, the present population of Japan, lived in such a small land area, nor have so many people ever died in such a short time with so few people to care for them.

Postindustrial countries will likely follow Japan in this aging pattern, especially ones from the Organisation for Economic Co-operation and Development (OECD), South Korea, and China, with its one-child policy. So the eyes of the world are watching Japan's experiment in aging. If Japan can manage aging and dying successfully, it will prove a model for the rest of the world. However, if the Japanese government poorly handles its elderly population problems, it will lose credibility with foreign cultures as well as with its own people. In this sense, Japan's management of its elder care and medicine is a critical issue, both internationally as well as domestically.

MEDICALIZATION OF JAPAN

A second major issue of relevance to the rest of the world is that Japan is the most medicalized society on earth. For example:

- Japan hospitalizes its patients an average of five times longer than America.
- Japanese visit doctors thrice as often as people from Britain and New Zealand, who share a comparable socialized medical system.
- Japanese spend thrice as long as the average European does sitting in doctors' anterooms, waiting for diagnoses and prescriptions.
- Japan prescribes an average of four to five times more medicine per patient than do other industrialized countries with comparable medical systems.

Ironically, the Japanese tendency to overmedicate is contradicted by a reluctance to prescribe palliative analgesics—particularly opioids, like morphine—even at the end of life. The combination of outdated bureaucratic legislation, lack of transparency, failure to document and prioritize patients' wishes, and economic incentives to prolong life frustrates a nationwide advance in palliative medicine.

Surveys document that most Japanese elderly do not want to have their lives artificially and mechanically prolonged. They want to know when further treatment is futile, so they can prepare themselves for a dignified departure. Yet the medical system wants to hospitalize them, and if they weaken in the hospital, to medicate them; if the medications fail, then to intubate them; and when all else fails, to sustain them on mechanical life support systems. Since the medical system reimburses doctors for services rather than for results, it is to their advantage to make patients dependent upon them. Many doctors' primary motivations have shifted—at least in part—from cure to profit or experimentation, which necessitates keeping patients for extended periods. Further, many Japanese hospitals have already bought so much expensive diagnostic machinery that even now there is not enough money to support them. Swollen by the policies and tax moneys of the Ministry of Health and the Japan Medical Association, the Japanese medical system has overridden the mandate of the people.

Economic Meltdown

This leads us to a third major problem: financing the medical system. In order to support a heavily socialized medical welfare system, the average income tax base in northern European countries like Denmark, Sweden, Finland, and France constitutes roughly 50 percent of their Gross Domestic Products (GDPs), while Japan's is about 23 percent of its GDP. Their income taxes and value-added sales taxes total anywhere from 50 to 70 percent of personal income, while Japan's is less than 25 percent. (While Japan's tax on industries has been high, average personal tax is low: about 18 percent income tax and 5 percent sales tax.) In other words, more than half of the European countries' economic activity is absorbed by taxes, largely in order to support their medical welfare systems. Yet even in tax-burdened Scandinavia, there are still patients who would rather die at home. Japan is trying to provide far more medicine and hospital beds on far less tax money, which is simply impossible and largely accounts for Japan's staggering national debt.

Scandinavian studies suggest that Japan has only two options: to raise its own taxes to roughly 70 percent, or to reduce its medical costs to one-third of present levels. There are many ways of doing the latter, but the Japan Medical Association and the Japanese pharmaceutical industry stridently lobby against cutting medical expenditures. Already, the bankrupt Minister of the Treasury is at loggerheads with the Ministry of Health, which is demanding funds on behalf of the Japan Medical Association. At some point, Japan will have no choice but to reduce medical expenses—preferably sooner rather than later.

The most practical and acceptable starting points for reducing medical expenditures are to begin by cutting counterproductive services, such as overlong hospital stays, and eliminating services that patients themselves least desire. Evidence-based medicine (EBM) already provides ample data that short hospital stays are preferable to long ones for a majority of physical conditions. Surveys of which medicines are being discarded rather than properly ingested can serve as one basis for reduced reimbursement for prescription of medicines that are not likely to be effectively used. Advance directives, designated decision-makers, Physician Orders for Life-Sustaining Treatment (POLST) forms, and living wills, which allow patients and their representatives to express their desires, should be the basis for reduced artificial life-extension for those who do not desire it. Significantly, most terminal patients themselves express more interest in quality of life than quantity of life—a fact brought out in the research by the Interdisciplinary Center for Palliative Medicine (IZP) at Munich University Hospital, detailed in the chapter on Germany.

A BUDDHIST REFLECTION

The situation described above epitomizes the Buddhist analysis of the human condition. Humans always want more than we have. Japanese medicalization shows that this is not only true of possessions like cars and cell phones but also true of health. We always want to be healthier than we are. Yet patients' desires perpetually exceed however much medicine and health care a system can provide. The only proper solution to this psychological tendency is to adjust our desires to sustainable levels. No population is ever as healthy as it would ideally like to be. Aging, sickness, and death are part of the human condition. The Buddhist prescription is to adjust our desires to reality.

The demographics discussed above will force Japanese to abandon their overreliance on medicine, because there are not enough caretakers, doctors, beds, nor money to enable eighty million patients to die in highly mechanized hospital settings—even if that were desirable. A growing percentage of Japanese elders will die at home—as had always been the case prior to the bubble economy of the 1980s. Home care will entail a less medical approach and a greater need to confront the elephant in the room that people have been trying to ignore—the reality of death. Japan can face this situation with tremendous social and political resistance, outraged at the idea of cutting medicare, or it can appreciate how other systems can complement and provide alternatives to this uncontrolled medical system. The Ministry of Health and Labor has already recognized this and is encouraging people to spend their last days at home, which is what most Japanese people have been saying they want.

THE DENIAL OF DEATH AND THE EFFECTS OF THE FEAR OF DEATH

Almost all Japanese, especially those hospitalized for slow processes like cancer and diabetes, know when they are dying. Typically, this is less from any clear discussion with their doctors or health care providers than from the following kind of dialogue:

"Please Doc, level with me. I've been lying here for months already. My hair is falling out. I've lost all my appetite. I know I'm weakening. Is it cancer? Is there something in my brain? What's happening to me?"

The doctor's subsequent pause is unnaturally short or long. With ill-concealed discomfiture, the doctor puts up a strong front: "No, no, no. Don't talk like that. You'll be out of here before you know it. Pick up your spirits. We're working on it. You've still got a way to go."

From the overly solicitous response of the obviously nervous doctor, the patient learns two lessons: The first is "Yes, I'm dying. My hunch was right." The second is "The doctor does not want to talk about it; dying is not a subject for conversation in this hospital ward."

The patient gets the same kind of response when he asks the same questions of his family who have already been informed that he is dying. They jump in with overreactive protests or furtive glances around the room like, "Who is going to respond to this, please?" This tells the patient, "Yes, my suspicions are correct, and no, we cannot talk about this."

In English, we distinguish "truth telling" from "informed consent." "Informed consent" means asking patients about their desires to receive medical procedures to cure their conditions. In terminal cases, however, the issue becomes less "informed consent" of how to cure them than "truth telling" about the end of life. Research on "truth telling" in Japan shows that doctors and families do not want to tell the patient the truth. Nurses often want to communicate more fully with their patients, but they are intimidated by the doctors not to do so.

The common fear that "truth telling" will depress patients is not totally groundless. Anyone suddenly informed that they had only two months left to live would be shocked and confused. However, the issue is not *whether* to tell the truth; it is *how* to tell the truth. Doctors have not been trained how to tell the truth about dying, because the taboo of silence over death and dying pervades Japanese medical education. As Rev. Tomatsu's chapter details, the six to nine years of medical education in Japan cover diagnosis, operations, treatment, and medical cures. Doctors are taught neither to communicate bad news nor to deal with patients' inevitable facts of death. These communication skills need more training, preferably during medical school, or at least in workshops after medical school. However, there is precious little room in the Japanese medical system for retraining or continuing education units.

The percentage of people in Japan who consciously prepare for death is extremely low. It is this denial of death that obfuscates and frustrates the natural dying process. As recently as sixty years ago, shortly after World War II, international surveys ranked the Japanese among the least death-fearing people in the world. Within the forty years between 1960 and 2000, among the dozens of countries surveyed, Japan became the most death-fearing country in the world. Fear is an indication of ignorance. For example, when we fear an interview, a contract negotiation, or a doctor's appointment, we are afraid because we don't know what will happen. If we know what is going to happen, then we can mentally prepare for it. It may seem difficult, challenging, or even attractive, but we are no longer afraid of it. This forty-year turnaround indicates that Japanese have changed from a people that understood death—and the hereafter—to a people that no longer understand death, much less the hereafter.

Since the 1960s, a culture of silence made death unspeakable. Nothing kills as effectively as deliberately ignoring something. If we ignore and ostracize death throughout education, adult professional life, eventual aging and illness, then death too becomes a black box—something we no longer understand. In turn, dying patients find that people no longer know how to speak to them, doubling the misery of their physical dying process through the psychology of estrangement.

In traditional societies, like Japan, one qualification for "coming of age" was having watched and cared for elders in the process of death—typically grandparents or great aunts or uncles. When people lived in large families and died at the age of fifty or sixty, by the time young people were fifteen years old, they had watched one or more members of their family die. They had helped in feeding, washing, and caring for them in that process. In the past few decades, due to extended life spans, nuclear families, and hospitalization of the infirm, young people in the process of growing up no longer care for dying people. The whole subject area of death has been excluded from their worldview. The resulting ignorance brings fear and further repression; a cycle of silence, fear, and avoidance. Observed directly, death can be sad, heart wrenching, sometimes peaceful or even uplifting, but not fearful. Like a child being born into the world, or like first love, death is a rare and precious event, a special sacred moment, a rite of passage. Rites of passage formed an integral part of traditional culture, as Philippe Aries (1914–84), the influential writer on childhood and dying, recognized fifty years ago.

Today, many Japanese youth display a fundamental inability to maintain intimate relationships. Electronic technology enables a lifestyle superficially connected with many people. However, when relationships become more complex, uncomfortable, difficult, or threatening, Japanese youth suddenly break off contact, like turning off their TV. They seem to lack the emotional strength to work through issues to develop more meaningful and intimate relationships. Many young people in Japan are obsessed with *jiga-sagashi*, or "trying to find themselves." However long they stare at their navels, trying to find themselves, they will never find meaning unless they step *beyond* themselves, into larger contexts, as members of families, contributors to larger projects, or club members aiming at a higher purpose. Meanings only emerge in relationships, so a self without relationships cannot find meaning. In terms of terminal care, this lack of intimacy in contemporary Japan can make the practice of truth telling harmful, if dying patients retain no close relationships either with friends, family, or caregivers, with whom to work out the issues of their final days. The structure of a good death as taught in progressive hospice care cannot proceed from the act of truth telling alone; it requires intimate relationships.

THE ROLE OF BUDDHISM IN FACING AGING, SICKNESS, AND DEATH

The great twentieth-century scholar of religions Mircea Eliade said that humans are not only *homo sapiens* but *homo religiosus*. In other words, a fundamental part of our nature is connected to the invisible, to the spiritual, to powers in the universe that we can only experience through synchronicity, dreams, and spiritual experiences. Eliade said that if organized religion is suppressed by government or society, it will emerge in countless less organized forms, such as fortune telling, because some part of our being needs connectedness with the invisible spiritual universe.[1]

Some twenty years ago, when Taiwan was just beginning to socialize its medical system, Taiwanese colleagues of mine in medical psychology surveyed about one thousand homes in rural Taiwan between Kaohsiung and Chiayi and one thousand homes in the highly industrialized Taipei area. One question asked respondents whether they would choose traditional Chinese medicine, Western medicine, or religious healing to treat an illness. In the countryside, each option was chosen by about 40 percent of the survey participants.[2] In Taipei, where the government was already subsidizing clinics using Western medicine, the choice of Western medicine rose from 40 percent to 80 percent, while the choice of nonsubsidized Chinese medicine dropped from 40 percent to 20 percent. Researchers had hypothesized that the more educated and wealthy urban Taipei people would rely less on religious healing than those in the countryside, but in fact the number of urban Taiwanese who said they would visit temples doubled from 40 percent to 80 percent.

Surprised by this finding, they sent graduate students to interview why more urban people relied on religion. The following story repeatedly emerged: When a person went to the hospital, she waited for two hours. Then in three to five minutes, the doctor looked at her tongue, checked her pulse, and wrote a prescription. Doctors did not ask about patients' lifestyles nor listen to their concerns. They neither counseled patients about how to avoid recurrences nor listened to the problems that the patients faced. Respondents said that their daily problems and maladies were inextricably intertwined, but their doctors only looked at symptoms and gave them something to cover the symptoms.

However, Taipei respondents reported that if they went up the back hill to an old temple and spoke to an old bearded monk, he would listen patiently and quietly for an hour or two as they poured out their hearts and described in great detail life's problems. The monk's brief sage advice at the end of their visit helped such parishioners regain faith and courage to persevere. When they left the temple, such clients gladly left offerings for the monks, unconnected to the national health insurance system.

Like religious healing, traditional Chinese medicine also allows time for the doctor to get to know the patient, in addition to examining the patient's tongue, fingernails, and pulses. As modern medicine becomes increasingly routinized, such spiritual interaction occurs less and less frequently. Feeling the need for this kind of interaction, Taipei respondents visited local Buddhist or Taoist temples where priests would listen patiently and give them a quotation from the Tao Te Ching or a Buddhist sutra, that would serve as a koan to contemplate until their next meeting.

In the time of the Buddha, Buddhist monks used local pharmacopeia to heal people physically as well as spiritually. Japanese Buddhist monks followed that tradition in the sixth and seventh centuries when Buddhism first came to Shitenno-ji in Osaka. Arguably, it was the superiority of Buddhist medicine and hygiene that forced the anti-Buddhist Mononobe clan to grudgingly acknowledge the value of Buddhism in the seventh century. In Japan, traditional rural doctors were typically priests as well. Like Dr. Red Beard from Shugoro Yamamoto's eponymous novel (and film adaptation by Akira Kurosawa), they counseled as well as cared for the families they visited. They served as healers for the ill and for the families of the ill, both while the patient lived and after.

By the seventeenth century, the words "monk" and "doctor" had become almost synonymous, because the only people with the time and education to read Chinese medical texts were Buddhist priests. These priests served not only to send off departing souls but also to purvey pharmaceutical, psychiatric, and acupuncture care for their parishioners. While providing physical care, Buddhist priests interacted with their patients on a personal and even philosophical level, helping them to understand that aging, sickness, and death are natural stages of the human condition. They visited homes not only to chant sutras after a death but to counsel their patients before their deaths, and to comfort the bereaved families thereafter. Instead of fighting death as if it could be overcome, Buddhists learned to accept reality for what it was.

Sadly, most Japanese people have lost this closeness to their temples. This is partly because temples were manipulated by the Tokugawa government and disbanded by the Meiji government. When General MacArthur arrived, he blackened out all discussion of Shinto. For over a century, the Japanese were taught that Buddhists were disreputable and subsequently that Shinto was false and dangerous. In the postwar period, education has emphasized the physical sciences at the expense of human cultivation, and mass media have been outspokenly antireligious. Over the past century and a half, authorities have repeatedly told the Japanese that religion is not a suitable source for spiritual consultation.

Since Buddhists were oppressed in the Meiji period—and indeed some did violate their vows and lost the respect of their parishioners— it has been a long and winding road to regain their prior social status. However, Buddhist priests are beginning to realize that they have important roles to play in this society. Today, a small but growing number of priests in Japan are visiting hospitals and lending ears to the concerns of dying people. Doctors who also happen to be ordained are "coming out" openly as Buddhist priests, to provide Buddhist counseling as well as *materia medica* for their clients. The Buddhist hospice movement in Japan—the Vihara Movement—and the growing role of priests as counselors are as welcome as they are overdue. As Rev. Taniyama, Rev. Sengoku, and Dr. Hayashi relate in this volume, Buddhist viharas in Niigata, Kyoto, and Tokyo are beginning to provide alternative venues for the dying. At the same time, Western scholars are rediscovering the wisdom of Japanese Buddhism in dealing with death and dying. Out of these movements may come insights that may help or heal people facing the care or departure of a loved one.

JAPANESE BUDDHISM'S SPECIAL SKILL IN GRIEF CARE AND "CONTINUING BONDS"

Medicine may be able to combat sickness, but medicine is virtually powerless in the face of aging and, ultimately, death. No industry can reverse aging or avoid death forever. A small but growing number of Japanese doctors are beginning to realize that aging and death are beyond their provenance. The shocking reality of aging, sickness, and death were what catapulted Gautama Siddhartha into his quest for enlightenment; the teachings of Buddhism begin not from myth, fable, nor faith, but from the suffering of aging, sickness, and death. So Buddhists have recognized and contemplated aging and death since the time of Buddha.

Caring for the aged and dying has been a concern of Japanese Buddhists for 1,500 years. From the ninth to the nineteenth century, Japanese priests kept records of the deathbeds of their most famous monks and parishioners.[3] This Buddhist tradition is not merely of historical interest; it holds tremendous resources for helping people to age and die gracefully, peacefully, honorably, in some cases even beautifully. In Japan, however, roughly 90 percent of the nearly two hundred hospices are Christian-based, while only 2 percent are avowedly Buddhist; this contrasts with roughly 90 percent of the Japanese people who desire to have Buddhist-type funeral rites and less than 2 percent who say they want Christian care at the end of life. Not surprisingly, Christian hospices emphasize salvation by faith, Biblical mythology, and even a spirit of celebration. Collared chaplains visit with Bibles or hymnals, while crosses adorn the halls, and muzak hymns pour from ceiling speakers. The Buddhist approach to death and dying is less celebratory and faith based. Buddhist viharas I have visited are more solemnly accepting of suffering, proffering hope without vivacity, endurance without celebration.

At the same time, the fact that people around the world attest to being met by a compassionate figure of light at their deathbeds is something that can unite different faiths in contemplating death. Compassionate figures of light have been documented in medical journals like *The Lancet* by Pim van Lommel, the *Journal of Resuscitation* by Sam Parnia,[4] and by many other medical doctors. Western physicians from Carl Jung and Elisabeth Kübler-Ross to Raymond Moody Jr. and Larry Dossey publicly acknowledge that meeting a compassionate light at the time of death is central to the dying experience. In fact, so many Western patients reported this experience that Western doctors had to coin the phrase "figure of light" simply to refer to this phenomenon. However, Chinese, Korean, and Japanese Buddhists had already recorded and named this experience for two thousand years; the figure of light is called Amida Buddha, which in Sanskrit means "Buddha of infinite light and life," and the coming of this light at the time of death is called the *raigo* experience. I have seen patients staring at a wall or a window with extreme joy in the last moments of their lives, so eagerly that I too looked at the wall to see what they were experiencing—but could only see the wall. Seeing the face of a dying patient who a moment before had been pallid or wrenched in pain suddenly glowing in anticipation was a very persuasive experience for me.

Buddhist discussion of the afterlife is not grounded on Maccabean myths of bodily resurrection and apocalyptic judgment. It is grounded on the understanding of the cycle of rebirth that we gain through meditation, and through the countless deathbed visions that report the coming of a salvific figure of light. Like others who have experienced this at death, Pure Land Buddhists believe that there is light at the end of our tunnels. We should walk every step of this tunnel, accepting it for what it is and learning what we can from it. Indeed, there may be commonalities between Christian and Buddhist myths that are worthy of more exploration.

Another important insight of Buddhism is that death seriously affects the bereaved and their society as well as the dying person. The Japanese Buddhist tradition of ceremonies following the wake, at one week, three week, and seven week intervals, followed by the first summer Obon celebration and periodic ceremonies thereafter, serve as valuable occasions to address the grief of the bereaved. If these ceremonies fossilize into rituals that no longer attend to the needs of the bereaved community, they lose this important function. However, longitudinal medical research on bereavement is documenting that bereaved people who participate in follow-up counseling sessions escape many of the problems that typically follow the loss of a loved one. Those problems typically include depression, reduced immunity, increased sickness, absenteeism, accidents, even sudden death and suicide attempts. This is a tremendous cost, not only to the people undergoing them but also to their caretakers and society who lose productivity and have to pay police, ambulances, hospitals, and caretakers to deal with the accidents, illnesses, or suicide attempts.

The Japanese Buddhist tradition of periodically convening bereaved people to reminisce about the deceased and reconsider their understanding of life and death is a brilliant traditional mechanism to avoid these tragic aftereffects. In premodern days, the Japanese labeled recurrent tragedies afflicting the bereaved with the word *tatari*—curses from the other world. If one did not sincerely perform the ceremonies and appreciate the meanings or messages of the deceased, it was believed that the deceased might respond with some curse. Today, we can interpret this curse not as some ghostly revenge, but rather as immune system depression leading to sickness, or lapses in concentration leading to a car accident or to cutting off a fingertip when chopping vegetables. This may be less a curse than our own failure to fully reintegrate after a period of mourning. Every society in the world has had a period of mourning followed by rituals of reintegration—a reunderstanding of the world after which bereaved people no longer are sick or suicidal. Temples effectuated these meaningful and valuable rituals in previous generations.

Another important insight of the East Asian Buddhist tradition concerns our indebtedness to former generations. In 1910, Sigmund Freud counseled widows deeply attached to their deceased husbands. Unable to cure them, Freud pontificated in *Melancholia and Mourning* (first penned in 1915, published in 1917) that the best solution to mourning was to degrade and forget the figure to whom one felt attached. In the wake of World War I, where virtually every family in Europe either lost someone or knew people who lost someone, posttraumatic stress disorder (PTSD) further encouraged Europeans to forget their dead—as Caroline Brazier discusses in her chapter. Hitler used this forgetfulness to his advantage when he extinguished millions of Jews and disabled people. For many tragic reasons in twentieth-century history, the message to "forget the dead" was imprinted on Europe. Freud's message was echoed by Americans, who are so geographically mobile that often they cannot even remember where they had buried their dead. Freud's admonition to forget the dead was compatible with the American ethos, since Americans had deliberately chosen mobility over attachment.

About twenty years ago, a brilliant psychologist of religion named Dennis Klass, educated at the University of Chicago under Mircea Eliade, visited Tokyo. He watched people talking and listening to their ancestors in front of Buddhist home altars and people reporting to their ancestors at gravesites. Klass concluded that, far from crazy, these were some of the wisest people he had met. When they faced challenges in their lives, they asked their parents or grandparents in their hearts how to deal with them. In quiet meditation, they listened to the voices of their grandparents or parents advising them. Relying on the wisdom of former generations, they dealt with serious problems in their lives without hiring psychiatrists. Their ancestors in their hearts knew better answers than any third-party psychiatrist could provide. Dennis Klass returned to the United States, and with Phyllis Silverman and others wrote *Continuing Bonds*. "Continuing bonds" is the idea that when someone dies, although their body is no longer present, their spirit remains connected to us. We can respect, appreciate, and even learn from them. We can no longer call them on our cell phone, but we can call them on the "cell phone" in our heart. If the cell phone in our heart has its battery charged—if our mind is receptive—we can get their messages even after their body is no longer with us.

Many readers in Europe and America rejoiced at the "continuing bonds" theory, for although their loved ones were gone, they too could hear their voices and feel their presence. Klass and Silverman depathologized mourning, overturning the Freudian psychology of grief by translating this Japanese Buddhist wisdom to the West: far from pathological, learning from our elders can be psychologically and ethically beneficial.

From Continuing Bonds to Interconnected (*en*) Society

Thirty years ago, the great Yale-educated scholar of Japanese religion Tom Kasulis concluded that the genius of Japanese Buddhism was "intimacy";[5] he developed this into a full-fledged philosophy of culture in *Intimacy or Integrity*. Ironically, the intimacy of relationships fundamental to the Japanese religious worldview that Kasulis experienced thirty years ago when studying in Kyoto and meditating at

Myoshin-ji Temple has largely disappeared. Just as Japan has reverted from the least-death-fearing to the most-death-fearing culture, it has moved from a culture centrally valuing intimacy and relationships to one that is all too frequently devoid of serious intimacy. Ironically, Japanese society depends on the Buddhist-derived concepts of *in* (causality/responsibility), *en* (interconnectedness), and *on* (sense of obligation or gratitude)—all basic to relationship and intimacy. When these values are forgotten, Buddhist society cannot function.

This has a further ramification for ethics education. Young people in both America and Japan ask why they should care about future generations when they inherit a world so full of problems. Many feel that they might as well just live for whatever they can get out of life and forget the next generation. However, if every morning we bow to our ancestors, expressing our thanks for inheriting their land, house, education, books—even for this body that we would not have if it were not for them—then we realize our interconnectedness to the many past generations that make the present possible. Only when we realize this dependency on the sacrifices of many previous generations do we also begin to think about what kind of world we want to leave behind after we are gone. If I am always aware that my ancestors restricted their own lifestyles in order to leave this forest or river in a relatively unpolluted state for my use, then the least I want to do is to preserve this same forest or river for my progeny. In technical terms, this is known as the problem of responsibility toward future generations, or intergenerational responsibility. The crisis of much of American education in failing to educate its youth in intergenerational responsibility is related to the American failure to recognize indebtedness to previous generations.

The way to teach the young about these concepts might begin by teaching them about family altars. It might also begin by taking class excursions to look at where our food comes from, how our water comes to us, and the whole process of how we are maintained. If we lose our *in*, *en*, and *on*, then there is no brake on suicide; there is no inherent reason to live if we are just meaningless atoms in isolation.

Japan's ongoing epidemic of more than 30,000 annual suicides since 1998 attests to this. It is the participation in larger structures and our interrelationships with other people that gives meaning to life.

Theology witnessed a long discussion in the 1960s and '70s about the grounds of ethics. The monotheistic stance typically held that divine command is the ultimate ground for ethics. John Hick argued that God's ultimate justice and judgment is clearly not evident in this life, so that without afterlife, there would be no ground for ethics. Against this, relativist and materialist East Asians argued that ethics is socially grounded; for society would collapse if ethical rules were not followed. Christians retorted that if ethics are purely social then, outside of their own societies, Asians would have no reason to behave ethically. The atrocities of Japanese soldiers, for example, illustrate the danger of socially dependent ethics when people are removed from their own social contexts. To this, East Asians responded that monotheist ethics can license brutality of the chosen "believers" against pagan infidels, from the crusades to Hitler's ethnic cleansing.

Ironically, the monotheists were right about ethics breaking down when society breaks down, but Asians were right about consciousness of interconnectedness being essential. If monotheists, who consider their ethics revealed from God, are the only people who can dictate ethics to the world, we will have wars until the end of time, because different revelations provide different realities. Whereas if we are aware of our interconnectedness, then the central ethical question becomes: how must humans cooperate to keep the planet sustainable? Sustainability implies reducing individual desires to a level compatible with the fulfilling of others' desires throughout the future.

In sum, Japan portrays a curious juxtaposition: On the one hand, in the face of changing demographics, medical technology, and welfare economics, it finds itself increasingly incapable of addressing the psychosocial needs of elderly patients. On the other hand, Japan's long-sustained Buddhist tradition includes rich resources for understanding and psychosocially supporting such elderly patients. This is not to critique either medical technology or welfare economics, but rather to suggest that a more humbly human approach to aging and dying is requisite for a sustainable future. Traditional Japanese Buddhism provides one such approach, based less on religious faith than on a sober contemplation of the human condition.

JAPAN
Tear Down the Wall: Bridging the Premortem and Postmortem Worlds in Medical and Spiritual Care

Yoshiharu Tomatsu

INTRODUCTION: THE WALL BETWEEN LIFE AND DEATH IN JAPAN

In a 2008 study by the Japan Hospice Palliative Care Foundation,[1] the question was posed to general respondents, "In the moment of facing death, which person would you most rely on?" Their answers, which allowed for multiple responses, were, in descending order, spouses (77.4 percent), children (71.4 percent), friends (30 percent), doctors (27.8 percent), fellow patients (20.8 percent), relatives (19.4 percent), nurses (17 percent), social workers (6.3 percent), religious professionals (4.7 percent), coworkers (2.7 percent), and no one (4.9 percent). Compared to the results from the same survey taken in 2005, there were significant increases for spouses (+8.2 percent), friends (+10.3 percent), nurses (+5.8 percent), and doctors (+4 percent).

This data brings out two significant points that my chapter will focus on. The first is the lack of reliance on religious professionals. Considering that death is usually thought of as a time of intense spirituality or religiosity when one confronts mortality and faces what lies beyond, it is rather shocking and alarming that in Japan religious professionals are at the bottom of this list with only a tiny minority showing faith in them. In recent times, there has been much negative propaganda around Japanese Buddhism for losing touch with society and becoming stuck in the moneymaking business of "Funeral

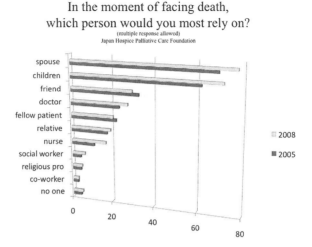

In the moment of facing death,
which person would you most rely on?
(multiple response allowed)
Japan Hospice Palliative Care Foundation

Buddhism" (*soshiki bukkyo*). This above survey is very concrete evidence of this situation and the loss of confidence by the public in Japanese religious professionals, who are in a high majority Buddhist priests as around 90 percent of the Japanese population is said to be Buddhist.

Over the past century and a half since the advent of the modern era in Japan, the role of the Buddhist priest has been circumscribed to the point where he is now mostly a ritualist presiding over funerals and memorial services. Unlike in the past, Buddhist priests and institutions no longer care for people before they get sick, while they are sick, and in their dying days and moments. Professionalization has increasingly relegated what were once the roles and activities of priests in general counseling, support for the ill and dying, funeral preparation, and so forth to licensed experts. Priests without the proper modern credentials and licenses are thus no longer respected or welcome in a world of highly trained experts and professionals that make up the modern medical system.

The second significant point for my paper that this survey brings out is the surprising reliance on medical doctors as perceived confidants for patients. There has developed a tendency for Japanese in recent times to depend on doctors not just for physical care but also for mental and emotional support. As we can see in the above survey, they are the first care professionals depended upon in the critical moment of facing death, surprisingly ahead of nurses who are usually the main medical caregivers. This data does not just apply to patients but also to families who rely heavily on the support and guidance of the doctor.

The problem with this structure and culture, however, is that doctors are not properly trained in providing such emotional and mental care and thus are unable to adequately deliver this service to their patients. This point is seen in the increasing number of lawsuits in recent years against doctors, which almost tripled in a ten-year span from the early 1990s to early 2000s.[2] Tellingly, suits were initiated most often because of emotional frustration by families with the attitude and manner of the doctor and the lack of mutual trust from little personal interaction, rather than actual medical malpractice.

In sum, the situation that we have arrived at in Japan is a strong wall between premortem and postmortem worlds. The premortem world is dominated by medical professionals, who focus solely on the physical needs of patients and very quickly remove themselves from the scene when a patient becomes terminal. The postmortem world is dominated by the religious professional, generally a Buddhist priest who enters the scene right after death and becomes very active; as the alienation between temple priest and parishioner deepens in Japan, it is only in unusual circumstances that a priest is on the scene before death occurs. As we will see in other chapters in this volume, this strong separation is not the case in other countries, including other Asian and predominantly Buddhist societies like Thailand and Taiwan. For example, the United States has developed a strong system of team care in hospitals that includes highly trained chaplains (of which Buddhists are a rising number), while Buddhist monks in other Asian countries are more closely involved in the dying process. In these Asian societies, secularization has not advanced as far as in Japan, so the role of doctor and priest is not so strongly alienated.

This specialization of roles, from the doctor as purely physical mechanic to the priest as purely spiritual mechanic, leads to a fundamental alienation from the human relationship with the patient. When one considers the work of doctors or priests, one might think that their intense experiential work with people in great suffering would deepen their awareness and create a critical wisdom and compassion. However, the opposite seems to be true. As mentioned above, there are an increasing number of lawsuits against doctors mostly due to their lack of feeling and compassion to their patients. A common scene today in Japan is a doctor staring into his computer screen reading off medical information and statistics on longevity and mortality as he attempts to communicate to a patient his or her illness. At the same time, there are an endless number of complaints about priests showing up for funerals, doing the necessary rituals, receiving their offering-*cum*-fee, and leaving without making any real connection with the grieving family. This situation is well illustrated by our Jodo Shu Research Institute's study that shows many priests do not even bother to give a Dharma talk at the funeral; that when they do, it is usually no more than five to ten minutes long; and that the impact of the service on the bereaved family is very little to none.

Survey on Dharma Talks at Funerals in Japan

#1   In general, about what percentage of priests give dharma talks at funerals?

		%	Number
1	0~20%	19. 8	20
2	20~40%	28. 7	29
3	40~60%	20. 8	21
4	60~80%	24. 8	25
5	80~100%	5. 9	6
	Total	100. 00%	101

#6   Objectively speaking, about what percent of these talks touched people's hearts?

		%	Number
1	0~20%	47	47
2	20~40%	34	34
3	40~60%	12	12
4	60~80%	6	6
5	80~100%	1	1
	Total	100%	100

This survey was given to 890 funeral homes in the Kanto area
by the Jodo Shu Research Institute in 2008

Doctors and priests both display very little communications skills. They have become master mechanics in their craft, but they have lost sight that their materials are living human beings whose mental, emotional, and spiritual needs have a fundamental impact on their physical well-being. It has become my personal challenge to break down these walls that separate the premortem and postmortem worlds, the medical and spiritual worlds, and the caregiver and patient worlds. Through the fundamental process of human relationship, I believe we can find the way toward authentic and holistic care for those in suffering. Concretely, I am trying to bring religious and medical professionals together to better understand each other's worlds, changes, and needs.

DEVELOPING DOCTORS AS COMPASSIONATE CAREGIVERS

Structural Barriers to Holistic Care in Japan

The problem of poorly trained doctors has its roots in the systematic reductionism of care in the Japanese medical system, which views and treats all forms of suffering (physical, social, emotional, and spiritual) as medical, as physical. For example, psychological care in Japan through trained psychiatrists and psychotherapists has been reduced to largely administering pharmaceutical medicine to reduce and sedate anxiety. Spiritual care needs are usually unacknowledged by not only medical professionals but also families and patients themselves. This situation explains why there is no system of trained spiritual care professionals or chaplains working in Japanese public medical facilities.

I have met a number of very concerned doctors with good motivation to provide personal emotional care for patients. However, the constraints and pressures of the present Japanese system make following such motivations almost impossible. One of the principal constraints is the case overload that doctors and nurses in Japan face, compared with other countries. Based on OECD statistics from 2008, Japan had 15.6 doctors and 69.1 nurses per 100 beds, while Germany had 43.4 and 130.2, England 76.8 and 280, and the United States 78.4 and 346.8 per 100 beds, respectively. What is interesting is that the amount of medical professionals is inversely proportional to the number of beds and average length of stay in each country—Japan has an average of 13.8 beds per 1,000 citizens staying for an average length of 18.8 days, while Germany has 8.2 beds for 7.6 days, England 3.4 beds for 7.1 days, and the United States 3.1 beds for 5.5 days. Thus, although Japan has proportionately a fifth of the number of doctors and nurses compared to the US, there are more than four times as

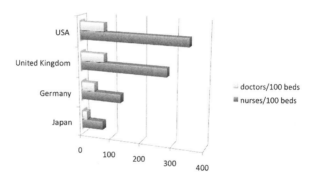

Comparative View of Doctors and Nurses
compiled from OECD statistics for 2008

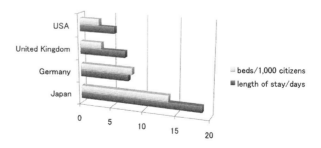

Comparative View of Hospitalization
compiled from OECD statistics for 2008

many available beds with patients staying on an average of more than three times longer during their hospitalizations.[3]

Carl Becker in his chapter has discussed this point in terms of the unnecessary overmedicalization of the Japanese health care system. The result of this system on the ground is that doctors and nurses just do not have the time to attend to the personal needs of patients as they frantically handle as many medical situations and emergencies as they can. This situation is exacerbated by the lack of team care in Japanese hospitals where other caregivers, especially chaplains, could play an important supporting role. One progressive response to this situation would be to divert financial resources away from maintaining so many beds and patients for long-term hospitalization toward paying for more professional caregivers, like chaplains, who could improve shorter term care for patients and support overburdened medical professionals.

Japan desperately needs to adopt the practice of team care in which doctors and nurses share their work with other care professionals, specifically spiritual care professionals. I use this term "spiritual care professional" in contrast to "religious professional," which I define as the average priest who is trained in the teachings and doctrines of a particular denomination and in the care of a congregation. Spiritual care professionals, on the other hand, are trained to go beyond sectarian and even strictly religious sensibilities. They are skilled in dealing with not only patients and their families but also medical staff. Spiritual care professionals, or what we call "chaplains" in the medical field, may spend as much time tending to the emotional needs of the medical staff as to their patients and families. Looking at the previous statistics on Japanese medical care, we can easily come to understand that stress, burn out, and ill health are common among nurses and doctors in Japan. Japan lags far behind much of the developed world in providing even competent psychological care much less spiritual care for its hospital patients, because the doctors and government bureaucrats who control the system are still deeply ingrained in Western attitudes toward medical care that are now at least twenty years out of date.

Another major cause of this situation had been the gradual adoption in Japan of the Evidence-Based Medicine (EBM) system for prioritizing types of treatment, allocating budgets accordingly, and receiving remuneration from the national insurance system for such treatment. Since mental, emotional, and especially spiritual care usually do not provide tangible physical and medical benefit, it becomes even more difficult for doctors to provide such care for patients, even if they have the time and interest to do so. Simply, a doctor who spends extra time getting to know a patient personally or trying to handle a patient's personal anxiety around his/her treatment will not only not be remunerated for such care but is technically wasting time since he or she could be administering actual medical treatment to another patient. Furthermore, while insurance will pay for a first psychological consultation, further psychological care is only remunerated when medication is given.

The hopeful news is that this situation might ironically lead to the kind of breakthrough that we need in Japan. Rev. Thomas Kilts, a Tibetan Nyingma Buddhist priest who trains religious professionals as chaplains for hospital work (profiled in a later chapter in this volume), reports that the widespread application of EBM in the United States forced doctors to abandon any attempts at mental, emotional, and spiritual care.[4] This led to a movement to prove the necessity of such holistic care and that such expertise could be provided, if not by doctors, by new groups of professionals in these fields. The key in the movement to legitimize such care was building the scientific data and evidence that showed that patients tangibly improved in their medical and quality of life conditions due to mental, emotional, and spiritual interventions.[5] The next important step was showing that this care saved hospitals, insurance companies, and governments money. These advancements became the tipping point in the present movement toward spiritual care facilities and integrated team care in hospitals in the United States. This movement has also assisted "spiritual care professionals" to overcome the reluctance of many modern families toward interacting with and depending on religious people in hospitals and medical environments. A similar situation exists now among many modern urban Japanese who generally have strong sentiments against engaging with Buddhist priests in medical environments and often look at them frocked in their black robes as omens of death.

Working with Doctors as a Spiritual Care Professional

These concerns have been fermenting in my consciousness over the years, and not just through my work as a Buddhist priest. From 1989 to 1991, I studied at the Harvard Divinity School, where I was able to take courses on medical ethics. I was surprised to find in the United States that there was cross registration for courses between the medical and divinity schools and that medical students could study about ethical, spiritual, and religious issues as part of their training. Furthermore, at Harvard particularly, we had very interactive and experiential courses that involved role-playing activities around how doctors handle difficult ethical and human issues. These are educational components that we cannot find in Japanese medical or divinity schools, even at elite ones like my own Keio University School of Medicine.

In 2004, after meeting and having discussions with the dean of the Keio University School of Medicine, I pursued a position as a lecturer for doctors in training. In Japan, there are a number of doctors who also are ordained Buddhist priests, yet their identity as priests is kept strictly out of view in their medical practice. In this way, although I have not done any survey, I am perhaps the only Buddhist priest who is teaching nonmedical subjects in a Japanese medical university *openly as a Buddhist priest*. I have brought my experience from Harvard to my classes in which the students engage directly in ethical issues and human relationships in medical care. In general, my courses are very unique in Japan where medical schools spend little or no time at all training their doctors in such ethical and human relationship issues. Even at the Keio University School of Medicine, young Japanese medical students typically spend day after day attending mandatory courses in the nuts and bolts of medical care and hospital management for the national exams for doctoral qualification. Furthermore, my courses are only part of a small elective curriculum. In this way, many students may graduate and become doctors with absolutely no background in how to actually deal with patients and their families as people. In the end, they will learn through a slow and difficult process of trial and error during their residency and eventual formal practice.

The two courses that I have been teaching are "Preparation for Death, The Situation and Issues in Terminal Medical Care: Thinking about Life through Looking at the Hospice Experience" and "The Expected Image of the Doctor: Thinking about Quality of Life and Bio-Ethics through Informed Consent." These classes are currently held on the one day per week that the medical school sets aside for all elective courses, which is only available for third-year students. We are now in the process of changing this system, which must be done under the guise of "medical professionalism," and will offer such courses to all six grades of medical students. With the entire day set aside for one class, I am free to organize my classes in a more experiential manner. In this way, my class is held over five hours from lunch to the evening, and we are able to delve deeply into a number of difficult issues in patient care.

For example, in my class on informed consent, I invited in a professional actress to play the role of a patient who must be told difficult medical news. I took this idea from one of my Harvard courses. Having a real actress instead of a fellow student in the role of patient enables the encounter to be much more intense and real. One role play revolved around the young doctors having to explain to a woman that she had stage four cancer and had six months or less to live. Another involved telling a woman that her six-month-old baby had congenital heart failure and would probably not live beyond the age of two. The young doctors varied greatly in their ability to communicate with the patient, and the actress also varied her responses from outright anger to silent shock. One particularly interesting interaction was with a young doctor who was very sincere and well intentioned but had very poor communication skills. As he stumbled to impart the news to this woman about her child, he made critical mistakes in his use of words and expressions. At one point, he recommended to her a bereaved family support group, even though the child was still alive. At this point in the interaction, the actress went into silent shock, and as this good-natured doctored continued to fumble about, she stormed out of the room.

After each of these individual role plays, I have the students evaluate each other's performance, and we then have time for a wide-ranging conversation on the issues that come up. Typically, we will spend an entire hour on one role play and ensuing reflection. I always emphasize to students that there are no fixed answers and that we arrive at solutions through sharing the feelings and the experience of suffering with patients and their families. On the day when we had the above-mentioned interaction with the well-meaning but unskilled doctor, I happened to have an Indonesian forensic doctor looking in on the class. Coming from a strongly religious country such as Indonesia, he was shocked to see that a doctor would try to impart this news without the aid and support of a religious professional, which he says is common in Indonesia. The young doctors in response were both surprised and curious to interact with this highly trained doctor, who also had a very strong religious faith and viewed the role of religious professionals in caring for patients and family members as a natural and essential part of the medical process.

At first, most of the role-playing exercises that I set up revolved around informed consent and telling bad news directly to patients. However, my students remarked that in Japan, while informed consent as a presentation of a patient's diagnosis has become quite common at over 70 percent,[6] truth telling as a communication of prognosis is still not commonly practiced. Doctors may outline a course of treatment directly with a patient and his or her family but in the case of a critical illness the doctor will initiate further consultations and decisions with the family only. Although the doctor may encourage families to tell their relative of his or her prognosis, the prevalent denial of death in today's Japanese society stops them from doing so. Therefore, through their recommendation, I developed some case studies and role-playing activities for dealing with families, which more directly address the present needs of doctors. Furthermore, the students felt that doing role plays in which one broke bad news to a patient or his or her family completely at one time was also somewhat unrealistic. Thus, I have also recently developed extended role plays in which doctors repeat an interaction with a patient or family over two or three meetings and thus practice divulging the full extent of their condition more gradually. In this way, I do my best to receive the student's critical viewpoints and provide them with skills that they can use in the present situation while also guiding them toward a more ideal situation in the future.

BRINGING PRIESTS BACK INTO LIFE CARE

Structural Impetus Toward Engagement

This chapter has thus far concentrated on how religious people, like myself, can influence the medical system and support medical professionals to better care for the holistic needs of patients. However, this is only half of the problem. Unfortunately, as resistant as medical professionals are to the idea of spiritual care, religious professionals in Japan seem to be as equally uninterested in offering genuine spiritual care to people who are ill and dying. As I outlined at the beginning of this chapter, many Buddhist priests are not able to satisfactorily care for the spiritual needs of their lay congregations, especially in their specialized role of providing postmortem rituals for the bereaved. Ironically, there is no comparative course at the Buddhist university where I teach young priests in training, Taisho University, to the one that I teach at the Keio University School of Medicine. Neither the students nor the administration seems interested in a program that trains priests to be chaplains or counselors to those in critical environments like hospitals, prisons, nursing homes, and psychological care centers. As we will see in Rev. Yozo Taniyama's chapter, the few such initiatives at Buddhist universities in Japan have generally failed.

The one hope at present is through the crisis facing many Buddhist temples of declining numbers of membership and followers seeking other alternatives to caring for the dead. In the next generation or two, many more temples will shut down due to depopulation. There is one estimate by Takanobu Nakajima, professor of business and commerce at Keio University, that by 2060 the present number of 76,000 temples will become as few as 6,000 due to population decline, disinterest in religion, and marginalization as a niche business involving funerals only.[7]

A second critical factor facing Buddhist temples is that the Japanese government, led by bureaucrats in the Ministry of Finance, is making the law under which temples attain their tax-free status—the "public benefit corporation" (*koeki hojin*) law—more strict. This movement is due to Japan's increasing public debt, much of which is caused by the intense strains in the medical and social welfare systems due to the growing number of elderly and the declining birth rate. Furthermore, many government officials no longer see temples as having a public benefit function, since they act as havens for tax-free earnings in a variety of business activities.[8]

While the headquarters of the major Buddhist denominations have shown increasing concern, especially over their legal status, a number of self-motivated priests at the grassroots level have actually begun to confront the role of Buddhism in society through activities in a wide spectrum of critical social issues such as suicide, youth problems, and poverty.[9] While this movement is encouraging, it reflects a small number of remarkably keen and motivated priests. A wider mobilization of average priests needs to take place to create a real paradigm shift. As part of an effort to effect such mobilization, our Jodo Shu Research Institute held a major public symposium in February 2010 on the suicide problem in Japan as well as grief care for the bereaved. The symposium was especially aimed at such rank and file priests and sought to introduce practical activities for priests to bridge the postmortem world of grief care with the premortem world of preventing suicide. In general, the average priest needs to first recognize how his role and the temple's role in society have become deeply marginalized. He then must make the extra effort to bridge the gap between the premortem and postmortem worlds and thus engage with people, because there is very little structure or culture left connecting priests with the common people.

Home Care: Re-engaging at the Grassroots

The first, most practical form of engagement is through visits by priests to the homes of parishioners and people in their general community. In urban areas like Tokyo, there are many people without a home temple in their community due to the relocation of their families from the countryside in the postwar era. However, there are numerous reasons why such people, as well as regular temple parishioners, need the support of a community temple.

One reason is the increasing demand for home care due to the increasing financial constraints in the public medical system that are pushing patients out of hospitals. This situation is creating a phenomenon called "hospital refugees." Under present regulations, a patient under full public insurance cannot stay in one hospital for over three months unless they pay up to $500 per day in separate room fees. For the growing number of economically challenged Japanese, this is not a choice they can afford. These patients end up being sent to rural hospitals, which are in financial crisis and need patients, far from where their families live, and then have to move again to a different hospital every three months.

These kinds of financial conditions, which Carl Becker has detailed in his chapter, restrict the development of palliative care wards, because palliative care does not bring in as much income as other units devoted to surgery and intensive medical procedures. As a result, the Japanese government plans to increase the number of elderly housing projects with doctors and clinics inside them. However, many patients will continue to be thrown back into the care of families, in which increasing numbers of wives who used to traditionally perform home hospice care need to work to help support the family.

A second major reason for engaging in home care initiatives as a first step is due to the marginalization and lack of acceptance of religious professionals in medical environments. In the three major Buddhist hospice and palliative care units in Japan that are profiled in this volume (Nagaoka Vihara, Asoka Vihara, Kosei Vihara), as well as at Christian hospitals, there are numerous testaments to patients showing no interest in using the trained spiritual care professionals on call. The Jodo Shin denomination has done incredible work through their vihara programs to educate and train over one thousand priests and temple wives in spiritual care for the dying.[10] However, these programs have not had a major effect, because there is no public medical or welfare facility that will accept them to practice. The priests and priest wives are educated, but due to a lack of places to do real residency and training, they lack fully developed care skills. On the other hand, Buddhist priests and temples still have the ability to connect to networks of parishioners and local residents. From this basis, priests can find out which households have the need for caring for an elderly or sick family member and take it upon themselves to engage with them, whether through actual spiritual support or more basic social and material support.

By entering the people's lives before they die, priests may widen their capacity to offer spiritual care at the time of death. From such a basis, priests can visit patients who request them individually in the hospital, although they are not part of the hospital staff. There are priests today, such as myself, who have strong bonds with their parishioners, are aware when they face a critical medical situation, and may come to their bedside to offer ritual, comfort, or simple presence with the family. The point is in order for priests and temples to gain back the confidence and trust of the common people, the government, and professionals in various fields, we must begin to engage in concrete activities that show our usefulness, or "public benefit character" (*koeki-sei*).

Building New Structures

The next level of engagement after this stage is for Buddhist denominations to build more hospitals, palliative care units, and hospices. At present, Buddhist denominations in Japan have been very active in building schools and universities, yet very inactive in comparison to Christian denominations in building medical facilities.[11] If they had their own institutions, they could work to mainstream spiritual care as well as team medical care. Though, as Dr. Moichiro Hayashi of the Buddhist-founded Kosei Hospital explains in his chapter in this volume, mainstreaming such care in a major hospital is still very difficult even when the facility has been created by a Buddhist denomination; the creation of such facilities should begin on a small, grassroots scale, such as the Saimyo-ji Temple-Hospital Care Facility run by Rev. Masahiro Tanaka, M.D., in Tochigi prefecture.[12]

In the case of my own Jodo denomination, we have begun to support a grassroots initiative called the One Spoonful Association (*hitosaji-no-kai*), started by a group of young priests to support the homeless in Tokyo with food, medicine, and funeral and grave services. With institutional support from the denomination, we are planning to expand the services to rent a small building as a temporary house with a small clinic where the dying homeless can spend their last days. As a private institution that receives no public funding and is not part of the national insurance system, we will have complete freedom for our priests to engage in the work in whatever ways they see as necessary. As some of the young priests who are leaders in this work have also been involved in activities to counsel and support the suicidal, they have an understanding of the core values and practices of chaplaincy, or spiritual care professionalism, such as the need to offer presence and deep listening to people rather than impose religious agendas on them. This project reflects the "ground zero" situation in Japan where we must begin to rebuild religious community structure and culture through working with the most marginalized people in society. It is similar to how Buddhist hospice work began in other countries profiled in this volume, such as Cambodia, Thailand, and the United States, where publicly ostracized AIDS patients were the first targets of the work.

Conclusion: Bridging the Gap between Worlds

A final level of engagement that I am pursuing is exploring how priests as death professionals can assist doctors to better care for patients and families as well as how to better take care of themselves. The one speciality in which Buddhist priests are recognized as professionals in modern Japan is postmortem death and memorial rites. Although the survey I cited at the beginning of this chapter indicates that many priests are quite ineffectual in the spiritual care of the bereaved, there are some priests who have become quite skilled through their activities as the head of temple communities in managing human relationships and providing grief care. From this basis, priests often have access to a number of important perspectives on medical professionals' premortem care through their relationship with bereaved families. Many bereaved families quickly lose contact with the medical professionals who cared for their family members after their deaths. They have little opportunity to express their honest feelings about the care, both critical and complimentary. Priests often hear these complaints and compliments and, if they had personal relationships with medical professionals, could share these reflections with them. On the other hand, doctors and medical professionals who have an intense experience with patients and families on the premortem side can offer priests important perspectives on their real suffering and needs before the wake, funeral, and memorial process begins.

One of the principal things we can do to influence and raise awareness about bridging the gap between premortem and postmortem worlds is to create mutual study groups that cross not only denominational lines but also professional ones by gathering together people from all types of caregiver backgrounds. In this way, I initiated the *Ojo* and Death Project at the Jodo Shu Research Institute in 2006. Thus far, we have held roundtables and public symposia to discuss these issues with medical professionals and Buddhist priests and laypeople interested in holistic care, as well as bringing in spiritual care professionals from overseas. Still, while there have been a number of conferences for religious and medical professionals in Japan in the last twenty to thirty years to explore how to help the dying, these conferences have not led to many concrete initiatives. As such, I would again like to emphasize taking on smaller, grassroots initiatives as a way toward building larger systemic change.

One such traditional Buddhist grassroots activity has been the community association (*ko*). The *nenbutsu-ko*, a particular association for developing faith in Amida Buddha, who guides people at the time of death to the Pure Land, has throughout Japanese history been an important community association for the elderly that transcended sectarian affiliations. The *nenbutsu-ko* has served as a traditional Buddhist support system for elderly people and the concerns they develop about their health and eventual death. In modern urban Japan, these *nenbutsu-ko* are neither numerous nor strong. However, I see their regeneration as an important piece to this puzzle of the crisis of health care in Japan.

About fifteen years ago, the core members of my temple here in Tokyo asked to start doing the special practice of one million recitations of Amida Buddha's name (*hyakuman-ben nenbutsu*) every month. This group also wanted to learn a more formal level of sutra chanting. This group consists of mostly retired businessmen and widowed women all over the age of sixty. At these events, we spend a short time chanting and then the real core of the meeting begins with teatime, chatting, and good food. We always have two lead speakers who rotate with each session. In their talks, they raise topics and concerns from their own experiences, and then we form a discussion. As can be expected from this age group, their main topics are about health, sickness, and critical family experiences that often include death. From these conversations, I could see that they did not want to talk just about spirituality but also wanted to talk about the specific aspects of physical health care. In fact, it was impossible to divide the two topics—the physical and spiritual aspects of health—as the professionalized medical system has worked so hard to do.[13] As a consequence, I began to invite doctors whom I have met at Keio Medical University to my temple to give the Sunday morning Dharma talk.

Instead of preaching about religion, these doctors give practical talks on medical issues that are of deep interest to my aging congregation. It comes as no surprise then that on these Sundays my temple is packed with attentive listeners busily taking notes. In this way, we have recreated a *nenbutsu-ko* here in downtown Tokyo.

In conclusion, the key point in this process is that the patients and family can serve as the bridge between the religious and medical worlds. If the people have a strong bond with the temple, they will carry that into the hospital and other medical environments and demand it as part of their care. As we have seen in other countries, the creation of spiritual support and care in medical systems has often come about from the demand of the consumers: the patients and their families. Beyond all the activities to prove to the medical establishment that spiritual care is scientifically verifiable as well as cost efficient and to train chaplains or "spiritual care professionals," the fundamental need is to engage directly with patients and their families. This is the most important step in creating change in the present structure and culture and, more importantly, to directly meeting the needs of people in suffering.

Indeed, through my reflections on all this research and work, I have come to see how this particular issue of death and dying in Japan serves as a microcosm for all the other social problems we have. In the true Buddhist view of interconnectedness, one can see directly, as Carl Becker has shown in his chapter, the connections to Japan's economic, human relationship, and spiritual problems. In this way, the wall between the pre- and postmortem worlds that serves as the central theme of this chapter is simply a reflection of our segmented and fragmented Japanese society. Today, people commonly speak of this situation as *mu-en shakai*—a society of no interrelationship. It is not ironic at all that one can see the Buddhist foundations in this term *mu-en*, in which *en* refers to the "karmic relationship" that we as Japanese have tried to preserve for generations upon generations through our Buddhist forms of ancestor veneration. Yet today, we have arrived at this place of *mu-en*, no relationship, where in particular people are dying alone without each other's support.[14]

From a Buddhist standpoint, I feel it is less important for priests to develop new doctrinal and ritualistic applications for dying than it is to become deeply involved with the very experience of death by engaging directly with people before they die. From each individual priest's own personal experience in such work, we will see the development of meaningful Buddhist responses and initiatives. This is the real way to recover the meaning and role of Buddhism concerning death and dying and in turn to recover Buddhism's role in Japanese society at large. As the dying issue is part of a much larger holistic social problem, by engaging in it actively and directly, we can touch the many other social issues that need our attention today and come to a much broader holistic solution to them.

JAPAN
"True Regard": Shifting to the Patient's Standpoint of Suffering in a Buddhist Hospital

Moichiro Hayashi

INTRODUCTION TO THE KOSEI VIHARA

Kosei Hospital, affiliated with the lay Buddhist denomination Rissho Kosei-kai, established its Fuyu, or "supporting friends," Center, which includes a Palliative Care and Vihara Ward, in April 2004. As of April 2008, there were 3,468 beds for palliative care in Japan with 331 in the city of Tokyo, which has a population of almost 13 million people. Kosei Hospital has a total of 363 beds, which means if we converted our entire hospital to specialize in palliative care and hospice we would roughly match the number in the entire city of Tokyo. This highlights the serious lack of palliative care and hospice facilities in Japan at this critical stage of our aging population. Out of Kosei Hospital's total of 363 beds, we have twelve private rooms with single beds in our Palliative Care and Vihara Ward.[1] Each private room also has a sofa bed that families often use for overnight stays. In one case, we had a female patient whose husband would commute back and forth from his job to her room at the Vihara. The Vihara also has a multipurpose room for social events for patients and families, training sessions for staff, and a Buddha image for religious services.[2]

The Vihara Ward is a place for those who desire to ease both the mental and physical pain caused by cancer. Treatment is decided in consultation with the patients and their families. We offer to palliate symptoms to the greatest extent possible but do not offer life-prolonging treatment. The Vihara Ward will neither speed up nor delay death. There is the possibility of using substitute or folk remedies within the Vihara's capacities. In general, our focus is to (1) get rid of the side effects of patients' previous treatments, (2) relieve their pain using morphine, and (3) support their appetite.[3] The Kosei Vihara uses an extensive team-care system of doctors, medical social workers, nutritionists, pharmacists, office staff, religious professionals, and other specialists as well as volunteers to support the patient and family.

The process for admittance to the ward begins upon receiving a formal request from a patient or family. The head of the nursing staff and a medical social worker (MSW) will inquire about the patient's condition and wishes while at the same time explaining about the Vihara Ward to the patient and his or her family. There is no charge for this initial consultation. Afterward, the Admissions Examination Committee conducts an external examination and decides on admission based on the following provisions: (1) due to national insurance regulations, the Vihara only accepts cancer patients with malignant tumors who no longer wish to receive active treatment; (2) the Vihara only accepts patients who wish to receive an explanation of the actual name and condition of their illness as well as make an acknowledgment of having received such an explanation after entrance to the Vihara; (3) the Vihara has no regulations to accept or bar patients based on their religious affiliation or general religiosity.

Once patients are admitted, there are no special limitations to their needs and requests, outside of our concern for the utmost safety of other patients and not imposing on them and their families. With the mutual consent of patients and their families, there can be visitation at any time. Families may also spend the night at the Vihara. There is the possibility for patients to go out on visits, stay out overnight, and be released entirely from the ward. Pets may be brought into the patient's room, and ways to accommodate a patient's lifestyle, like drinking alcohol, can be considered.

Cancer is an awful disease, but it is also wonderful in that after receiving a terminal prognosis there is usually time to attend to matters with one's leftover time. On average, a patient will stay for one month in the ward, though our policy is to admit patients who have a prognosis of six months or less to live. In the first stage of this time, patients have to reevaluate who they are and decide how they will spend this time. In the next stage, they have to make a decision on where they want to be, either at home with hospice care or here at the Vihara. In the final stage, life is lived slowly and final conversations with loved ones take place. About 70 percent of our patients experience their final moments surrounded by their families. However, we also feel strongly that vihara and hospice are not just for helping patients die but also for helping families with the grieving that comes afterward.[4]

PALLIATING PHYSICAL PAIN AND CONFRONTING SPIRITUAL PAIN

In general, health is defined by the medical studies field and is, thus, based on a scientific perspective. The World Health Organization (WHO) has defined health:

> Health is a state of complete physical, mental, and social well-being, and not merely the absence of disease and infirmity.[5]

Recently, there are also people who have made definitions in which health is not just about being blessed with mental well-being but also spiritual well-being. If we regard health not so much as a field of medicine but rather as an art or a problem of the heart and mind, then perhaps the conventional understanding of "health" might not reflect what health really is. In Japanese, we use the term "complete health" (*kenzen*) when speaking of a healthy person.

In this way, when we consider the condition of the patients who enter the Kosei Vihara, we have those who cannot walk and even those who cannot speak. However, these people are able to demonstrate their intentions. They may not be able to live beyond one month, but if you remove their pain, they can spend this time freely on their own. They might fear death, but these kinds of people are in a much healthier situation than those in the everyday world who have physical health but are stressed, have anxiety, and think every morning that they want to die. While trying to fight their illnesses, our patients are not filled with anger or malice toward other people and can thank the people who are close to them. In this way, can we call them sick people? I think the phrase "sick people" does not fully describe them. If you can call this state of positive intentionality "healthy," then you can say they are healthy. I think that is what the WHO definition of health is trying to say. In this case, even though they are looking death right in the eye, it is quite irrelevant to their overall health condition. What is more important is the manner in which these people can continue to live.

It is quite easy to remove physical pain by using morphine, contrary to what people would think. We have only been running our palliative care unit since 2004, yet we have enough practice to remove the physical pain of patients 99 percent of the time. The pain can be removed unless a mistake is made in preparing the treatment. The more intense problems we face are the mental ones, especially regarding problems between families. We are really unable to solve these matters. No matter how much anesthetic we use, we cannot remove this pain. When this kind of pain appears, we cannot remove it from the specified place, because it comes from words. The more you remove the physical pain, the more patients' daily lives settle down. However, their spiritual pain may not go away and may actually increase. Therefore, when patients know that their families are there to support, it really helps them to calm down. When I say this kind of thing, people ask me, "Is it good or bad to remove pain? Is it then better to have some physical pain?" Of course it is better not to have physical pain. If patients are enduring serious physical pain, they will want to die quickly and will not have any free time to think about spiritual pain. It does not make sense to call such a physical situation a kind of spiritual pain.

However, even if a patient is physically falling apart, he or she may be able to say to his or her family members that it is all right for them to go home, because the patient is mentally and emotionally fine. I think the ability to make this point is important, and it happens more often than you would think. In one such case, there was a patient who said such a thing while he was breathing in great distress. Why did he say he was okay? Everyone in the family could clearly understand that it had become impossible for him recover. Yet his family was able to share his thinking with him, because of how close they were; they understood he was departing this world. Because of this kind of family, it is certain that this patient could say, "There is nothing to worry about; it's okay." There was only this thought in the end. Because the family relationship was fulfilled, he was "okay."

This is something that Rev. Yoshiharu Tomatsu, whose writing also appears in this volume, has talked with me about. In coming to face death, patients who have a connection with their family, the doctor, or a nurse, can die peacefully. Even if they do not have family on hand at the time of death and are alone in bed staring up at the ceiling, they are not lonely at the time of death. Rev. Tomatsu said that from our own perspective, we probably think that if no family is there at the moment of death, then it is a pity. In reality, however, people who die understand their own death from conversations with their family. By coming to such an understanding, there is no such sense of loneliness. If there is a patient who has come close to and had real communication with a caregiver, then even when directly facing death that person can have peace of mind. Humans after all will live their lives, and then they must die.

If you work in medicine in general and especially in dealing with the final moments of dying people, I think "loneliness" becomes a common way of speaking about the situation. But I do not think terminal patients are *necessarily* lonely. The important thing is the promise that is made between a patient and his or her family or caregiver. For example, when a patient says it is okay for his family to go home, they still need to make a promise to come back, such as the next morning at 9:00 a.m. At all costs, they then must come the next morning at 9:00 a.m. If they cannot come the next morning at 9:00 a.m., then it is okay to promise to come the next day, as long as a promise is made and fulfilled. As we observe patients and families, there are families that only come once a week to visit but are still firmly bonding. On the other hand, there are those families that come quite often but go home quickly. In this case, if I say to the patient, "Your son came to visit today. When is he coming next time?" the patient says he does not know. He wonders whether his son will come the next day or not, and then suddenly he becomes anxious. Therefore, I always ask families to please be punctual in their routine. If they do not keep their promises, in the end the patient will become lonely and will increasingly complain of pain.

DEALING WITH SPIRITUAL CARE IN A SECULAR ENVIRONMENT

In the WHO's definition of palliative care, there is the addition of a spiritual element:

> Palliative care is an approach that improves the quality of life of patients and their families facing the problems associated with life-threatening illness, through the prevention and relief of suffering by means of early identification and impeccable assessment and treatment of pain and other problems, physical, psychosocial, and spiritual.[6]

The problem for most Japanese, however, is that they cannot understand why the term "spiritual" should be added to the definition of health. In general, it is said that religion provides an answer for people about what to do in difficult times. When I see Christian patients, they almost always have an icon, a statue of Mary, or a cross. In this way, I can understand how Christians do little things. I think this is quite different from typical Japanese Buddhists. On the other hand, the patients at the Kosei Vihara who are Rissho Kosei-kai members tend to be more openly religious, such as having sutras and a rosary at their bedside. There was once a patient who was a member of Tenri-kyo, a Shinto-based new religious denomination, but he was not as overt in showing his faith. In general, we, the Kosei Vihara, stay out of these matters, because we feel they are personal.

The Kosei Vihara is the first hospice in Japan owned by a Buddhist denomination. The Vihara Ward at Nagaoka Nishi Hospital in Niigata is well known for having Buddhist priests on call, especially ones from the Jodo Shin Pure Land denomination. However, the ward does not belong to this or any other religious group; it is a standard medical institution. Almost all of the people who come to the Kosei Vihara ask about our relationship to religion. They do not know that we actually do not allow religious professionals open access to enter this place. It is not that we reject them but that the patients simply do not request them. When we established this vihara, we listened to the vihara priests and the thinking of people who visited us from Nagaoka Nishi Hospital. We thought we needed chaplains on call twenty-four hours a day, 365 days a year, and so we were able to create such a system with everyone's cooperation. However, after a year or two had passed, we found that there was no demand from anyone to talk with such chaplains.

Certain requests, though, did come out little by little. For example, a volunteer might be pushing a wheelchair when a patient would say, "Excuse me but . . . can I say something?" and would share a personal trouble or worry. The volunteer would then respond, "You seem to have some spiritual pain. I know someone who you can talk with about this. The person on that photo there that says 'mental counselor' will listen to you," and indicate a psychological professional. However, Japanese dislike psychological professionals peering into their inner life. Many of them do not express this directly but simply say that they don't want to see them and that they are happy just talking with the usual volunteers.

The problem with bringing up religious or spiritual topics is that if people do not accept these topics when they are healthy, they don't have any room to accept them when they become sick either. By that time, they are just struggling to live. After becoming hospitalized is not the time to begin religious dialogue. For example, we had a patient who was the head of his temple parishioner's association (*danka sodai*). Once he was hospitalized, he talked about such matters as his temple undergoing reconstruction and so on. We thought that he was somewhat interested in religious conversations and that it would be nice to have someone for him to do that with. Thus, for the first time at Kosei Hospital, we called in a mental counselor. However, the conversations became too difficult for the patient. He complained that he was tired and had had enough already, so we stopped. For this person, rather than talking about such inner matters, talking about something more concrete, like taking a pilgrimage to the one hundred famous Buddhist temples in Japan, would probably have been best. For a patient staying in the hospital, talking about "What does it mean to live?" can get complicated.

There are occasionally traditional Buddhist priests among the patients who have entered Kosei Hospital. One time we had a patient who was a Soto Zen priest and the father of my senior colleague's wife. He was really an authentic monk, so when he arrived, I wondered what kind of things he would do in this situation. However, it ended up not mattering that he was a priest. He did not chant sutras in the morning or do any such overt religious practice. I guess that he could have been chanting in his mind, but he did nothing that was obvious. We often say to the families of patients that even a doctor is not treated as a doctor when he becomes a patient here. If there is a patient who is a medical professional, we do not want him to ask other family members medical questions. We are the medical professionals. Therefore, it is our job to speak about what we know and not the role of the family. In the same way, I think that for us to talk about religion with a patient just because he or she is a religious professional is not appropriate. Even though a person is a priest, it does not make a difference once he or she becomes a patient. We treat that person just as one of the patients.

When the founder of Rissho Kosei-kai, Rev. Nikkyo Niwano (1906–99), entered the hospital here during his final days, I do not know whether he was reciting the sutras or doing anything overtly religious. At that time, though, a member of the staff asked him about the purpose of the daily morning service and sutra chanting, saying,

"What should we pray for and why?" He answered, "It is like brushing one's teeth every day. If you don't do it, then the mind does not become clear, and you cannot proceed with your daily living." I think this expression sums up the point that religious practice is not about thinking about what one should do externally but rather internalizing practice as a part of one's own body. In reality, a person who is a religious leader never dies like "a religious leader." I think that each person dies in his or her own way.

At the same time, I have increasingly come to believe that it is important to be open about the religious base of our hospital and to know the religion of our patients. Here at Kosei Hospital, there is a questionnaire that nurses must give patients when they first arrive. One of the questions at the end asks, "What's your religion?" There was one nurse who said, "Dr. Hayashi, we have to ask people about their religion, but it's hard to do so." Then I asked her, "Why?" The nurse replied, "It shouldn't matter what religion the patient is." But that's not true. For example, if a patient is Muslim, there is a chance that this person will want to pray five times a day in the direction of Mecca. He or she may also have particular requests about food or something else. This kind of person may not come to our hospital, but if one does, we have to think about what to do about such things. The reason why we ask about religion is not because we are a religious hospital. Although we have a principal religious image in the Buddha, we are not focused on emphasizing our religiosity. However, I want us to be careful about respecting the religion of the patient. Therefore, we ask patients in order to respect their religion.

I have asked a number of Buddhist priests whether it is all right to speak this way to patients. Even they quickly retorted, "Dr. Hayashi, it is strange to ask what religion they have." They have also said, "This question is strange. Everyone is free concerning religion." If I argue that we need to know in order to respect their practice, they say, "Well yes that's true, but I dare say, isn't it all right not to ask?" I think that is strange, maybe because I'm not a priest. It seems Japanese do not like to show their religiosity for fear of the opinions or judgments of others.

Religion is nothing more than the entrance into the truth of all things. We Japanese have received explanations on this matter by such great teachers as Rev. Niwano, the thirteenth-century reformer Nichiren, and Saicho, the founder of the Tendai denomination in Japan. Yet every religion is leading us to the very thing that Rev. Niwano said is "true regard" (*shinkan*). This is the essence or spirit of the universe. We are nothing more than interpreters of this essence, so in a way, any religion is good enough. That is why for me it is not strange to ask about religion.

THE ROLE OF BUDDHISM FOR MEDICAL PROFESSIONALS

As someone who has been the head of a hospital owned by a religious group, I have been asked the difficult question of whether we have a different mission than other hospitals. The Kosei Hospital holds as its founding principle one verse from chapter 25 of the Lotus Sutra called "The All-Sidedness of the Bodhisattva Regarder of the Cries of the World." This verse speaks about the five different ways that the bodhisattva regards the world and the suffering of sentient beings, the first being "true regard." Rev. Niwano offered this verse on the founding of this hospital, explaining that "true regard" is to perceive the form and the situation of the suffering of humans in this world as well as to discern the true nature of suffering.[7] After receiving this message from him, I made the vow that this hospital should have doctors who work with the aim to not only treat the illness of the physical body but to diagnose and heal the illness of the spirit as well. I have also developed a feeling for the importance of coming into contact with patients moment by moment by being present with them, deeply listening to their feelings, and deeply perceiving them.[8]

From this basis, if I were to say what is unique about this hospital, it would be the general atmosphere. Every year when I greet all the new staff members, I can recognize if they are Rissho Kosei-kai followers as soon as I hear them speak. When other doctors come here, they always say the nurses are kind and laid back—in a good way.

They are not as strict and tense as nurses from most other university hospitals. Our nurses are honest and have had a laid-back rhythm ever since they were Kosei students. I think this is a good point of our hospital. A person who, like myself, has spent time here since residency would never feel uncomfortable when another staff member speaks about the founder of Rissho Kosei-kai, Rev. Nikkyo Niwano. That person might have curiosity aroused by such conversation and take a look at the Buddhist sutras.

This reminds me of one case with a family who were shown the Vihara and also our statue of Shakyamuni Buddha. They remarked, "Yep, this place is run by a religious group. Let's go somewhere else." According to the people who gave the tour, their reaction was probably due to thinking we would thrust our beliefs upon them. At the other main Buddhist vihara in Japan, Nagaoka Nishi Hospital, they also feel that having an image of Shakyamuni Buddha is important. Nevertheless, people who go there still ask, "Is this place religious?" On the other hand, if you go to St. Luke's International Hospital in Tokyo, people do not ask if the place is religious. Of course they know it is. These are the kinds of irrational attitudes toward religion that people have in Japan. In this way, we are carrying on somewhat single-handedly. We feel that we should have a system in which at least the people who work at our hospital can feel proud about what they do. We want the people on the inside of our hospital to carry on with nursing while also thinking in a traditional Buddhist manner of gentleness.

However, the feeling of a doctor who has come here from a university hospital, who was not raised as a follower of our denomination, is indeed totally different. In this situation, it is difficult for that doctor to understand terms like "true regard." For example, at first we would not show young doctors applying as clinical interns the seventh floor where the Buddha Hall and altar are located. At that time, the Vihara still had not been established on that floor either. If we had shown them that floor, they probably would have had some uncomfortable feeling, since it is rare to have religious facilities in Japanese hospitals. However, over time I have begun to develop a different feeling about this. Now I make sure to show the interns the Buddha Hall on the seventh floor. Every year there are at most two new interns, and when they get the tour, none of them say they feel uncomfortable and just leave.

When we visit the Buddha and look at the statue, I ask them, "Do you notice anything particular in the Buddha statue?" They mostly say they do not know. I tell them that when patients look at the statue, they often do not say that the face is tender or the gaze is kind. Rather, they say that the hands are tender. Undoubtedly, this indicates their sense of pain in the body, and their desire to be caressed to make the pain go away. Then I ask these young interns about the meaning of treatment in terms of how much a doctor listens and becomes familiar with a patient's point of view. The point I want them to see is the more you know, the more you may understand. When patients say they don't like some treatment but don't explain how they dislike it, if you cannot persuade them that there is enough personal benefit in the treatment, you had best not do it. You have to say to them, "Since you don't want to do it, then we won't do it." Similarly, patients often tell us, "I'm fine with the treatment. I'm fine with the surgery. In any case, I'll be asleep. But one month after the surgery, will I have returned to normal?" That is the viewpoint of the patient. We medical staff want to talk all the time about surgery, but patients want to know about the return to their way of life. In the end, only a few doctors are able to develop such an attitude toward patients' needs.

I think by going back to our Buddhist origins we can support the salvation of the mind and heart of our patients by entering into their daily lives and those of their families. If we, who have come to work in medicine, do not look at it from the patient's viewpoint, we have undoubtedly entered the issue "with our shoes on"—that is, we've been selfish and rude. The people cannot accept this from us. This is the experience I have had since starting here five years ago. There is certainly no textbook at present in Japanese about hospice wards like our vihara unit. In textbooks, this kind of space is not taught.

THE FUTURE ROLE OF TRADITIONAL JAPANESE BUDDHISM IN SPIRITUAL CARE

Buddhism was introduced to Japan in the sixth century and gradually entered into the lives of all Japanese. However, for various reasons, it has become distant over the last sixty years, and now everyone speaks of how Buddhism is no longer a part of daily life. In the past in Japan, when one was suffering, one first went to talk with someone. My grandfather was a village doctor, and people came to consult with him about anything. In his generation, the wisest people in the village were the schoolteacher or the doctor. However, even in those days, there were also people who would go to see the Buddhist priest. Nowadays, the social community, which includes the family, has become dispersed. There are no bonds. There are no traditional hospitals. Even memorial services are now not being done, especially by the young generation. The old system of delivering mental and spiritual care has collapsed, or we can at least say that the number of people who perform such roles has decreased. In short, the organic culture of the traditional Japanese system is rotting away.

Nowadays in a family, if a son becomes out of control, there is no support coming from the temple. So who will help resolve this matter? Are Buddhist priests or organizations making an effort to help this situation? Religion, which originally bore a central role in this matter, does absolutely nothing now. The center of every denomination has withdrawn from such work. They are simply focusing on maintaining their own organizations. Rev. Tomatsu and others have talked about the problem of "Funeral Buddhism," in which priests and temples seem only concerned with making their living off of people after they have died.

Contrary to Japan, Buddhist monks in Southeast Asia must go out every single day to beg for alms. In those countries, Buddhism is internalized through such daily living. Because of this, if a monk asks a common person, "What's the matter?" he or she will probably answer straight away. However, in Japan, if one day a priest suddenly appears and asks, "What's the matter?" the response will be something more like, "If you are asking about the funeral, we have prepared for that." If Japanese priests suddenly start coming to hospitals to visit patients, the patients may naturally respond in an unwelcoming way saying, "What does he want? Money for a posthumous name (*kaimyo*)?" If the patient's condition is not good, he or she might say, "Why does the priest come today? I'm still alive, damn it!" In this way, Buddhist priests must first show the people how Buddhism can have meaning in the midst of everyday life.

It has come to a point that all patients including those with cancer have begun wanting spiritual care from medical institutions that deal with total, not just physical, pain. Doctors as well as all nurses increasingly understand this sensibility. At viharas, more than at usual hospitals, there will be such people, and that is the reason these places get such a high evaluation. In this way, I think the demand for hospitals with vihara facilities will tend to increase from now. Citizen volunteer groups have also emerged, and there are now groups like bereaved family support associations. However, it is certain that these groups are not enough to meet the demands. In this way, when we think about Japanese religious culture as a whole, we should ask, "Can it respond to the 'wants' of the people, especially those who are ill?" If the present situation continues, I think there will not be any such demands made of religious organizations in the near future. Rev. Tomatsu and others have said that this is something that they have to confront. He said to me, "Dr. Hayashi, it will take hundreds of years, but we are already moving in that direction." I think that there are Buddhists who are working hard to enter this field, like Rev. Tomatsu and Inoue Vimala of Koyasan University. However, are priests really going to be able to become clinicians?

In terms of pallitive care, I really dislike the use of the term "needs." I first heard this term about twenty years ago. We always speak about necessity, but necessity is different from what is being requested by the patient. Needs and wants are different. In the Kosei Vihara, we thought we *needed* a mental counselor. However, the reality has been that, from the patients' standpoint, they do not have such demands or "wants." The thing to do is to understand the patients' point of view to learn what they want in addition to what they need. At hospitals that are doing an incomplete job, they say to patients, "If you need anything, just give us a call." I think this is not something to be satisfied with, because normal people do not know how to ask for what they want. They do not know the proper way to ask. Therefore, we have had to figure out how to handle this situation. It is not good that a patient's demands become a justification for any kind of need, but it is all about the patient's point of view in the end. I have specialized in prenatal care and now in hospice care, but I still do not have the answers regarding life and death, so I have to continue to work to understand the patient's own point of view.

I also have reservations about the terms "spiritual pain" and "grief care," which many people in Japan now talk about. I feel like they do not know what they are talking about, because Japanese Buddhism, with its wakes and funeral ceremonies and so forth, is all about grief care. As Carl Becker points out in his chapter, we Japanese have been doing it already for centuries. Every single year, Japanese make a large fire at the summer Obon festival to welcome back for a few days the spirits of dead ancestors and relatives. As long as we treasure these traditions, then specialized grief care programs should not be needed. The reason this has become an issue today and that people say we need "grief care" is because we are not taking care of these traditions.

Here at the Kosei Vihara, we still do not have a bereaved family support group. I continue to wonder what that means, because in the public documents provided by the government on the establishment of hospices, it is written that bereaved family support groups and grief care are necessary services. In this situation, we must again return to the real demands of the patients. I think we have to create a system that enables us to take action immediately. However, we cannot just present Buddhism in a rather direct and artificial way. We should move toward thinking in a more natural manner. I do not know how many years this will really take, perhaps one hundred or even two hundred to three hundred years. However, in the process, we can steadily borrow from all standpoints, such as, of course, celebrating traditional Japanese New Year, putting up a Christmas tree, singing Pure Land hymns, and celebrating Hanamatsuri, the flower festival that is Buddha's birthday. When we do such things, there will be the elderly who say, "This brings back memories," but the young may not understand. However, all we can do is to try our best by properly carrying out such traditional-style grief care.

I would not say this is a small endeavor. However, the first generation of patients and families have passed through here now, and the second generation is starting to come back. There was a person who thought this would be a good place to come to die, because his older brother died here. There were other people who thought that since their own grandmother or father died here, they also want to come here. There was a person who thought, "Since my aunty came here, why not my uncle too?" Up to now, three such people have come back. For us, those people are three very major achievements. If you ask us about the level of care at Kosei Hospital, we can definitely say that over a period of three years, we have had three family members of three people who died in the Vihara come back here to die. Of the five hundred people who have been here, there are only three, but those three are very profound.

I think that from now other people will also want to return when they have such an experience. I do not really know to what extent people will return. It depends on how much energy we put into the process. Therefore, it undoubtedly depends on how we cultivate the second generation. Hospice is about getting intimate with patients. It is the ultimate form in that everything from catching a cold to having a pain somewhere to cystitis to tonsillitis involves palliative care. That is the palliation we must do. Doctors have so many ideas about palliative care, but it is not such a difficult matter. The basic thing is making the patient the center of things.

The main text, except where noted in footnotes, comes from an interview conducted January 14, 2009, from 1:00 to 3:00 p.m. at the office of the Director of Kosei General Hospital by the following staff members of the Rissho Kosei-kai magazine Dharma World: *Kazumasa Osaka (editor), Katsuyuki Kikuchi (editorial staff), Toru Nakagawa (senior staff writer). The text was then edited and translated by Rev. Jin Sakai and Jonathan S. Watts.*

JAPAN
The Vihara Movement:
Buddhist Chaplaincy and Social Welfare

Yozo Taniyama

THE EVOLUTION OF FUNERAL BUDDHISM IN JAPAN

Funeral Buddhism (*soshiki bukkyo*) is an important keyword in considering Japanese Buddhism. In the Japanese religious tradition, ancestor worship was syncretized with Buddhist rituals by the Middle Ages, and the form was further fixed by the time of the Edo Shogunate (from the seventeenth to the nineteenth centuries). In this system, more than 90 percent of funeral services were carried out in a Buddhist style at home or at a temple until the twentieth century. The income from funerals eventually became the basis for temple management. However, Funeral Buddhism has faced a turning point in recent years. The number of funerals now held at funeral homes and performed in a non-Buddhist style has increased, as well as the performing of a *chokuso*, a simple cremation without rituals. The Buddhist temple was traditionally one of the centers of the community; priests carried out funerals in cooperation with the local community. However, now some of the roles of priests have been taken over by undertakers and the many different kinds of funeral homes.

As part of the customs of Funeral Buddhism, people automatically participate in the weekly, monthly, and yearly memorial services after the funeral—that is, every seventh day until the seventh week or forty-ninth day; the hundredth day; every month on the date of death; the first anniversary; and the anniversaries of third, seventh, thirteenth, seventeenth, twenty-third, twenty-seventh, thirty-third, and fiftieth years. The monthly memorial service was an especially important function to develop the relationship between the priest and his parishioners. In this system, a priest would visit the parishioner's house to chant sutras in front of the home Buddhist altar (*butsudan*) in which mortuary tablets (*ihai*) of deceased family members are installed. However, this custom, and thus also the relationship, has become weaker, principally because many people have relocated to other regions and do not know the name of the temple to which their parents belonged. Consequently, when a new death in the family occurs and they are introduced to an unknown priest through the intermediation of an undertaker, they may not ask for such extended memorial services after the funeral. Thus, the relationship between Buddhism and funerals is changing.

Many priests have not been able to find concrete solutions to this crisis. According to a questionnaire of Buddhist priests that the Japan Young Buddhist Association carried out in 2003,[1] about half of the respondents criticized Funeral Buddhism, making remarks like, "I am not actively concerned with living people," and "My activities incline toward funeral services." Of these respondents, 85 percent were priests less than forty years old. They feel more a sense of impending crisis in comparison to elderly priests. Their reflections that rituals are heavy and human relationships are thin is the focal point of the criticism. Before modern times, priests were concerned with the deathbed process of common people. Deathbed rituals had been required by devoted laypeople. Priests also gave the certificate of death and executed the funeral. In the twentieth century, the number of people who die at hospitals has increased so that now 78 percent meet their end there.[2] On the other hand, the role of the priest at the deathbed has declined. When a priest enters a hospital in black robes, he is evaded. He is only called in after the death of the believer to chant sutras. This indicates why priests in the questionnaire said they are not "actively concerned with living people."

The main purpose of this chapter is not to deny Funeral Buddhism itself, but rather to introduce the Vihara Movement as a response by some priests to the criticisms from society. The idea of the vihara priest

or Buddhist chaplain has been an indispensable part of the development of the Vihara Movement, and therefore, a training program for
chaplains was necessarily created. However, I feel their field of work
should not be limited to only medical settings. If an organization
could be established that is linked with local temples, such chaplains
could play an active role as health care specialists, not only at hospitals
but also in the local community.

WHAT IS THE VIHARA MOVEMENT?

Vihara is both a Sanskrit and Pali term that means "temple," "monastery," or "place of the rest." Rev. Masashi Tamiya, a priest of the
Higashi Honganji or Otani branch of the Jodo Shin Pure Land
denomination, proposed it in the early 1980s as a substitute word
for "Buddhist hospice," and the term came to indicate "terminal
care based on Buddhism and the institution that provides it." Since
vihara usually means just a "temple" or "monastery," especially in
Theravada Buddhist countries, some of the readers might feel some
incongruity. However, monasteries in ancient India had lodgings for
pilgrims, and large ones had facilities for medical care, social welfare,
and education for local people. The Jetavana Vihara was established
during the lifetime of the Buddha, and after centuries, it came to
house medical facilities, including a "house for the dying" or "abbey
of impermanence" (*mujo-in*) for terminal nursing care.[3] This background of the term *vihara* reminds us of the history of hospice in
Buddhism. Hospices in Europe during the Middle Ages also started
as lodging places for pilgrims and then developed into medical and
social welfare facilities. Therefore, *hospice* and *vihara* have a common
point in their development and function. Japanese Buddhists who
first participated in the hospice movement here were reluctant to use
the word "hospice" as it is derived from Christianity. Therefore, they
chose the Buddhist term as a banner for their movement.

Although the Vihara Movement is not a complete response to the
criticism of Funeral Buddhism, its concept includes the reformation
and the reactivation of Japanese Buddhism. Rev. Tamiya was affected

by the hospital sermons started in 1984 by the Kyoto Young Buddhist Association (now called Bhagavan Kyoto), which is an ecumenical Buddhist group. He then began to promote the Vihara Movement as an ecumenical activity in 1985. After him, the Nishi Honganji or Honpa Hongwanji branch of the Jodo Shin denomination created vihara activities in 1986. Rev. Shunko Tashiro of the Higashi branch then started vihara activities at the Nagoya Higashi Betsuin headquarters temple as a foothold in 1988. The Nichiren denomination started their vihara activities in 1994. Aditionally, volunteer organizations of the Vihara Movement were formed in many cities. Some are denominationally based while others are ecumenical. There is no particular difference between the terms "Vihara Movement" and "vihara activities."

The starting point of the Vihara Movement was terminal care. In total, there are 208 certified palliative care units in Japan as of December 2010, yet only two of these are Buddhist based. The first one was created at the Nagaoka Nishi Hospital in Niigata in 1993 and is nonsectarian. The second was created at Kosei Hospital in Tokyo in 2004 and is run by the Rissho Kosei-kai denomination. The third will be the Asoka Vihara Clinic in Kyoto, which was established in 2008 by the Nishi branch of Jodo Shin, but is not yet certified as not enough of the patients have cancer or are terminal. However, besides palliative care units, there are several vihara institutions and organizations for the welfare of the elderly, disabled persons, and children, as well as for counseling. Most of them are grassroots based.

In this way, I have defined *vihara* in three ways:

Narrow Definition: Terminal care based on Buddhism and the institutions that provide it.

Wider Definition: Activities and institutions managed by Buddhists that are focused on aging, sickness, and death in the fields of medical and social welfare.

Widest Definition: Social activities managed by Buddhists and non-Buddhists that support the lives of people and provide opportunities for the contemplation of "life," such as disaster aid, education for children and youth, and cultural programs.[4]

Although many Buddhists and concerned people use both the narrow and the wider definitions, my investigation has shown that the actual activities of vihara institutions fit the wider and the widest definitions. Therefore, we will mainly use the wider definition in this chapter; in the future, it may be possible that the widest one will be mainly used. In the development of the Vihara Movement, it is the chaplain who forms the core. In the next section, I will describe the situation, surroundings, and education programs of chaplains in Japan.

The Role of the Vihara Priest

At vihara institutions, the Buddhist chaplain is called a "vihara priest." Unfortunately, at most such institutions, most of the staff are not believers of the related religious group; thus, the religious idea is not thoroughly understood, and the chaplains do not always have a role of authority. However, chaplains can show the characteristics of Buddhism through their actions just as much as they might show someone the Buddha hall. Their role is thus very important.

Rev. Masashi Tamiya's brother manages the Nagaoka Nishi Hospital, which serves as a symbol and exemplar of the Vihara Movement. Local priests have been cooperating with the activities there even before the establishment of the Vihara Ward, a Buddhist hospice. One chaplain is a full-time employee, and ten to twenty volunteer chaplains also play active roles. They have a volunteer group that is financially supported by over one hundred priests and laypeople from several denominations. At the hospital, 27 out of a total of 240 beds are used for the Vihara Ward, and the chaplain belongs to only this ward. There is not a chaplain for the other wards. The roles of the vihara priests at Nagaoka Nishi Hospital are as follows:

(1) Religious Services: A chaplain will chant sutras every morning and evening as well as holding seasonal religious events. When a patient wants a chaplain to chant a sutra for him or her or to have a religious talk, the chaplain is available to do so at any time at the Buddha hall or at their bedside. I remember an extraordinary patient who had a small Buddhist altar (*butsudan*) in her room to worship and to communicate with her late daughter. She welcomed any chaplain to chant in front of the altar. There are volunteer chaplains from several different denominations, so that if a patient wants to see a priest from a specific denomination, the full-time chaplain will arrange for that. Unfortunately, at almost all hospitals in Japan, patients' daily religious activity, like chanting Amida Buddha's name, is kept private and hidden by the patients themselves, even though chaplains can help with many kinds of religious services. As I mention below, it is a Japanese custom to hide religious matters in public places.

When a patient dies, a chaplain is called on at any time of day. If the full-time chaplain is out, a volunteer one will come to the hospital. The dead patient is given a bath by the hands of their primary nurse and the bereaved family, which is similar to a Buddhist ritual called *yukan*. After the deceased is dressed, the bereaved and staff gather at the Buddha hall. A chaplain will do sutra chanting and give a sermon, after which all participants will offer incense in turn. The deceased is then taken away, usually by undertakers, but sometimes by the bereaved family itself. The staff sees them off at the door of the hospital.

(2) Spiritual Care: A chaplain provides spiritual care for patients and family members. When a patient wants a chaplain to provide spiritual care, the chaplain does so according to the patient's faith and not his or her own. A nurse may also come to talk with a chaplain, when he or she gets very tired with his or her job or daily life. A physician may seek advice from the chaplain on sedation, intravenous control, notification of the limit of lifetime, and other ethical matters.

I had one interesting and impressive case with a patient who was born into a Catholic family. At one point, she became devoted to a new Christian denomination, but she eventually left the sect after several years. She continued to believe in many of the sect's teachings, however, and this lead her to fear that she might cease to exist after her death. I wondered why she did not believe in heaven, even though she appeared to believe in Christianity. I asked her, "You said that you will cease to exist after your death. Don't you believe in the Resurrection and Judgment Day?" She answered, "I was instructed that we must wait for the Resurrection, but that 13,000 chosen people have already been resurrected soon after their death, so I don't know what will happen to me if I'm not one of the chosen." I said, "Well, some resurrect quickly, while others take a rest for some time." She said, "Yes." I said, "I see. The chosen people will resurrect and work for this world. That's great. But those who want to take a rest can do so in another world for some time." She said with a smile, "Wow, this is the first time I've heard such an interpretation. So I can take a rest for some time then, can't I?" I said, "Yes, you can." Then she seemed relieved and thanked me by putting her hands together. While the content of the conversation was religious, our faiths were different from each other. It was an ecumenical experience for both of us.

(3) Grief Care: Days after a patient passes away, some of the bereaved family may come to the ward to have a talk with the staff, including a chaplain. Some of them may stay hours there with the chaplain. The Vihara Ward also hosts gatherings of bereaved families. One gathering is for the bereaved of less than one year. Another is for those over one year and is managed by people concerned for the bereaved members of the group. Both meetings have sutra chanting and incense offering at the Buddha hall as well as a tea party on another floor of the hospital. Former Vihara staff members are also invited to these meetings. The tea party is not structured like a self-help group, and the attendants talk freely.

(4) Cultural Events: Chaplains and staff plan and prepare seasonal events: cherry-blossom viewing in the spring, fireworks shows in the summer, colored-leaves viewing in the autumn, and an end-of-year

party in the winter. Each of the volunteers, and sometimes patients and their family members as well, play strong roles in these events—acting as drivers, cooks, waiters, builders, wheelchair attendants, and so on. For example, Nagaoka city is well known for its fireworks show, which serves as not only a cultural festival but also a memorial service for the victims of the air bombing in 1945 and of the earthquake in 2004. The Vihara Ward has a good roof from which to see the show where several beds can be set up. During this event, patients can forget their pain. In this way, patients aim to survive until such seasonal events.

(5) Team-Care Approach: A chaplain attends meetings for daily and weekly updates, for reviewing recent deaths, and for the multidisciplinary team. He provides new information about patients if needed. When a meeting with a patient, family members, nurses, and the presiding doctor is held, a chaplain will also attend. Sometimes a chaplain will help patients with decision making. For example, in the case of an old man with terminal cancer, the patient asked to stop his intravenous fluids. The doctor and the nurse in charge called for his wife, his relatives, and a chaplain (myself in this case). The patient said in a calm voice, "I don't want to prolong my life anymore. I want my intravenous fluids stopped now." His relationship with his family was not so good and his attitude was strong, so there was a tense and unpleasant atmosphere in the room. Then I said to him, "Life is not only for you. Life is shared by everyone. Shall we talk about it more? After talking more, we can make a decision." After a while his niece said, "We want you to live as long as possible." He in turn softened his attitude, and at last concluded, "Okay, I understand all of you want me to live more. I will prolong my life ten more days," after which he decided to reduce his fluids by half.

(6) Troubleshooting (between family members, staff members, and so on): Here I will show three cases of dealing with a patient's family, a chaplain in training, and the medical staff.

There was a case of the grandson of an old patient. He was a young adult aged twenty and emotionally unstable because of overlapping stresses, including anticipation of his grandmother's death. He began squealing in the ward, picking fights with staff members, and stalking a nurse. I confronted him, and fortunately we could develop a good relationship. He then began come to my room every day to talk about many issues and never made any more trouble. I did nothing more than act as his sitter for some weeks.

Another time, a monk came to our hospital from South Korea. He wanted to train as chaplain at the Vihara Ward, so we arranged everything for him. When I met him, we encountered some problems: first, he could speak little Japanese and only some English; second, he was overly aggressive and compulsive in attending to patients so that we worried he would become a bother to them; third, he told me that he wanted to preach to the patients. I became upset, especially with this last point. I explained that, in the concept of vihara, our aim is not to spread faith. However, he was too stubborn to understand our concept, so I actually had to ask him to leave. In Korea, it seems priests are respected and allowed to preach anywhere. The religious environment in Japan, however, is far different. He could not understand the simple maxim: "When in Rome, do as the Romans do."

Looking back on my three years at Nagaoka Nishi Hospital, one of my important failures as a chaplain is that I could not have good relationships with all the doctors, nurses, and volunteers. When I was employed as a chaplain, I did not understand what chaplaincy was really about. There were few notes and instructions at that time about being a full-time vihara priest. The role of the chaplain was vague among all of the staff, except for some routine work. I had to begin by clarifying the role of a chaplain as part of the medical team. I managed to clarify the nature of chaplaincy and reform its role. In short, I tried to increase the time spent seeing patients and their families, while skipping some of the routine work the medical staff expected of me. From the view of medical staff, it seemed that I was negligent and perhaps arrogant, since I did not share enough time to talk with them about my intentions to clarify and reform the role of the vihara priest.

Such misunderstandings seemed to have come from both my immaturity as a coworker and by the lack of understanding of chaplaincy.

THE WORKING ENVIRONMENT OF CHAPLAINS IN JAPAN

The term "chaplain" is not well known in Japan; it is generally only known to Christians—who only constitute 1 percent of the population. The chaplains at Christian medical, social welfare, and educational facilities are often given the title "director of religion." There are some examples of those with the title "vihara priest" at some Buddhist palliative care units. There are very few "chaplains" at non-religious medical and welfare facilities. The other kinds of terms used are "spiritual care worker," "pastoral care worker," "counselor," or "clinical spiritual care counselor." There have been prison chaplains in Japan since the nineteenth century, but they are not called "chaplains," rather they are called *kyokaishi*, which literally means "clergy who provides instruction and preaches." Since the name *vihara* is new even for Buddhists, few know that both vihara priests and *kyokaishi* are "chaplains."

Apart from the problem of the name, Japanese medical facilities are not an easy place for chaplains to work. An understanding of the roles of a chaplain is not shared among either medical staff or patients. A chaplain's work is not counted in the point system of public medical insurance, so the merits are not clear from the viewpoint of financial management.

Furthermore, most Japanese are not conscious about their own religion, although they are influenced by it. In a public opinion poll by the national *Yomiuri Shimbun* newspaper from May 30, 2008, about the outlook toward religion, responses to the question "Do you believe in any religion?" were 26.1 percent "yes" and 71.9 percent "no." However, to the question about participating in religious activities, most people said that they visit their family graves (78.3 percent), pray at Shinto shrines (73.1 percent), and pray before Buddhist and Shinto altars at home (56.7 percent). Only 3.9 percent answered that they do not engage in any religious activities. About three-quarters of the respondents were not active members of a specific religious community, yet most of them do worship ancestors or pray in a Buddhist or Shinto manner. In contemporary Japanese society, which has been heavily secularized, we refrain from talking about religious and spiritual matters in public places. It is the same in hospitals, where it is extremely rare for patients to appeal to medical staff about their own religious needs. In addition, the hospitals with no religious affiliation do not have chapels or a place to pray calmly. On the other hand, some patients do wear Buddhist rosaries, have sutra texts or the Bible at their bedside, and pray under the glancing eyes of medical staff. Once in my experience as chaplain at Nagaoka Nishi Hospital, there was a terminal patient at the vihara ward who, although he did want to have a conversation, was always counting numbers under his breath like, "245, 246, 247 . . ." I asked the reason for this of his family, and they answered, "When he was at the other hospital before, he recited Amida Buddha's name, *Namu Amida Butsu*. However, this was not appreciated by the other patients around him, so he began to recite numbers instead." In this way, patients will hide religious practices at hospitals in Japan in the same way they might hide alcohol or cigarettes.

One way that chaplains in Japanese hospitals can create a good working environment and perform their duties well is to be mindful of aggressive religiosity. People hate a pushy priest, and I have heard that some priests were forced to leave certain hospitals since they had given unexpected, unwelcome sermons to patients. We should think carefully about what it means to "save" a person. When we face a suffering girl, how can we answer her? It may be arrogant to answer, "I will save you." It is easy to answer, "The Lord will." It is difficult to answer, "I cannot." However, we can answer not just in words but with actual actions. If there is something we can do, we just do it. If not, we just listen to her, pray in silence, or seek the help of others. In this way, chaplains must distinguish between religious care and spiritual care. Only when a patient asks for a religious need can we respond to it. This is a very simple but important motivation in the Vihara Movement.

Another way is in their relationships with nurses and doctors. Who will call in a chaplain if he does not have any relationship with the medical staff? A basic relationship as a coworker with other medical staff members is very important. Chaplains must show other staff members that they can play a positive role for the whole hospital, especially in taking care of the stressed-out staff. Healing the staff can help the patients to heal.

Another thing to remember is that a well-trained priest has many skills to help people, but he is never almighty. When he faces a difficult case, he might become burned out. Who can help this priest? I feel a support network can help him before he becomes exhausted. We need a safety net for suffering priests in order to help suffering people.

EDUCATION AND TRAINING FOR CHAPLAINS

Some Japanese clergy are developing a system for the training of chaplains. Although Clinical Pastoral Education (CPE) is a common mandatory course at Christian theological schools in the West, unfortunately, it is offered at only a few schools in Japan. From the 1960s to 1980s, Protestant clergy played a key role in establishing a few institutions for CPE in Japan, but their work did not spread through the country. Rev. Tsugikazu Nishigaki, who is one of the pioneers of this work in Japan, emphasized that it is important to introduce CPE in theological education.[5] The Clinical Pastoral Education and Research Center of Japan directed by Rev. Fr. Waldemar Kippes has provided some courses and developed pastoral counselors since 1998. Led by the Catholic Church, it has made a large contribution toward pastoral care and counseling, but it is still not widely accepted among the medical community in Japan.

Some kinds of programs that are distinct from CPE are provided by Buddhists. Both the Nishi branch of the Jodo Shin denomination and the Nichiren denomination have training programs for volunteers of their vihara activities. The Nishi branch started their program in 1987, which includes clinical experience at elderly homes. Ryukoku University, which was established by the Nishi branch, cooperates with this program. Ryukoku University also established the Graduate School of Practical Shin Buddhism in 2009 and aims to educate priests as experts in social activities, including vihara activities.

In 1993, Rev. Tamiya played a key role in establishing a one-year graduate course in Buddhist nursing at Bukkyo Unversity, which is affiliated with the Jodo Pure Land denomination. It aimed to train vihara priests. However, it was closed down in 2006, because they could not attract enough students. I surmise that the program offered insufficient clinical experience and that the image of the vihara priest, of Buddhist nursing, was too obscure for many. Furthermore, the university did not seem to have a full understanding of this course, and they seemed to switch their policy away from a Buddhist approach.

In 2002, the Koyasan branch of the Shingon denomination opened courses for counselors and spiritual care workers under the direction of Rev. Daien Oshita. This served as an opportunity to establish the Department of Spiritual Care at Koyasan University in 2006. However, prospective students found attending the course in the remote mountain area of Mt. Koya unappealing, and student recruitment was stopped in 2009. In this brief period, although they did attract some adult students as well as teenagers, I think that an undergraduate course is not appropriate for training chaplains, which is a specialized and intensive field. The program could also not bring in compelling specialists as instructors. Rev. Oshita has since left the university, continuing on with the Japan Spiritual Care Worker Association. Many of the students at this association are medical staff while some are priests and lay Buddhists.

The Japan Association for Buddhist Nursing and Vihara Studies was established in 2004 by Rev. Tamiya, Akiko Hujihara, and some scholars, including myself. The name of this association shows its aim. The field of endeavor is not necessary limited to medicine and nursing; social welfare and education are also included.

The Professional Association for Spiritual Care and Health (PASCH) was established in 2005 and carries out the Program for Spiritual Care Chaplains, which can be said to be a Japanese version of CPE. PASCH is a unique association as it is managed by

Christians, Buddhists, and nonreligious persons; its supervisors are Rev. Toshiyuki Kubotera of the Free Methodist denomination, Rev. Taka-aki David Ito of the Anglican Church, and myself, of the Higashi Jodo Shin denomination. Rev. Kubotera and Rev. Ito were the second generation of Japanese chaplains developed by CPE who followed the lead of Rev. Nishigaki and others. As they are conscious of the problems in the spread of CPE in Japan, they have the following goals: to be ecumenical and multifaith, to have cooperation with public hospitals, and to join hands with Buddhists, since they comprise the majority among Japanese religions. In addition, because changing jobs and leaves of absence are not easy to obtain in Japan and the scholarship system is not well developed, full-time programs that last a month or a year like those in the United States are not appropriate. Therefore, they have developed short programs that attempt to condense fifty hours of instruction into one week.

The Grief Care Institute of Japan was established in 2009 at St. Thomas University and funded by the West Japan Railway Foundation. It was then transferred to Sophia University in April 2010, because St. Thomas University was in financial difficulty and stopped student recruitment in 2010. This institute has opened a Grief Care Worker training program under the direction of Rev. Sr. Yoshiko Takaki, who is one of the pioneers in grief care in Japan. I have also been invited to join the institute for this program. We train facilitators for self-help grief care groups and chaplains for professional grief care and spiritual care. We also provide continuing education for health care professionals. Our courses include PASCH's one-week short program and a four-month extended program. More than twice as many students as available openings took the entrance examination in 2009 and 2010. About one-third of the students are nurses, a few are Buddhist priests, and some are Catholic and Protestant laity. However, most of them have "no religion."

The task of chaplain training in Japan is to be ecumenical and to form a consensus about the role of spiritual care in health care, to create a place where religious persons and health care professionals can make a sincere connection to the spiritual needs of people, especially ones in suffering. The Japan Society for Spiritual Care was established in 2007 to take on such a role. Most of the members are medical professionals and experts in social welfare, psychology, and education. Christian, Buddhist, and Shinto clergy also participate.

What is the turning point between success and failure in these projects? I think the key points are market analysis, accessibility to the program, and clinical experience. For instance, Rev. Kippes has a large market for Catholic pastoral care; Rev. Kubotera and Rev. Ito have a good discernment of Japanese society. These groups are small nonprofit organizations, target working adults, and provide short-term programs. In addition, the trainers are clinically experienced. In contrast, Bukkyo University and Koyasan University failed to gather students because they are incorporated educational institutions concerned with profit making, were targeting young students, and provided long-term programs in which students had to resign from their jobs before entering the school. Furthermore, few of the trainers/teachers were clinically experienced, and many were rather academic.

The Future of the Vihara Movement

As seen in the chapter by Joan Halifax, the concept of Buddhist chaplaincy is beginning to transcend the field of terminal care. In Japan, the Vihara Movement is growing and is linked to the wider field of social welfare. However, the recognition and understanding of the role of the chaplain is still quite narrow. Therefore, I will not consider the future of Japanese Buddhism from the concept of chaplaincy; I would rather like to start from a wider view by considering it from the daily practice of a priest participating in the suffering of the people.

Funeral Buddhism Becomes Grief Care

In early Buddhist scriptures, the Buddha instructed the monks not to busy themselves with arranging and conducting his funeral, but to leave it to qualified laypeople and to continue on diligently with their practice.[6] However, even Theravada Buddhist monks, who are seen to follow early Buddhism more closely than Mahayana ones, do involve themselves with such funeral services. Of course, in Japanese Buddhism, the syncretization with ancestor worship since the Middle Ages has developed the performance of funeral services. As such, we should recognize that there is an inconsistency in the significance of funerals between Buddhist doctrine and folk religion. Rev. Kokan Sasaki, a Soto Zen priest, comments on this issue from the viewpoint of religious anthropology:

> Japanese society is beginning to cope with the significance and the role of funerals, which has been considered just as a tradition and custom. Now, people are asking these questions: Why is a funeral necessary? Why is a priest necessary for it? Buddhist denominations and priests must answer them. They should revise their doctrines and practice sincerely. This can answer the criticism of "Funeral Buddhism."[7]

When we consider grief care, we may also answer this question. As Carl Becker describes in his chapter, in the psychoanalytic view of Freud, attachment with the deceased is considered to be a pathological attitude; Freud advised that one should forget the dead. However, recent studies show that it is better to reconstruct the "bond" with the deceased. Dennis Klass took notice of the Japanese prescriptions for ancestor care:

- Take good care of a Buddhist altar and a mortuary tablet, and talk with the deceased as if he or she exists there.
- Do so in front of a grave as well.
- Invite the souls of those who have died to one's house during the Bon Festival, and see them off after hosting them for a few days.[8]

Klass went on to argue that such practices eased the grief of the bereaved, and that Buddhist death rituals, which maintain the "continuing bonds" with the bereaved, could be a form of grief care. Such a reconceptualization of traditional practices coming from an overseas researcher is a powerful call to Japanese Buddhist priests to not just blindly continue funeral rituals simply because they have always done so. Each denomination must reexamine its doctrine and rituals, while considering the grieving process. Although Funeral Buddhism is often used in the context of criticizing contemporary Japanese Buddhism, there are some priests, like Rev. Yoshiharu Tomatsu in his chapter, who have a positive way to look at their funeral work. It is, therefore, more constructive to reform Funeral Buddhism in line with real social needs rather than to seek to get rid of it.

The Temple as a Social Welfare Center

In the study of Buddhist social welfare in Japan, it has been shown that a temple has several social resources and that it can be a center for community welfare, nursery schools, and elderly homes. On the other hand, the research on Buddhist temples done in 1992–93 by Kairyu Shimizu and Tei-ichiro Hoshino reported that only 15 percent of the respondents, who were associated with temples but may not have been the chief priest, "engaged in social work." Concerning "problems when a temple performs social work," the following frequent answers were given:

- There is not enough manpower or funds.
- All of Buddhist society should engage in social work.
- There is not an incentive system offered by the denomination.
- Efforts by at least some temples / parish units are necessary.
- Operations adopted with a stronger Buddhist mind are necessary.[9]

A typical chief priest is very busy with religious services, duties as a member of the community, and his family; priests can only be active in vihara activities after having fulfilled these duties. Because most temples are managed by only one or two priests, when various new functions are added at a temple, like vihara activities, the burden is shouldered by them, and this never turns out well. In this way, one wonders, "Can we lighten the duties of priests to make their social work more active?"

Traditionally, priests have given advice or consultation to local people and members of the temple. This is a kind of social work or coordination work. When the matter is beyond the ability of a priest, he introduces an appropriate expert from his own connections. If every priest can share such connections at the local temple or parish level, he can cope with these problems more effectively. Temples can be more effective windows to care than other types of social work facilities; through the close relationships between priest and parishioner that Funeral Buddhism has promoted for hundreds of years, a priest can access a temple member and connect him or her to care more easily. A priest can intervene in various domestic problems that are hard for other social workers to do. In this way, more people will be helped without increasing the burden on a priest if such particular social resources are connected to a network of services.

I would like to suggest that we establish regional centers of Buddhist social welfare, so that each temple can become a window to a social welfare network. Social workers, health nurses, lawyers, and chaplains can be posted at a regional center, which links to a network of many priests and public resources as well as providing direct support for temple members in trouble. The types of services that could be offered are (1) counseling on psychosocial, spiritual, religious, economic, and legal issues; (2) self-help groups of the elderly, disabled, bereaved, abused, alcoholic, and so on; (3) dispatch of chaplains to medical and welfare institutions; and (4) referrals to outside specialized agencies. In this way, we could realize the aim of the Vihara Movement and activities as well as Buddhist social welfare. Such a network can help with spreading this movement, and the inheritance of Funeral Buddhism can be turned into practical use in the present age.

Conclusion

A quarter of century has passed since the Vihara Movement began. Meanwhile, Funeral Buddhism has changed greatly, and Japanese Buddhism has been driven into a corner. The result of the Vihara Movement has appeared at the grassroots level. However, it cannot be said that the whole of Japanese Buddhism has been influenced and reformed by this movement. An understanding of chaplaincy, which should form the core of the Vihara Movement, is not yet shared. Concerning the education of chaplains, some clergy are continuing efforts in multifaith cooperation. It may be a long path, but it is an important contribution to Japanese society. Change will happen gradually, but I feel more priests are now engaged in social action. While many people are still unconscious about their own religion, they are seeking something spiritual. Buddhism has unique resources that can meet the psychosocial and spiritual needs of suffering people.

USA/JAPAN
One Dies as One Lives:
The Importance of Developing Pastoral Care
Services and Religious Education

Mari Sengoku

INTRODUCTION

As a minister of the Nishi Honganji or Honpa Hongwanji branch of the Jodo Shin Pure Land denomination, as well as a hospital chaplain and psychotherapist, in Japan and Hawaii, I like to reflect on the words of the founder of Jodo Shin, Shinran Shonin (1173–1262): "Know that the Primal Vow of Amida makes no distinction between people young and old, good and evil; only *shinjin* (entrusting faith) is essential."[1] This quote makes me think about all the terminally ill patients and elderly people whom I have met at hospices, viharas, and nursing homes. Unlike sects that emphasize strict practice to gain enlightenment, Jodo Shin Buddhism teaches that Amida Buddha will ultimately save everyone, including persons who are dying or suffering from dementia. Jodo Shin Buddhism has great potential to bring peace and comfort to such patients. As the death rate from cancer and numbers of elderly people in nursing homes increase in both Japan and America, it is the special challenge and responsibility of Jodo Shin ministers to address their spiritual needs.

From 1994 to 2007, I served as a hospital chaplain and psychotherapist, and as a minister of the Jodo Shin Honpa Hongwanji Mission of Hawaii. Living in the United States, I learned that providing counseling for our congregations is one of the ministry's most important services. Regardless of denomination, chaplains play a very important role wherein ministers can serve the spiritual needs of hospitals, nursing homes, prisons, the military, and the police. In Japan, however, Buddhist ministers rarely provide such services. Generally, Japanese people have the impression that Buddhist ministers only perform funeral rites and memorial services and have nothing to do with their daily lives. Although more than one million people suffer from depression, and more than thirty thousand Japanese have been committing suicide annually since 1998, it is rare for a Japanese to seek out a Buddhist minister for spiritual guidance.

Upon my return from Hawaii to Japan, I was honored to serve for a year as the first Buddhist chaplain at the Vihara Hongwanji Nursing Home and the Asoka Vihara Clinic for terminal patients in Joyo City, Kyoto, which was established by my Jodo Shin Honpa Hongwanji denomination. It was a dream come true to introduce chaplaincy to Buddhist organizations in Japan that were dealing with patients' spiritual pain and elders' spiritual needs. Unfortunately, I soon discovered that chaplaincy rarely reaches the majority of Japanese who ignore Buddhist teachings while they are well. If patients are unfamiliar with the ideas and teachings of the Buddha, it may be too late to help them when they are confronting death or suffering from severe dementia. In this chapter, by presenting case studies and a survey comparing Hawaii with Japan, I would like to stress the importance of early religious education and urge the establishment of a systematized Japanese Buddhist chaplain program and services.

THE INTEGRATION OF CHAPLAINCY IN MEDICAL CARE IN HAWAII

Most large hospitals in Hawaii welcome chaplain services in sickrooms, hospices, ICUs, and emergency rooms, where their patients confront death and dying.[2] American chaplains are pastoral care counselors licensed by the Association of Professional Chaplains (APC) after completing all necessary curricula and training. Chaplains are required in emergency situations and when patients or families request spiritual services. Chaplains are often asked to pray for patients' recovery, to provide bedside services, and to comfort troubled patients or grieving families. Since Hawaii is a multicultural society, chaplains encounter a wide range of cultural customs and religious beliefs; the Christian-Buddhist encounter is especially noteworthy. Sometimes Buddhist chaplains conduct services for Christians and vice versa.

The Queen's Medical Center, where I served as a chaplain, was founded in 1859 by Hawaii's King Kamehameha IV and Queen Emma. The Queen donated her property and solicited contributions for Hawaii's first hospital when foreign-bred plagues endangered the Hawaiians' very existence. In the century and a half since its founding, the original hospital of 124 beds has expanded to 560 beds, employing over 1,000 doctors and 3,500 staff members. The chapel that chaplains, patients, and their families use to fulfill their spiritual needs, such as prayers, services, and counseling sessions, shows the dynamics of multiculturalism and spirituality in Hawaii. When you open the Christian-style stained glass doors, you find a statue of Amida Buddha inside. When I first entered this chapel, I felt that everyone was welcome, regardless of religious or ethnic background. As a Japanese, I had never been exposed to multicultural and religious differences until I started to work in Hawaii. Through my activities as a chaplain, I learned the importance of empathetic listening and showing understanding toward patients and their families. Many feelings and emotions transcend ethnicity; hospitalized patients and their families particularly seek salvation and comfort as they confront death or tragedy.

As we will see in greater detail in later chapters in this volume, American hospitals treat chaplains as medical staff, who work with doctors, nurses, therapists, and social workers. For instance, when a family has to decide whether to remove a patient's life support, the doctor and chaplain discuss the feelings and best interests of the patient and the family. Americans do not consider body, mind, and spirit divisible; illness is not only a physical problem. Since body, mind, and spirit influence each other, they must be treated simultaneously. The chaplain is crucial not only for providing spiritual guidance but also for advising medical staff. Whereas Japanese associate priests with death and funerals, Americans see them as caregivers, sources of spirituality. As examples, let me present some cases of my patients in Hawaii.

Case 1

This case involves a thirty-nine-year-old Japanese male instructor at a Japanese medical school, conducting research while on vacation in Hawaii. He had had cardiac and kidney trouble for fourteen years, but things took an unexpected turn for the worse on this trip. He was admitted to an ICU unit in Queen's Medical Center. When his doctor and nurses asked me to visit him, they told me that they had contacted his family in Japan, for he was expected to die in a few days. When I visited him, he was sitting upright in a chair, but he had so many tubes connecting him to machines that looking at him was painful. When I introduced myself as a chaplain, he did not understand the term. I explained the role of a chaplain as a spiritual caregiver, a part of his medical team. The patient was surprised but understood about chaplaincy and asked me if he could be cremated in Hawaii. Shocked at his request, I inquired why he so desired. He replied that he knew he would die soon, so he did not want to burden his family who were on their way from Japan. Contemplating his pain and feelings confronting death alone in a foreign country, I did not know how to comfort him. "We will take care of everything. Please do not worry, but trust yourself to the Buddha," was all that I could respond.

When his family arrived in Hawaii, he was already unconscious. When I visited the family, his irate father berated me, "You came too soon! My son is still alive!" thinking that a priest should only be summoned after the decease. When I explained chaplain services in America, the family understood and was relieved that I had talked to the patient before he went unconscious. The father regretted not coming sooner, for he had never imagined that his son would die so suddenly.

Although they were not Jodo Shin Buddhists and planned to have a funeral at their family temple as soon as they returned to Japan, they requested my services at the bedside and cremation. At these services, I met the patient's wife and two little boys. None of the family could accept the sudden death of this medical doctor. At the service, I preached, "Using his own body as an example, he has revealed the truth that everything is impermanent. Don't take his death only as misfortune, but rather as an occasion to listen to the teaching of the Buddha."

This happened many years ago when I had just started as a chaplain. Even now, I clearly recall that incident, and sometimes remember that patient and his family. This story illustrates how Japanese in tragic situations avoid ministers. Since then, I have met countless families of Japanese tourists encountering traffic accidents or unexpected strokes or heart attacks in Hawaii. They do not understand chaplaincy at first, but some feel encouraged by meeting a Japanese minister concerned about them.

When I was young, I lost my own fiancé to a brain tumor. It was this spiritual crisis that led me to move to Hawaii, where I later learned about chaplaincy as a Jodo Shin minister. In Japan, few medical staff members perform spiritual care for patients and their families. I wish I had been able to see a chaplain for my own spiritual comfort when I was grieving. Bereaved without spiritual support, I suffered depression for three years. However, I now appreciate the incident, because it gave me the opportunity to think about what I could do as a minister and spiritual caregiver.

Case 2

This case involves a ninety-year-old female, second-generation Japanese-American from a Buddhist tradition. Doctors, nurses, and chaplains visited her home regularly, caring for her terminal cancer with Hospice Hawaii's home care service. When I visited her for the first time, she delightedly reminisced about her family and departed husband. She related the rigors of laboring on the sugar plantations as she struggled to establish a better life.

Suddenly serious, she queried, "Reverend, I have lived a long and satisfying life. I am happy to be surrounded by my beloved children and grandchildren. I have no regrets, but I have one concern. Will it hurt when I die?" Unprepared for her question, I leveled with her, "I am sorry; I cannot say whether you will feel pain or not when you pass. But you are embraced by Amida Buddha, here and now, and at the moment of your death. Your staff, including me, are always by your side. Please do not worry, but entrust yourself to the Buddha and to us." Upon hearing this, the patient seemed relieved, and retold some other people's experiences of meeting angels before they passed. A few days later, she passed away peacefully at home, surrounded by her children, grandchildren, and medical staff.

Case 3

This case involves a sixty-five-year-old Caucasian male with lung cancer who was admitted to the medical center and requested a chaplain through a nurse. A Baptist but open to Buddhist teachings, he tearfully lamented, "Reverend, I am ready to die. I had a wonderful life. However, I have one regret. My daughter is pregnant, but I won't be able to see my grandson. In fact, I won't be able to do anything for him." I suggested he might write or record a message to his grandson. Delighted with the idea, he recorded how much he wanted to see his grandson and promised to watch over him from heaven, exhorting him to live the best life that he could. He asked his daughter to play the message for his grandson when he became ten years old. His nurses informed me that he passed peacefully a few weeks later.

Japanese medical professors, such as Kazuko Kikui of Kawasaki University of Medical Welfare and Mieko Yamaguchi of Hiroshima State University College of Health Sciences, have visited Hawaii to observe hospice care and have highly evaluated chaplaincy as an integral part of the medical system. They report that patients' spiritual pain is not fully considered by most Japanese terminal care services, but Hawaiian chaplains fill indispensable roles as spiritual caregivers transcending ethnicity, culture, and religious denomination. For terminally ill patients, pain is not only physical but psychological, social, and spiritual. To respond to patients' total pain, caregivers should work as a team with doctors, nurses, social workers, chaplains, counselors, and volunteers. In Japan, although social workers and volunteers play important roles in terminal care, chaplains are rarely involved, except in Christian hospices and Buddhist viharas. This is despite the fact that spiritual pain is the most fundamental pain of all.[3]

In a recent book popular in Japan entitled *Healing through Words*,[4] Dr. Minoru Kamata, professor of clinical studies at Tokyo Medical and Dental University, advocates improving doctors' attitudes and communication skills with terminal patients. He advises Japanese medical doctors to be more considerate when they talk to terminally ill patients and their families. Dr. Kamata deplores the many doctors who are so busy that they forget their original reasons for becoming doctors. He urges that doctors and nurses learn communication skills, lest patients feel ignored or abandoned by their medical staff. These are all points strongly echoed by Rev. Yoshiharu Tomatsu in his chapter in this volume. Finally, Dr. Kamata also recognizes the importance of teamwork among the doctors, nurses, therapists, and social workers to deal with patients' needs.

Dr. Kamata explains that in his use of narrative therapy with terminally ill patients, he acknowledges the difficulties of attending patients confronting death. However, he proposes that listening to patients' stories and feelings may gradually help them to accept their deaths. Indeed, it is crucial to listen to patients nonjudgmentally, and this can be a first step for patients dealing with life and death. However, Dr. Kamata discusses neither patients' spiritual pain nor chaplaincy. For peace and comfort toward the end of their lives, some patients need more than Dr. Kamata's narrative therapy. Patients need heartfelt satisfaction, a sense of gratitude, and acceptance or forgiveness. I admire Dr. Kamata's wonderful work and compassion for his patients and hope that young Japanese doctors will follow his path. At the same time, the conspicuous absence of discussion of spiritual pain and its treatment indicates how far Japanese hospitals lag behind in terms of spiritual care.

"People Die as They Lived": Experiences with Patient Religiosity in Japan

In April 2008, the Jodo Shin Honpa Hongwanji denomination founded a terminal care clinic, the Asoka Vihara Clinic, and an adjacent nursing home, the Vihara Hongwanji, in Joyo City, Kyoto. Unlike regular clinics, hospitals, and nursing homes in Japan, both facilities have altars to Amida Buddha, where Hongwanji ministers and chaplains conduct morning and evening services, monthly Dharma services, and special major Buddhist services for patients, residents, and their families. Until March 2009, I served as one of the first Buddhist chaplains in these facilities. The chaplains who serve for the Asoka Vihara Clinic and the Vihara Hongwanji are called "vihara ministers." The Asoka Vihara Clinic has the capacity for nineteen terminal patients, while the Vihara Hongwanji accommodates one hundred permanent residents and eight persons for short stays. Surrounded by beautiful wooded hills, these facilities provide a quiet relaxed atmosphere for patients and residents.

Volunteer musicians, dancers, and storytellers periodically provide entertainment. Besides my regular routine as a vihara minister, I played the harp and sang for patients in music therapy sessions. Harp music has been shown to ameliorate depressive disorders, cardiac and blood pressure problems, and other somatic and psychological problems.[5] This is hardly news; the Book of Samuel relates that the psalmist David played his harp to relieve King Saul's manic depression three thousand years ago. Playing the harp for the patients, elderly people, and their families is a great method of communication. My patients often cried, "I never expected such beautiful harp music here." Unlike America, however, Japanese patients and elderly do not comfortably express their feelings about their lives and deaths to chaplains.

"People die as they lived" is the motto of Dr. Haruhiko Dozono, physician for countless hospice patients in Kagoshima, Japan.[6] He holds that patients who live their lives with appreciation end their lives with gratitude and satisfaction, while inappreciative or troubled patients have difficulty dying peacefully. Observing and communicating with patients and the elderly in Hawaii and Kyoto, I would add, "People die as they lived, and they also grow old as they lived." I have observed that whether or not a person has a religious practice (regardless of domination) makes quite a difference in how one grows old and dies. In the nursing home at the Vihara Hongwanji, about 80 percent of the residents have dementia or Alzheimer's disease. The 10 percent of the residents who do join in the daily Dharma services rarely complain about their lives, and instead help the ministers and staff as much as they can. They usually smile and put their palms together in *gassho* to show their appreciation. Some have dementia or Alzheimer's so severe that they cannot even remember their own relatives, but they still show their appreciation to the staff. On the other hand, residents lacking religious faith and practice tend to complain about their lives and blame the hospital staff. Some become violent, causing trouble for other residents; others suffer fits of anxiety, repeatedly summoning "Help! Help!" Although we have a beautiful altar where we hold services every day, people lacking childhood religious education never join our daily services. Conversely, those raised in a Buddhist tradition join the services even though they may have dementia or Alzheimer's. Observing them, I concluded that religious affiliation from a young age inculcates an appreciative and happy attitude even for people suffering illnesses. My observation coincides with the theory of Person-Centered Care developed by Tom Kitwood (1937–98), whose work on care for those with dementia has stood out as the most important and creative development in a field that has for too long been neglected. Person-Centered Care means providing care, especially for those with dementia, through making the patient the central focus, respecting him or her as an individual and seeing things from his or her perspective.[7] My understanding of his theory is that what we think and how we act throughout our lifetime contributes to what we will become when we get older. Thus, "People grow old as they lived."

In terms of "People die as they lived," in America the acceptance of chaplaincy allows chaplains to talk sincerely and deeply with patients concerning their lives and deaths. In Japan, most patients avoid serious conversations with chaplains. I have listened to some who said, "I hate my daughter-in-law who took my son" or "I hope my boyfriend never forgets me" or "I have many concerns, but I do not want to mention them to anybody." Their comments display reticence both to admitting their own mortality and to communicating heartfelt concerns while there is still time. In contrast to America, where people usually know of their impending deaths, many patients in Japan are uninformed of their brief life expectancies. This frustrates chaplains' full spiritual support toward the end of their lives. Still, I was able to connect deeply with Japanese patients in a few cases.

Case 4

This case involves a seventy-six-year-old female cancer patient. Raised in a Jodo Shin Buddhist family, she had grown up watching her mother reciting Amida Buddha's name—*Namu Amida Butsu*—at their home altar. Encouraged by that memory of her mother, the patient joined our morning and evening services regularly, reciting the sutras along with the ministers and staff, and attentively heeding the minister's sermons. As her condition worsened, she joined the services in her wheelchair or on her bed, accompanied by her family or a nurse. Visiting her bedside, I listened to her stories, especially about her grandchildren. She enjoyed my harp and voice when I played for her. I performed "Sakura Sakura" ("Cherry Blossoms"), "Kojo no Tsuki" ("Castle Ruins in the Moonlight"), "Furusato" ("My Old Home"), and other songs familiar to her from youth. She enjoyed my music and even sang with me, saying, "These really take me back." However, when a nurse asked her which song she liked best, she answered, "Sen no Kaze ni Natte" ("A Thousand Winds"), a hit song expressing that the deceased are not in a grave but always by your side, like sunlight on a ripened grain, a gentle autumn rain, or a thousand winds.

A few days before her departure, she complained of severe pain, beseeching the nurses "Please help me!" Although she had enjoyed the Dharma services so much, she showed how difficult it is to die peacefully in the face of physical pain. When I visited her bedside, I proposed, "Your cry for 'help' and '*Namu Amida Butsu*' are the same. Why don't you recite Amida Buddha's name instead of screaming 'help'?" Thereafter, the staff and I heard her continuously reciting "Namu Amida Butsu!" The next day, she passed away repeating, "I am saved! I am saved!" Although others could not see it, I believe that the path to the Pure Land was opened to her.

Case 5

This case involves a seventy-one-year-old male with kidney cancer. Estranged from his daughter and ex-wife since his divorce, he was cared for by his two sisters who visited him frequently. Since the patient was informed of his diagnosis, I conferred directly about his life and death. He joined daily services with his deceased parents' picture, and we enjoyed talking about the Pure Land. He loved singing the song "Furusato," or "Home Town," to my harp. Once I averred, "The Pure Land is our wonderful *furusato*. Whether I precede or follow you, we can rendezvous in the Pure Land." Imagining that we might marry in the Pure Land, he often regaled his nurses, "I will marry Rev. Sengoku in the Pure Land." I wondered about his notion of marriage, but since he believed he would go to the Pure Land, I did not worry about him. Before he passed, he reiterated, "Thank you. I am happy and satisfied to die here." When he passed, I missed him, but I was gratified that he had died peacefully and gratefully, and I felt rather relieved that he was reprieved from his severe physical pain. What disturbed me about this case was that, although the patient passed with gratitude and satisfaction, the doctor still lamented, "It's too bad." For that doctor, any patient's death was a defeat, despite the fact that no one can avoid death.

In my understanding of chaplaincy, gentle but correct communication of diagnosis and prognosis is essential. Anyone would be shocked to learn that his or her condition is terminal. However, contemplating their own mortality, patients can reflect deeply and resolve unfinished business before their departure. Some may want to convey thanks or apologies, or to see long-lost friends or relations, in order to leave this life without regrets.

Some Japanese patients ostensibly prefer not to know the facts, but their feelings may be assuaged if they are assured of sufficient spiritual care. Even at hospices and viharas in Japan, many doctors and nurses lack an understanding of life and death. One doctor confided that he would conceal his patients' diagnoses since he felt sorry for them. I reproved, "If someone else could die for them, they do not have to know. But it is they who will die, so they have to confront their own deaths." The shocked doctor admitted that he had never thought about it in that way; in fact, he had never contemplated his own mortality.

I believe it is very important that medical staff members develop their own understandings of life and death and respect the spirituality of their patients. Otherwise, staff members will suffer burnout, burdened by stress and harboring regret when all treatment proves futile. Regardless of personal religious differences, unless the staff supports patients' spirituality collectively, no hospice or vihara can fulfill its mandate. Instead they will be reduced to simply performing like any other hospital that addresses patients' physical problems alone.

Case 6

This case involves a ninety-one-year-old male nursing home resident who was a retired high school principal. Confined to a wheelchair by a stroke, while fighting diabetes and minor dementia, he showed no problematic behavior. He voiced his concern, "Reverend, please do not think I am crazy, but I saw a host of ghosts marching from the entrance to the statue of Amida Buddha, where they disappeared. It made me fear that I may die soon. Then, last night in my dream, I heard the voice of Buddha saying *anjin-ritsumei*. What do you think of that?" I told him that *anjin-ritsumei*, which literally means "secure-mind-establishing-life," describes the Buddha's state of mind, for *anjin* means "mentally peaceful and stable," and *ritsumei* means "constantly guiding sentient beings."[8] Hearing my explanation, he rejoined, "Now I understand. The Buddha was instructing me, 'Do not worry. I am here with you.' I feel ashamed that, although I was born into a Jodo Shin family, I was not an earnest practitioner and have never joined the services here. Nevertheless, Amida Buddha shows me his compassion. Now I believe it is my great karma to live in this nursing home." Starting that very day, he joined in the Buddhist services. I was happy that his anxiety transformed into gratitude to Buddha, because he had encountered Buddhism when he was a child.

Importance of Religious Education for Youth

Through such encounters with patients and elderly as I have described above, I have concluded that it is too late to develop a spiritual life when you start to suffer from dementia or just before you die. Each of our days alive affects how we grow old and how we die. No matter how beautiful the buildings at the Asoka Vihara, this beauty cannot function fully in the patients' benefit unless people desire to learn and appreciate the Dharma. Buddhist education from an early age is crucial in guiding people toward a meaningful life and a peaceful death.

According to world-famous professor of psychosomatic medicine Dr. Yujiro Ikemi, the human neocortex completes its development by the age of fifteen to sixteen, so personal character formation is very difficult to change thereafter. The paleocortex is even more fragile and sensitive to stress than the neocortex. Infants' interpersonal emotional stresses greatly influence the formation of their paleocortices and hence their personalities.[9] Ikemi's perspective suggests the importance of providing a warm spiritual environment for children from infancy. Many mental patients do successfully complete long-term psychological therapy and transform themselves from negative to positive and appreciative ways of thinking. However, unless they continually repeat the therapy by themselves, they are drawn back to their previous habits and perspectives.[10]

In the 1990s, I conducted a survey entitled "Evaluating Jodo Shin

Buddhism as a Potential Tool for Coping with Spiritual Decline in Modern Japan"[11] to discover how Jodo Shin Buddhists educate children in their homes and how Buddhist teachings affect the relationships and understandings of parents and children. Using questionnaires given to Americans of Japanese ancestry living in Hawaii and to Japanese nationals, including parents and children (fourteen to eighteen years old), I surveyed three types of families: (1) "religious" families who highly respect Buddhist teachings in their daily lives; (2) "cultural" families who visit temples periodically for cultural association; and (3) "secular" families disinterested in Buddhist teachings. Sixty families (ten from each group in each country) completed my questionnaires.

The questionnaires included the questions "How important is religion in your life?" and "How often, and on what occasions, do you go to temple or church?" The survey concluded that, regardless of religious or cultural background, children were strongly influenced by their parents' attitudes. For example, one question asked: "Do you know the meaning of the Japanese word *itadakimasu*, which is said before meals? If so, explain." *Itadakimasu* is a very important term expressing gratitude for the sacrifice of plants and animals and respect for the labor that raised and prepared the food. When the parents knew the meaning of the term, so did the children; when they did not, the children did not either. This question revealed that parents' attitudes—and indeed Buddhist spirituality—affect children in their daily lives.

Today, Japanese temples rarely hold the Sunday services, camping or sports activities for children, or volunteer activities or conferences for adults and seniors that are so common in America. My survey confirmed that, regardless of the strength of their religious orientation, Japanese people seldom visit their family temples. On the average, they attend temple only two or three times a year, on special occasions such as the Obon summer festival for the dead, memorial services, or funerals. By contrast, religious Japanese-American families in Hawaii regularly attend Sunday as well as annual Buddhist services. For many Japanese nationals, religion provides no spiritual guidance for daily life, but only a connection to their deceased, whereas many people of Japanese descent in Hawaii rely on their religion for spiritual guidance. Admittedly, some of these enjoy the temple as a venue to socialize with other people who share their cultural heritage, yet many admirably plumb their ministers' sermons for spiritual guidance. These families typically answered that Buddhism teaches respect for individual differences, the preciousness of life, and appreciation of the environment sustaining all people and animals.

Generally, American Buddhist ministers communicate with their parishioners at Sunday services, at other Buddhist and interfaith services, at individual pastoral counseling sessions, and as chaplains at hospitals or nursing homes. This variety of religious outreach is conspicuously lacking in current Japanese society. Nuclear families constitute the norm in both countries, but in Hawaii, parents, grandparents, and children gather at Sunday services and other temple activities. The lack of such opportunities for Japanese families may be a factor in the weakening of their intergenerational relations. Rev. Tatsuya Konishi, director of the spiritual care department at Higashi Sapporo Hospital in Hokkaido, stresses the importance of introducing chaplaincy to Japan with an eye to cultural sensitivity.[12] However, unless patients themselves seek the benefits of chaplaincy, it will not fully function.

Shinran Shonin wrote, "Although we *bonbu* (ordinary fools) cannot live without accumulating karmic evils, encountering the *nenbutsu* allows us to live our lives fully, accepting death and being embraced by the light of Amida Buddha." Shinran's master Honen Shonin (1133–1212) taught, "Since the world we live in is the *dojo* (practice hall) of *nenbutsu* practice, we can cultivate ourselves by reciting the *nenbutsu*. When we die, the door to the Pure Land opens up for us by eliminating our bodies of earthly desires."[13]

I believe that conveying the words of these masters is the greatest mission of Jodo Shin Buddhist ministers. The Asoka Vihara in Kyoto provides a wonderful spiritual environment conducive to peace of mind. To facilitate this, the effort of ministers to develop religious education and pastoral care services is especially urgent in Japan.

CONCLUSION

Comparison of religious practices and end-of-life care in Hawaii and Japan demonstrates the importance of introducing religious education at an early age and of spreading pastoral care services. Grounded in the customs of Sunday services and pastoral care, many Americans have their own religious practices. When they confront spiritual crises, they welcome pastoral care or chaplaincy for spiritual guidance. Since few Japanese consciously embrace Buddhist teachings, even when hospitalized in clinics or nursing homes with a Buddhist chaplaincy, they are uninterested in pastoral services. Many pass away with unresolved problems, anger, anxieties, and fears.

In vihara activities, including those at the Asoka Vihara, medical staff members should reflect on their own lives and deaths before dealing with dying patients. Even for those uninterested in Buddhism, Buddhist teachings foster spiritual development and comfort. Buddhist ministers must hasten to develop religious education, a systematized Buddhist chaplaincy program, and services responding to Japanese patients' spiritual pain, aiding people through the Buddhadharma to achieve meaningful lives and peaceful departures.

TAIWAN
The Development of Indigenous Hospice Care and Clinical Buddhism

Jonathan S. Watts and Yoshiharu Tomatsu

INTRODUCTION

As we have seen in the opening chapters of this volume, although Japan is considered a predominantly Buddhist country with a long and deep tradition dating back to the sixth century, Buddhism has been in decline there in the modern era. The advance of modern, secular culture has driven it out of most public places and facilities. Taiwan, on the other hand, presents us with an interesting comparative case in that it too has inherited a deep Buddhist tradition from Mainland China as well as developing a strong modern, secular culture from both the West and Japan. Taiwan, as a relatively new nation, however, exhibits some fascinating trends in the development of Buddhism in the social sphere.

With the weight of ancient Chinese traditions being somewhat lighter in this new nation state and little influence from communist China's strong antireligious sentiment, Taiwanese Buddhism has been able to recreate itself and its role in society. Since the 1960s, a number of large and prominent new Buddhist denominations have arisen in Taiwan, most conspicuously the "Four Mountains" of Fo Guang Shan, Tzu Chi, Dharma Drum, and Zhongtai Temple. They have revived a rigorous monastic study and practice that has been largely lost in Mainland China and given birth to the strongest movement of fully ordained women (*bhikkhuni*) in the Buddhist world. At the same time, these groups have developed very robust lay memberships. In general, this revival movement has paralleled Taiwan's rise as one of the Asia's economic tigers. In this way, many Taiwanese, monastic and lay together, find no apparent separation or alienation between their Buddhist faith and practice and their daily lives and work. Indeed, many of these new Buddhist organizations have promoted civic participation and volunteerism as a core value to their monastics and lay followers. These trends are in great contrast to the wide chasm between the Japanese Buddhist world and mainstream Japanese society.

In this chapter, we will look at one of the most compelling forms of this integration of Taiwanese Buddhist practice and modern, secular culture—the clinical Buddhism movement. It is fair to call this an actual movement as the training and dispatch of Buddhist monks and nuns in hospice and end-of-life care has spread throughout the country and is being sponsored by numerous different medical and Buddhist organizations. In this chapter, we will focus on the most prominent and compelling example of this work: based out of Taiwan's largest and most prestigious hospital, the National Taiwan University Hospice and Palliative Care Unit.

PREPARING THE GROUND

The National Taiwan University Hospice (NTUH) and Palliative Care Unit, established in Taiwan in 1995, was the first public unit in Taiwan, after private hospices had been established at the Christian Mackay Memorial Hospital in Tamsui in 1990 and the Catholic Cardinal Tien's Hospital in Hsindian in 1994. At this time, Prof. Rong-chi Chen was the vice superintendent of NTU hospital and had become aware of the need for Buddhist monastics to be involved in patient care. He explains, "Although spirituality doesn't necessarily pertain to religion, if religious representatives can become fully involved, the spiritual care that they could provide would be much more effective."[1] Prof. Chen also notes that Christian denominations have specific training programs for chaplains to serve in hospitals and other places yet comparable Buddhist groups have not. As 70–80 percent of Taiwanese are Buddhist, he and his colleagues thought it would be good to identify some enthusiastic monks and nuns to begin such training. The major obstacle they discovered, however, was that Buddhist monastics were not used to working in such intensive medical environments. Eventually, everyone in this first training group of candidates dropped out. From this experience, Prof. Chen and his colleagues realized they needed a systematic form of chaplain training.

In the previous year, 1994, a group of people from Buddhist universities, both ordained and lay, created the Buddhist Lotus Hospice Care Foundation (BLHCF) to promote hospice and palliative care and life and death education. Prof. Chen was serving as the President of the BLHCF and together they began a systematic plan for a full-fledged clinical Buddhist, monastic hospice training program. They asked Dr. Ching-yu Chen, the head of the department of family medicine at NTU hospital who oversees the hospice there, to design, coordinate, and run this training program. Dr. Chen sees himself as a mediator helping to merge Buddhism and medical science and to provide monastics with proper clinical training. He remarks that 10 percent of the Taiwan population is now elderly but that this will climb to 20 percent in the next twenty years. In this way, the issue of death is becoming increasingly important, yet education about life should also be developed. Thus, Dr. Chen feels monastic clinicians with their grounding in a traditional and deep understanding of life based on Buddhism can offer Taiwan's industrialized society something very important in these coming years.[2]

Finally, Ven. Huimin, the president of Dharma Drum Buddhist College, was brought in as Dr. Chen's spiritual counterpart. With the support of BLHCF, they began an initial three-year period of preparatory work in 1995 that focused on developing doctrinal and teaching standpoints from Buddhism for hospice and palliative care. Besides training and supporting Buddhist clinical chaplains, BLHCF also works to educate the larger public through seminars on death and dying issues. This education of the general public is equally as important as some Taiwanese, like Japanese, fear the sight of religious professionals in the hospital as harbingers of death. Eventually, this collaboration between NTUH, BLHCF, and Ven. Huimin and other Buddhist monastics led to a national program for training monks and nuns in hospice and terminal care through the establishment of the Association of Clinical Buddhist Studies in 2007. The mission of this association is:

(1) To integrate medicine with Buddhist studies, develop a spiritual care model indigenous to the culture of Taiwan, and enhance the quality of palliative care for terminally ill patients.

(2) Plan and host research activities, education programs, and training courses with a focus on clinical Buddhist studies.

(3) Incorporate hospice/palliative care and life education as integral components of health promotion activities and courses.

(4) Assist in the professional education of clinical Buddhist chaplains and expedite ongoing development and research.

DEVELOPING AN INDIGENOUS SPIRITUAL CARE MODEL

The senior doctors at NTU who established this hospice, specifically Dr. Chen, received a strong influence from the hospice tradition of the United Kingdom after visiting and studying at St. Christopher's hospice with Cecily Saunders. They have also been influenced by hospice care in Hong Kong and Singapore, which was also influenced by the UK hospice movement. The deputy superintendent of NTUH, Prof. Rong-Chi Chen who established this hospice, received a strong influence from the hospice traditions of Japan after visiting several hospice and palliative units in Japan in 1994. On the other hand, Ven. Huimin has been one of the leaders in the group to develop an indigenous spiritual care model that better suits the style of Taiwanese culture that is predominantly Buddhist. At the same time that NTUH was set up in 1995, Ven. Huimin and his colleagues began to look for a pattern and vocabulary that would fit the cultural background of Taiwan and the needs of this region. Defining "clinical Buddhism" was an important first step, and they eventually developed the following: clinical Buddhology is the contemporary excellence of integrated medicine with the Buddha's teachings for end-of-life care. This work covers six areas: (1) end-of-life suffering, (2) death preparation, (3) life meanings and affirmation, (4) clinical practice of the Buddhadharma, (5) fear of death, and (6) spiritual and life education.[3]

Another important task was addressing the differences in the occidental and East Asian view of the person and the self. Ven. Huimin explains that when the idea of "whole person care" was introduced to Taiwan, medical care was developed that addressed "physicality, mind, and spirit." Ven. Huimin remarks that occidental thought typically separates the person into either body and mind only, or into body, mind, and a "spirit" that transcends the body and exists separately. For example, in cases regarding the administering of euthanasia, curative medical care that believes that the essence of life is nothing but the body and mind will emphasize prolonging life in the case of a patient with terminal cancer.

In contrast, Buddhism sees the person as consisting of body, feeling, mind, and dharma—the Four Foundations of Mindfulness, as taught in the Satipattana Sutta. This approach focuses more on "awareness care" than "spiritual care." The two core Buddhist teachings of not-self and dependent origination offer a different view of life from the ones that posit the separate existence of a "true self" or a "spirit" that eternally never changes, or the idea that the body and mind both totally extinguish at death. From the viewpoint of Buddhism, the essence of life comes down to a middle way of seeing the reality of life as neither total extinction nor everlasting eternity. Following this middle way of thinking, in addition to the body and mind there is an object (not a "spirit") that can experience absolute illumination of the dharmas of reality, law, and duty. Further, the necessary condition for the arising of "mind" is "feeling," which changes in suffering and happiness and in life and death. In terms of hospice care, euthanasia and assisted death can be performed in accord with the concern for the person whose feeling and mind are experiencing unsuitable symptoms and levels of pain. Through deeply recognizing the four aspects of a patient—body, feeling, mind, and dharma—health care professionals can support a patient to develop a keen awareness and equanimity and help the dying person to purify his or her mind and at the same time enter the dharma of the fundamental practice of Buddhism.[4]

Ven. Huimin and his colleagues have developed a process for engaging in such awareness care based on the Buddha's Four Noble Truths as follows:

(1) Suffering: Because of the comprehensive suffering of a terminally ill patient, clinicians must engage in "truth telling," that is, inform the patient and his or her family of the patient's terminal prognosis. At NTU Hospital, they push doctors to engage in such practice, and approximately 50–60 percent of patients do know their prognosis. In Taiwanese culture, however, 80 percent of families tend to not want to have this information communicated to the patient.[5] Since they feel this is essential at NTUH, they communicate such news through a family conference with the patient, family, and the entire clinical team assigned to that patient.

(2) The Cause of Suffering: If a patient's health continues to deteriorate, they are encouraged to accept death. On a passive level, this means that working with patients' physical and mental pain and suffering and helping them come to an acceptance of death can help relieve this pain. On a more active level, such an acceptance of death can lead to seeing death as part of the continual learning process of the journey of life. In this way, the team tries to fulfill the patients' final wishes and to affirm the meaning and value of their life (strength from inside), and to affirm the care of the medical team (strength from outside).

(3) Nirvana: Suffering ends with the development of a sense of spirituality, which in passive terms means achieving relief of physical pain and tranquility of mind, and in active terms means a change in one's behavioral patterns through cul-

tivating buddha nature, nurturing compassion, and letting go of possessions. In the following chapter on Thailand, we will see a similar emphasis on the potentiality of people to continue to grow spiritually in their final days even as their bodies completely deteriorate.

(4) The Path to Nirvana: The path involves the practice of Buddhadharma, which in passive terms means the feeling of being guided toward salvation, and in active terms means one's own attainment of salvation. The result is a "good death," which includes awareness of death, accepting death peacefully, preparing properly (including arranging one's will), and timing the death appropriately.

Dr. Ching-yu Chen recalls one patient suffering from terminal oral cancer as a good illustration of this above process. The primary care Buddhist chaplain in this case designed many survey methods to communicate with the patient and to evaluate his physical and mental conditions every day. The patient had his first contact with Buddhism upon arriving for palliative care at NTUH, but quite shortly he became a very active practitioner, either reciting Amitabha Buddha's name or listening to Dharma talks on tape everyday. He developed great confidence in the Buddhist chaplain's care and dreamed one night that the chaplain led him to Amitabha's Pure Land. On the day before his death, he took formal refuge in the Triple Gem of Buddha, Dharma, and Sangha, even managing to chant out loud through his severely damaged throat. On the day of his death, his consciousness was very clear. About an hour and half before his death, he knew his time was coming and, under the guidance of the Buddhist chaplain, he lay on his bed and peacefully passed away. Dr. Chen notes that this patient reaffirmed their belief that palliative care provides one of the best chances for spiritual cultivation not only for patients and families but also care staff; the patient becomes a teacher for the care staff in the practice of dying. Dr. Chen concludes that the Palliative Care Unit "is a vihara or practice hall that encourages the patients, the relatives, and the team members to grow together."[6]

CLINICAL MONASTIC TRAINING PROGRAM

In 1998 the training program for clinical Buddhist chaplains began, sponsored by the Buddhist Lotus Hospice Care Foundation. BLHCF continues to support these students and the already-certified chaplains with small stipends for transportation, since it is widely believed that monks and nuns should not receive salaries. Monastics ranging in age from twenty-eight to forty participate in nurse training and receive academic credentials. The program lasts over five years with more than sixty hours of hospice and palliative care study. Candidates are first interviewed about their motivation and education level and then are selected for the program. The training consists of four stages:

(1) General Education: a twenty-eight hour course delivered by the experts in the hospice care team on the meaning of hospice and palliative care and the roles played by each and every member of the care team, which includes physicians, nurses, psychologists, social workers, monastics, and volunteers.

(2) Shared Courses: a sixteen-hour course open to Buddhist monastics and also to clinical professionals, which communicates the definition, meaning, and working of spiritual care developed in their research system.

(3) Profession 1: a fourteen-hour course only for monastics who have undergone the first two courses. It covers key issues for working in hospice and palliative care environments, such as how spiritual care works; learning how to read, understand, and make use of a patient's medical record; how to use Buddhadharma to care for the patient; and what dharmas are frequently used.

(4) Clinical Internship: a four-week course in which the monastic must be involved in one complete case. He or she must keep records of his or her dialogues with patients that are then given critical comments and suggestions by the instructors and professors. There is then an assessment of the student's qualities and fitness for the work. After passing this assess-

ment, the student may proceed to clinical training, which involves fuller participation as a member of the care team. The clinical experience follows a self-learning, problem-oriented model. The trainee should continuously assess what problems need to be solved and carefully evaluate problem-solving priorities. During the process, students observe and determine by themselves whether they have to go further. They are supported in this process through small-group discussion and sessions focused on the integration of clinical medicine and Buddhadharma with leading staff at NTUH.

Over the last ten years, seventy-three monastics have been involved in the training program, beginning with just two in the initial year of 1999 but quickly growing to seventeen by 2002. By 2009, twenty-nine had completed the full internship, all of whom are now working as clinical monastics in hospice and palliative care wards across the country, such as at Chungshan Medical University Hospital, Chinese Medical University Hospital, and Veterans General Hospital Taichung.

Bhikkhuni Tsung-Teung was the first monastic to be trained in this program, under the guidance of Dr. Ching-yu Chen, and she is now the secretary general of the Association of Clinical Buddhist Studies. She has been a nun since 1987 and has been involved in this training since 1999. She recounts that she had a hard time adjusting from a monastic environment to a hospital one. She had to learn how to interact and communicate with people in a way very different from interactions at the temple. At first, this is a big challenge for monastics. The monastic clinician must learn to refer to the physicians and nurses to find out about the patient's family and their needs. By developing a relationship with the family, monastics can better make a connection with the patient. The monastic clinician also develops a care plan, which is reevaluated and altered as needed before continuing on. Despite these challenges and new skills that must be learned, Ven. Tsung-Teung says that the role of religious professionals in a hospital is an ordinary thing. She notes that patients will usually ask more from a religious professional than from a nurse or social worker and that 71 percent of patients will ask for spiritual care from monk or nun.[7]

Bhikkhuni Der Chia completed the training in 2005 and became chief instructor responsible for training and assisting Ven. Tsung-Teung at NTUH. Ven. Der Chia also speaks of the difficulties for monks and nuns to learn how to do this kind of work. She says that many monastics, even high level ones, may just offer the dying very standard phrases like "Just think positive" or "You have to let go" or "You cannot do anything now" or "Just try to clear your mind for birth in the Pure Land of the West." She says, "Before I came to the training program, that was the method I used to treat a patient. Even though I knew that at that time and situation this method was incorrect, I was at a loss for what was the correct thing to say and consequently had a lot of apprehension. . . . When speaking those phrases, I feel like I'm walking upon clouds with a large sense of disconnection. Even to the point that, when I finish those phrases, I feel very sad deep down." This way of dealing with a patient may often neglect the emotional support and recognition a patient needs. Thus, in the training program monastics learn how to listen and to empathize with the patient's predicament and then guide the patient through a more realistic process to eventual death.[8]

In this way, the program has the stated goal that every fully trained monastic clinician must have the following qualities:

- Possesses a full understanding of hospice and palliative care
- Respects medical teamwork and the need to develop various clinical skills
- Capable of rendering care as a listener, supporter, and provider of new ideas
- Enthusiastic and eager to serve people as a life-death explorer

These competencies, especially the shift from the method of preaching like a temple minister to the method of listening like a hospital chaplain, are fundamental points for the training of chaplains, which we have seen across cultures in the chapters presented in this volume.

BUILDING A TEAM-CARE SYSTEM

At NTUH, there are seventeen beds, which are almost always full and are predominantly for cancer patients in the final stages of the disease. Liver cancer and lung cancer are the most common forms. Patients with ALS (or Lou Gehrig's disease) are also admitted, though these cases represent only 1 percent of the patients. Taiwan's national insurance system limited public hospice care to these two diseases until September 2009 when it expanded care to cover almost all terminal illnesses, such as the terminal stages of organ failure of the brain, heart, lung, liver, or kidneys. Seventeen days is the average stay at the hospice, and this short period is partly because of the misconception by people of what palliative care means. There is still fear and stigma among Taiwanese regarding admission to a hospice, so many do not want to come any earlier. At NTUH, the staff does not perform resuscitation, and the patient's family must sign a waiver upon the patient's entry. In Taiwan, such decisions are still usually the role of the family rather than the patient, since many Taiwanese, like Japanese, do not believe in "truth telling." In this way, patients may not really know they are dying when they are first admitted to the hospice. Dr. Rong-chi Chen and the NTUH team have thus been promoting the Do Not Resuscitate (DNR) advance directive in order to change both the modern medical culture of heroism and the traditional Chinese culture of filial piety that chooses saving a person's life at all costs over compassionately guiding him or her to death.[9]

NTUH has two senior doctors on call, out of a pool of fourteen. There are two to three third-year residents, who do a two-month residency and a one-month home care residency. There are seventeen nurses, one per bed according to national regulation. There are also three to four clinical psychologists who are still in training and shift every six months. They do psychological assessments, give advice to the team on care, and deal with patient depression and anxiety, etc. They will also seek help from their supervisor who may come to the hospice to assist. There are two art therapists who do bereavement support and help for the families as well as the patients; for example, supporting an elder sister who was feeling neglected by her parents because they were attending to the younger sister who was dying. The art therapists may guide patients in copying pictures of Kannon Bodhisattva, and the patients may add their thoughts to these pictures or actually speak to Kannon through them. There is also the sense of traditional Buddhist merit-making from copying such pictures. There is a pool of seventeen to twenty monastic chaplains with two to three on call in the ward at any one time. The team is rounded out by a base of fifty volunteers who work in shifts of five in the morning and five in the afternoon. They assist the medical professionals, cook food that may include Chinese medicinal herbs, read the patients books, help organize special events at the hospice like concerts and birthday parties, and help patients with special requests like facilitating a visit by a particular person or taking the patient on a final visit somewhere.

The core principle of NTUH is team care among the doctors, nurses, social workers, psychiatrists, and clinical chaplains. Every Tuesday morning for two hours the entire team goes on rounds together to all seventeen beds. Dr. Chien-An Yao, the head doctor and director of NTUH, relates that, "Our team does an assessment of good death after each patient's death, usually every week, to audit the quality outcome of the patients' dying process. At that time, clinical Buddhist chaplains often give important information about spiritual well-being. They also help the palliative team learn how to approach a good death by spiritual care."[10]

Dr. Yao also notes that it has not been easy to build this team-care model. He says, in order to introduce this system, they had to prove that spiritual care is effective. He says that since NTU medical school is considered the top in the country, the students have a high level of pride. They think proper medical education is very important, so it was necessary to make an impression on them concerning the integral nature of spiritual care. Therefore, this was another one of the key areas of research in which they engaged during the formational period of 1995–98. Dr. Ching-yu Chen notes that no medical education in Taiwan has tried to incorporate all four aspects of holistic care: the physical, social, psychological, and spiritual. Taiwanese medical doctors generally do not learn about spirituality at all in their medical training. Therefore, they have difficulty facing death and talking to the dying. Palliative care training exposes them to these issues. Dr. Yao notes that mutual respect for the rest of the team by the doctor is a key element, and now every doctor at NTU hospital must study end-of-life care. However, in other hospice units around the country, the lack of a complete care team that includes chaplains and doctors trained and engaged in holistic care means that an inordinate amount of the emotional and spiritual care of patients falls on the nurses. Thus, some hospices, like the Buddhist Tzu Chi Heart Lotus Palliative Care Unit at Tzu Chi General Hospital in Taipei, cannot operate at full capacity due to a shortage of nurses who are reluctant to enter such a demanding field.

Indeed, stress and burnout are common problems among clinicians working in this field. Priests and doctors, especially, tend to neglect their own health. They work hard for their patients but neglect their own well-being and development and, in turn, the well-being of the team. Dr. Yao says, "Ongoing involvement with dying and bereaved persons may cause a severe drain of energy and uncover old and new spiritual issues for the caregiver. As such, spiritual education, growth, and renewal should be part of a staff support program as well."[11] In this way, NTUH feels it is important to teach and develop such self-care: NTUH team members will often consult the monastic chaplains when they have their own personal problems, and nurses attend spiritual care programs for their own well-being. However, since doctors tend to avoid such issues, they have started to include such issues and study as part of the training for medical students. Sixth-year medical students take courses in spiritual studies, ethics, and counseling as basic knowledge in their education, while also studying outside of class in the NTUH ward. Concerning self-care for the monastic clinicians themselves, Ven. Tsung-Teung says there is training for chaplains to control and deal with the strong emotions that come up in hospice work. The Lotus Foundation and the Association of Clinical Buddhist Studies have also created their own internal counseling sessions. As an extension of the team-care ethos, the NTUH team participates in a biweekly video conference with palliative care units around the country at which they present case reports like truth telling and informed consent, symptom control, spiritual care, and success and failure stories. These conferences began twelve years ago with only four hospitals but have now grown to include forty.

MEDICAL ETHICS AND THE FINAL MOMENT OF DEATH

As in the Tibetan Buddhist tradition, Chinese Buddhists believe that moving the deceased's body or causing any abrupt environmental change will disturb the deceased's subtle consciousness. Thus, the body should not be disturbed (in some cases not even touched or moved) for at least another eight hours after it has gone cold. The part of the body where warmth lingers until the rest of the body has become cold is called the Gate of Death, since the consciousness finally leaves the body through this spot. Its relative position on the body is believed to indicate to which realm the consciousness has migrated. In general, higher spots on the body such as the crown of the head indicate heavenly realms while lower ones such as the feet indicate unfortunate realms.[12]

In this way, it is ideal for a person to die in a sitting posture so that the consciousness may more easily leave the body from a higher place. In contrast, dying in sleep, in unconsciousness, under the influence of drugs, or in other such abnormal or violent ways is dangerous to the migrating consciousness. The state of mind of the dying person is considered most crucial to his or her transcendence or rebirth. Therefore, the family should withhold expressions of grief that will disturb the dying and offer them encouragement. As is done in the Japanese Pure Land tradition, many Chinese perform a traditional Death Bed Ceremony practice (Ch. *lin-zhong-xing-yi*) in which a monk and groups of laypeople come to chant the name of Amitabha Buddha for the benefit of the dying person. In East Asia, there is a strong popular belief that says Amitabha Buddha will arrive at the moment of death to guide the deceased toward rebirth in his Pure Land. However, since the dying person may be too lost in the pain of death or his or her own delusion, all persons involved in the moment of death should chant Amitabha Buddha's name to assist the dying's transcendence. Volunteer groups, usually called "Help Chant Group" or something similar, and even audio tapes may be used to continue with the chanting of the Buddha's name.[13]

In this regard, one of the distinctive innovations of the Buddhist terminal care movement in Taiwan is the spiritualization of dying rooms in hospices in both private and public hospitals. Regulations in Taiwan require that hospices and palliative care units have a special room to move patients for their final moments. However, it was a Buddhist chaplain at NTUH who came up with the idea for putting up a large painted image of the Amitabha Buddha to assist in the special deathbed practice outlined above.[14] These rooms are also used for special counseling and for housing religious images for people of different faiths to pray. NTU hospital also developed special rooms in the basement called literally "Rooms for Rebirth in the Pure Land," which have become common in hospitals across Taiwan. Here the deceased's body may remain undisturbed for the traditional period of eight hours during which Buddhist priests, family, and members of the care team may join together in the chanting of Amitabha Buddha's name. There is also a room for observances by families who are not Buddhist. For Westerners used to morgues that are nothing more than a room of drawers for dead bodies or for Japanese whose Buddhist sectarianism and general social secularism have led to the elimination of all vestiges of religion from hospitals, this spiritualization of death is incomprehensible in a public medical facility.

ORGAN TRANSPLANTS AND GRIEF CARE

Unfortunately, this belief and practice of not disturbing the body after death has also been an impediment in Japan and Taiwan to the modern medical practice of organ transplants and of donating organs at death by common citizens. In Japan, organ donation by common citizens is not a common practice and can be problematic; in general, Japanese Buddhist organizations and priests have been very slow to adopt more modern views on such practices. It was this way in Taiwan until recently when certain Buddhist institutions and teachers, such as Master Cheng Yen and the Tzu Chi Buddhist denomination, began promoting organ donations and transplants as a bodhisattva act of compassion and self-sacrifice. Indeed, numerous well-known Tibetan Buddhist masters, who share the same tradition of leaving the dead body undisturbed, have commented that the power of people's intention to help others with their leftover organs will protect and override the negative influences of disturbing their body in order to harvest the organs.[15] In this way, many Taiwanese Buddhist organizations have begun to support and promote organ donation by their followers. NTUH supports this movement as well through holding a large annual memorial service for all patients who have donated their bodies for research or organ transplants. The families and monks are invited to attend as well.

The Tzu Chi Buddhist denomination has taken this movement a step further by encouraging whole body donation to their new medical school through their Silent Mentors program, which began in 1996. Because of the Chinese and Taiwanese traditions of "maintaining a whole body" and burial, there has always been a lack of cadavers for medical study in Taiwan. The founder of Tzu Chi, Master Cheng Yen, responded by trying to shift this traditional culture to a new one grounded in the Buddhist ethics of compassion and self-sacrifice. She notes that, "We do not own our lives. We only have the right to make use of them. . . . Turning the useless corpse into teaching materials is a liberating experience from life and death, as well as the wisdom of knowing how to teach selflessly."[16] To further these aims, Tzu Chi Medical College does not simply collect bodies and use them in the typical way that most hospitals and medical schools use cadavers. They have instituted a highly creative and systematic method of putting teachers, students, bereaved families, and the bodies of the donors in intimate contact to encourage the development of what they call "humane doctors." Tzu Chi has coined the phrase "Silent Mentors" to describe this use of the cadaver as a basis for not only imparting medical learning but also emotional and spiritual learning.

Before beginning the anatomy course at Tzu Chi Medical College, students will visit the families of the donors on whom they will operate to learn more about their lives. They look at photos and listen to stories by the family members. Afterward, the family members provide a photo of the donor, and the student writes a short biography of the donor, both of which are posted on the program's website, in the hall outside of the dissection room, and in front of the dissection table itself. At the beginning of the course, an opening ceremony of gratitude is held that includes the families of the donors. A Buddhist funeral rite is conducted at this time in order for the bereaved family to have peace of mind and for the donors to rest in peace. The ceremony is then moved to the medical operating classroom for surgical simulation, where the donor's bodies are uncovered, and the bereaved family members may face their departed loved ones for the last time. The medical students are actively involved in this moment, learning to be present and to comfort these families. In turn, the family members may also ease the nerves of the young students by reminding them of the vow of their loved ones to be used for this very purpose. This personal connection with the donor's bodies and their families is meant to emotionally move and thus encourage the students to develop themselves as more humane doctors.

The students will use this one personalized cadaver for the whole semester. Then, at the end of the semester, the students sew up the bodies, dress them in clothes and shoes, and place them in coffins. A public funeral ceremony with the coffins is held in front of the medical school attended by Buddhist nuns, the school president, faculty, students, volunteers, and the bereaved families. After cremation, the students and the families attend an internment ceremony for each individual's ashes at a special shrine called the Great Giving Hall housed within the medical college itself.

The comprehensive nature of this program shows the great meaning that can be created from building not just Buddhist but general spiritual mechanisms into the often-alienating, secular culture of modern medicine. The program clearly has a powerful effect on the students who are deeply exposed to the emotionality and spirituality connected with medical work—an aspect that is usually totally neglected in modern medical education. The effects span out further in (1) providing the dying with a sense of meaning to their deaths and personal value that will extend beyond their deaths; and (2) providing bereaved families a sense of continuing value to their loved one's lives as well as offering them a very profound form of extended grief care through participating in the program.

Conclusions and Future Directions

The NTUH, Buddhist Lotus Hospice Care Foundation, and Association of Buddhist Clinical Studies program have developed monastic clinicians who are serving all over the country. This work has now been expanded to include another hospital besides NTUH where monastic candidates can train. The Jinshan Hospital, located on the northern coast near Dharma Drum Temple and Buddhist College where Ven. Huimin serves as the dean, became an official branch hospital to NTUH in 2010. They have one hundred beds in a rural setting, in contrast to NTUH's downtown Taipei setting. With a more natural setting and fresh air, this hospital will specialize in patients with chronic diseases as well as supporting a hospice and palliative care unit. With its location within eyesight of Dharma Drum Buddhist College, it will also be tied into the educational program for monastics at the college.

This is a development of which Prof. Rong-Chi Chen would like to see more, especially since BLHCF struggles to fund this work. BLHCF has brought together different groups of Buddhists to appeal to society for donations, and the new reductions on income tax for making such donations have made doing so more popular, especially at the end of the fiscal year. However, without the generous donors behind the foundation who come from the laity and general public, this work could not continue as hospital insurance does not pay for chaplains. On the other hand, while the large monasteries and denominations, like Tzu Chi, Dharma Drum, Fo Guang Shan, and Zhongtai Temple, have well endowed Buddhist universities, they have no systematic programs for chaplaincy. Prof. Chen notes that in recent years there are many freelance monastics engaging in this issue of terminal care, but that it would be better if the major Buddhist universities would incorporate chaplaincy and clinical studies into the curriculums. Such curriculums would encourage and guide some students into the profession, since after their university training they could directly proceed to internships.

THAILAND
The Seven Factors of a Peaceful Death: A Theravada Buddhist Approach to Dying

Phaisan Visalo

Care for the Dying in Thailand

In the past, most people in Thailand died in their own houses. When a person was going to die, a monk or a group of monks would be summoned in order to guide him or her to a peaceful death. Monks would perform Buddhist chanting or remind the dying of the Three Refuges of Buddha, Dharma, and Sangha as objects of veneration. The dying person, with the help of relatives, would perform a last act of merit-making by giving offerings to the monks. In some parts of the country, such as the Northeast, the dying would hold flowers to pay homage to the Buddha's sacred tooth relic believed to be located in heaven where they were hoping to be reborn.

Cultivation of a peaceful mind at the moment of death for leading to a beneficial next life and belief that a negative state of mind will contribute to a harmful one was also a common belief in Thailand. If the dying were conscious enough, they would sit upright, leaning against a pillar, and meditate or chant to calm the mind—the ideal form of dying in the Buddhist tradition. The atmosphere around the dying, therefore, was to be peaceful. Cousins would gather around the dying, reminding them of their good deeds in the past and helping to relieve them of all anxiety. Some would ask forgiveness from the dying or vice versa. Everyone was discouraged from crying near the deathbed, much like in the Tibetan Buddhist tradition.

However, nowadays the pattern of dying in Thailand has changed.

There are more industrial diseases that require long and intense hospitalization. Thus, there is an increased need for palliative care, and this changes the sense of how to care for people in general. There is an increased focus on terminal care and so an increased need for spiritual and psychological care in hospitals. The concept of holistic health—physical, social, psychological, and spiritual, as defined by the WHO—is becoming part of the mainstream and part of actual Thai law. Many hospitals are speaking about these four aspects, and the larger hospitals and those associated with universities are beginning to put them into practice, especially for the terminally ill. However, it is still difficult to provide such care because of a lack of understanding and skills among staff.

Palliative care is still centered in the hospital in Thailand, not in the home or in hospices. Some hospitals have programs for psychological and spiritual care without religious connections, especially for children. At Chulalongkorn University Hospital, there is the "Wishing Well" program, through which children are granted their last wish. Other large hospitals have encouraged some religious support by providing space for nurses or monks to do this work since doctors cannot do it.

In Thailand, in both the ICU or in a regular room, monks are typically invited to come and to provide the opportunity for the patient to "make merit" (in Thai, *tan-bun*) or perhaps to guide the patient in meditation. Nurses also have begun to take charge in offering psychological and counseling care. Such counseling often involves calming patients or helping them find reconciliation with their family. Nurses may also be active in getting the family more involved in supporting the patient, which helps the family with their guilt in not being able to do more. Nurses may even offer spiritual care, like meditation.

Recently, there is more encouragement for doctors and nurses to support home care and to be involved in home care, especially for pain control. Pain care management skill is important so as to enable patients to maintain clarity without pain. Doctors may also predict what physical stages will come next. For example, a friend of mine died at home from breast cancer a few years ago with good home support from her doctor. At a certain point, her doctor told her that her breathing would get difficult, so then she began to change her meditation method away from mindfulness with breathing (*anapanasati*) to contemplation of Buddha images.[1]

In Thailand, there are only a few hospices. They are not so popular, because the Thai health system is still centralized, and there is not the appropriate infrastructure for them. Today, only the rich can afford to pay for a hospice. The most famous and largest, with over two hundred beds, is the Dhammarak Niwet Hospice, which was established in 1992 and is located on the grounds of Phrabat Nampu Temple in Lopburi, a few hours north of Bangkok. This hospice is specialized for destitute and abandoned AIDS patients and thus is not an appropriate place for common citizens. There are also a few Christian and private hospices, but in general home care is more popular than hospice care.

After the success of the Dhammarak Niwet Hospice, other temples began establishing hospices, but they are now on the decline because it is quite difficult to maintain them. Monks still do such work, but on a small temple-by-temple level, mostly in the countryside and mostly through home visits. In some ways, this a continuation of their old, traditional roles. However, this tradition is weakening as monks tend to focus now more on funerals, even in the countryside.

In hospital settings, medical professionals and monks unfortunately do not collaborate well. There is a gap between doctors and monks. Doctors do not know how to treat or talk with monks properly. Unlike Japan, monks are welcomed into hospitals as ritualists or advisors. However, like most other Buddhist countries, they have not been integrated into the care team or the advising medical team. They have to be invited first, usually by patients or their family, and are not part of the system. They are not on call, but they do often visit hospitals during festival seasons. Unfortunately, not many monks are interested in this kind of work. More and more, monks are being seen as harbingers of death. Thus, like in Taiwan or Japan, some people feel uncomfortable when they appear. In this way, families are actually better than monks in providing spiritual guidance since they have a close, personal relationship with the patient.

The End-of-Life Care Network, established in 2004, coordinates between the personnel of various hospitals and other concerned people like monks to amass and share knowledge on how to take care of the terminally ill. Every two months, this network holds a study session to develop skills and knowledge. Its goal is to promote change in the medical system for more spiritual care for the dying and in the curriculum in the medical schools. Spiritual-care training is not provided by medical schools, but this network has begun to offer such training for nurses of all units and some doctors. There is increasing demand but limited human resources in this area. Our network also initiated the Facing Death Peacefully Project, which aims to educate Thai people about peaceful death. Books and other media have been produced to give advice about this topic. It is interesting to find that many hospitals need such advice. Our workshops on peaceful death are now in much demand by many hospitals all over the country.

BUDDHIST SPIRITUAL CARE FOR THE DYING

Illness not only affects the body, but also the mind. Thus, when most people fall ill, they must contend not only with physical pain, but also mental pain. Especially in the case of patients who are close to dying, mental anguish is no less a cause of suffering than physical pain, and indeed it can even be the greater cause. This is because what these patients face right in front of them is death, along with a separation and loss that is final. All this provokes feelings of fear, anxiety, and isolation to surge up very intensely in a way they have never experienced before.

For this reason, patients need their spiritual well-being taken care of just as much as their physical well-being. Especially in the case of final-stage patients, whom doctors have determined to have no hope of recovery or improvement, taking care of spiritual well-being in fact becomes more important than physical well-being. This is because even though the body is irrevocably breaking down, the mind still has the opportunity to improve. It can cease its agitation and reach a state of peace, even in the last moments of life. Even though the body and mind are closely related, when the body suffers, the mind does not necessarily have to suffer too. One can take care of one's mind such that it does not suffer along with one's body. This understanding is consistent with the interpretation of Ven. Huimin and the Association of Clinical Buddhist Studies in Taiwan as outlined in the previous chapter.

In the time of the Buddha, there were many occasions wherein the Buddha and his disciples helped those who were sick and close to dying. The kind of help they gave directly focused on treating the suffering of the mind. In the Pali Canon, there are several stories of people on the verge of death who were told by the Buddha to contemplate their imminent death and the true nature of all conditioned things and who eventually came to realize high levels of attainment. Some even became fully enlightened. From these stories, there are two major points to consider:

(1) Being ill and close to dying is a time of crisis and physical disintegration, yet at the same time it can also be an opportunity to liberate the mind or elevate one's state of mind. Being ill and close to dying are thus not conditions that are negative in and of themselves. If one knows how to use them well, they can be of great benefit.

(2) The Buddha's teachings on illness and dying can be classified into two main parts:

- Incline the mind to have faith in the Three Refuges and confidence in the morality one has upheld or good deeds one has done in the past. In other words, recollect that which is good and wholesome.

- Let go of worries and all things, having seen with wisdom that there is nothing at all that one can hold on to.

These teachings of the Buddha provide an excellent model of how to give spiritual help to dying persons in ways that are applicable to the present day. This chapter will show how these principles put forth by the Buddha can be adapted for use by doctors, nurses, family, and friends in helping dying patients. Experiences from real-life cases have been drawn on to create the following guidelines.

1. Extending Love and Sympathy

Dying persons not only have to contend with physical pain but also fear: fear of pain itself, of dying, of abandonment, of dying alone, or of what will come after death. The fear may cause even more suffering than the physical pain. Love and moral support from family members and friends is very important during this time, because it can reduce the fear and help patients feel secure. One should remember that patients in their final stages feel very vulnerable. They need someone they feel they can rely on, someone who is ready to be there for them during times of crisis. If they have someone who can give them unconditional love, they will have the strength of spirit to deal with all the various forms of suffering that are converging on them at this time.

Being patient, forbearing, sympathetic, gentle, and forgiving are ways to show your love. Physical pain and a vulnerable state of mind can make patients act out in ill-tempered and abrasive ways. We can help them by patiently bearing these outbursts and not reacting in negative ways, as well as by trying to forgive them and sympathize with them. If we are peaceful and gentle, it will help them calm down more quickly. Pointing out their negativity may be something we ought to do sometimes, but always in a gentle and loving way. Family and friends need to have mindfulness at all times, which helps us not to lose control of ourselves and keeps our hearts filled with kindness, love, and restraint.

Even if you don't know what to say to make them feel better, just physically touching them in a gentle way will enable them to feel your love. We may hold their hand or touch their arm and squeeze it gently, embrace them, or touch their forehead or abdomen with our hands, while sending them our good wishes. For those who have some experience practicing meditation, while touching the patient, bring your mind to rest in a peaceful state. Loving kindness (*metta*) that emanates from a mind that is peaceful and concentrated will have an energy that the patient will be able to feel.

For example, when two volunteers from my network came to visit a patient, they found him screaming out of suffering from the pain in his abdomen. They asked if the patient would allow them to receive (or share) some pain from him. After getting permission, they asked the patient to close his eyes while they touched his body gently with their hands. They began visualize his pain as grey smoke emerging from his body and entering theirs before being transformed into a white ray emitting back to him. After about five minutes of this compassionate practice, the patient said that he felt much better. This practice mirrors the *reiki* practice described in the chapter on Cambodia as well as the Tibetan Buddhist *tonglen* practice popularized by Christine Longaker and the Rigpa Spiritual Care Programme, as outlined in the chapter on Germany.

2. Helping Patients Accept Impending Death

If patients do not have long to live, letting them know that will give them time to prepare themselves while they are still physically able to. However, as seen in numerous cultures throughout this volume, there are a great many patients who have no idea that they have a serious terminal illness and are in their final stages. To let time pass while keeping them in the dark will leave them with less time to prepare themselves. In Thailand, the patient's right to information is not respected very much. Many cancer patients are not informed about their real situation, because their families are afraid that doing so will cause the patient's situation to worsen. Since the doctor wants to have a good relationship with the patient's relatives, he or she has to conform to their wishes. In Thailand, relatives have a big say in dealing with the patient's situation. Volunteers from my network often find that informed consent and "truth telling" are not practiced when they visit hospitals. However, this right is becoming increasingly known and exercised by patients, especially those who have a high level of education. Furthermore, living wills and advance directives by patients are now legal and are being promoted in Thailand.

Still, telling patients bad news without preparing them psychologically in some way beforehand may cause their condition to worsen. When patients are told the bad news, they need to be given moral support and reassurance that family, friends, doctors, and nurses will not abandon them but will stay by their side and help them to the utmost of their abilities until the very end. In general, doctors play the important role in telling the news, especially if they have built up a close relationship with patients and earned their trust.

Sometimes, however, it is up to the family to break the news. Many families tend to think that it is better to conceal the truth from the patient. However, according to a survey done of patients in Thailand, the majority responded that they would rather be told the truth than be kept in the dark. Even when relatives try to conceal it, ultimately the patient can discern the truth from the changed manner and behavior of family and friends, such as unsmiling faces, softer speaking voices, or greater effort made to please the patient.

Nonetheless, a patient's acceptance of his or her impending death involves a process that takes a long time. Not all patients can accept the truth after they are told. Some patients may become angry at doctors, nurses, and family members for telling them the bad news, or concealing the bad news from them for a long time. There could be several reasons for these emotions, besides the fear of death; for instance, they could have some unfinished business or other worries. Caregivers must learn to be understanding of angry outbursts. If the patient is able to get past anger and denial of death, he or she will be more able to accept the reality of the situation. Relatives ought to help the patient express any concerns. If patients feel they have someone ready to listen to them and to understand them, they will feel safe enough to confide their inner thoughts. Posing appropriate questions can also help them identify what it is that is preventing them from accepting death or help them realize that death may not be so fearsome. As spiritual care professionals do, relatives can listen to the patient with an open, nonjudgmental, and sympathetic heart. They should focus more on asking questions rather than lecturing or sermonizing. Helping patients lessen their worries about their children, grandchildren, spouse, or other loved ones may help them accept death.

3. Helping Patients Focus Their Minds on Goodness

Thinking of goodness helps the mind become wholesome, peaceful, bright, less fearful, and better able to deal with pain. The Buddha and his disciples often recommended that those on the verge of death recollect and have firm faith in the Three Refuges. These can be thought of as something virtuous or sacred that the patient can worship. The Buddha also had the dying reestablish themselves in the observance of morality (*sila*) as well as recollect the good deeds they had done in the past. There are many ways to help incline patients to recollect these things. For example, you can:

- Place in the patient's room a buddha statue, other sacred objects, or pictures of respected spiritual teachers to serve as aids to recollection
- Invite the patient to chant or pray with you
- Read Dharma books out loud to the patient
- Play recordings of Dharma talks or chanting
- Invite monks, especially ones the patient has a connection with, to visit the patient and provide counseling
- Encourage the patient to do good deeds, such as offering requisites to monks and making charitable donations

In applying these ideas, one should keep in mind the patient's cultural background and personal habits. For example, patients of Chinese background may respond best to pictures of Bodhisattva Kuan Yin. If the patient is Christian or Muslim, one may use the appropriate symbols of these religions instead.

Encouraging patients to think of the good deeds they have done in the past does not necessarily have to mean religious activities only.

Pride in the good deeds they have done and faith in the beneficial effect of such deeds becomes very important for those close to dying. At this time, it is becoming clear to them that they cannot take any of their material wealth with them when they die. It is only the merit they have accrued through good intentions and actions (*karma*) that they can take with them.

Everyone, no matter how rich or poor or what mistakes they have made in the past, has to have done some good deeds worth recollecting. No matter how many terrible things they have done in the past, when they are close to dying, what we should do is help them to recollect their good deeds. If they are overwhelmed with feelings of guilt, they may not be able to see any of their good deeds. However, any good deeds, even small ones, will be valuable to them if remembered during this time of crisis. At the same time, patients who have been doing good deeds all along should not let any unwholesome deeds overshadow all the goodness they have done, making them feel badly about themselves. In some cases, family and friends may need to list out their past good deeds as a way of confirming and reiterating them, giving patients confidence in the life they have led.

One example that I learned from our network concerned a policeman who was trembling despite being in a comatose state. Witnessing this situation, his wife burst into tears, but the attending nurse warned her that her crying would make things worse. She was encouraged to speak good things about her husband. After composing herself, the wife told her dying husband that she was proud of him as a good policeman and loving husband who eagerly helped her to sell food in the market. His son also told him how good a father he had been. Gradually, the patient's trembling calmed, and he died in peace.

4. Helping Patients Settle Unfinished Business

One major cause of suffering that prevents people from dying peacefully is unfinished business. Such anxieties or other negative feelings need to be released as soon as possible. Otherwise, they will cause the patient to suffer, feel heavy-hearted, and push away death, thus making him or her unable to die peacefully and resulting in an unfortunate rebirth. A patient's family and friends should be very concerned about these matters and be quick to act on them. Sometimes patients may not bring the matter up directly. Those who are around the patient should thus be very sensitive to it and ask the patient about it with genuine concern and kindness, not annoyance.

Some of the kinds of unfinished business a patient may hold on to are the following:

- Remaining work, responsibilities, or a will that has not been settled. Families should do their best to find a way to help bring these matters to a conclusion.
- Seeing someone for the last time. If possible, it is best to hurry and contact that person.
- Angry grudges against someone or hurt feelings and grievances against a close intimate. In this case, it is best to advise the patient to forgive that person and let go of any anger.
- Nagging guilt over some wrong the patient had done. This is a major area, which requires further explanation.

Asking for forgiveness is not easy to do. One way to make it easier for dying patients is to have them write down their apology and everything they wish to say to the other person. They can have someone deliver it to that person or choose to keep it to themselves. The important thing is that by doing this exercise they have begun to open their hearts. Even if no real communication has ensued with the other person, there has still been some release of those feelings of guilt. If at some point they feel more ready to talk to that person directly, they may decide to do so on another occasion.

Oftentimes the person from whom the dying patient seeks forgiveness is someone close, who is right by the bedside, such as a spouse or a child. In this case, it is easier if such people initiate the conversation by offering their forgiveness first and telling the patient they do not bear any ill-will toward the patient for his or her past mistakes. However, in order to do this, such people must first let go of any pride or anger they may feel. By making the first move, such people open the channel for the dying patient to ask for forgiveness more easily.

In Thailand, oftentimes children do not dare to open up to their parents even when they are about to die. This might be because they may not be accustomed to talking to their parents openly. It also could be because they think their parents do not hold their misdeed against them or do not even know about it at all, which could be a serious and irreparable miscalculation. In the case where the dying person is a parent or elder relative, the children, grandchildren, and other family members may join together to hold a ceremony to ask forgiveness at the person's bedside and select a representative to speak for the group. They can begin by speaking of the dying person's virtuous qualities and the good things he or she has done for his or her descendants. Then they can ask for forgiveness for anything they have done that may have caused harm or offense.

5. Helping Patients Let Go of Everything

A refusal to accept death and the reality of its imminence can be a great cause of suffering for people who are close to dying. A reason for such refusal can be that they are still deeply attached to certain things and unable to be separated from them. A feeling of deep attachment can be experienced by people even if they do not have any lingering feelings of guilt in their hearts. Family and friends as well as doctors and nurses should help dying persons let go of their attachments as much as possible, such as by reassuring them that their children and other descendants will be taken care of and reminding them that all their material possessions have to be given to others to take care of.

In giving spiritual guidance to the dying, the Buddha's deepest advice was to let go of all their concerns, even any aspirations for rebirth in heavenly realms. The belief that heaven exists helps satisfy the deep-seated need for the continuance of one's self. However, anything that remains as a basis for attachment will hold their minds back, make them resist death, and be agitated until the end.

Thus, when death approaches, there is nothing better than to let go of everything, even the notion of self.

For those whose experience of Buddhism has been limited to rituals or basic forms of merit-making, however, it is probably not an easy matter to understand the concept of no-self (*anatta*). Nonetheless, family, friends, doctors, and nurses who have an adequate understanding of this truth can advise dying patients to gradually let go of their attachment to self by advising them to first let go of the body, recognizing that we cannot control our bodies to be as we wish them to be. The next step is to let go of their feelings, to not identify with or attach to any feelings as being theirs. Doing this will help greatly to reduce their suffering and pain, because suffering tends to arise when one attaches to pain and identifies with it as being ours. One holds that "I" am in pain instead of just seeing that the condition of pain has arisen.

To be able to let go in this way requires considerable experience in training the mind. However, it is not beyond the reach of ordinary people to do so, especially if one starts training the mind when one first becomes ill. There have been many cases of people with serious illnesses who have been able to deal with extreme pain without using any painkillers at all or only small doses. The method that is widely suggested is the practice of mindfulness of the breath (*anapanasati*), which helps to calm the mind and keep it from identifying with the pain. By keeping their minds focused on the breath or abdomen, they ended up needing to use very little pain medication. Moreover, their minds were clearer and more alert than patients who used many painkillers.

For example, a good friend of mine named Supaporn who had developed terminal breast cancer preferred clear awareness over painkillers. Her regular practice of meditation helped her to withstand the pain with very few painkillers, much to the surprise of her doctor.[2] In the past, there were many people in Thailand who died peacefully in an upright sitting posture, because they were able to let go of their identification with the pain as being theirs. It could be said that they used spiritual medicine to heal their minds.

It should be noted that a large amount of pain is caused by anxiety, fear, and other negative emotions. Pain can be reduced if the patient is thus relieved of these emotions. In one example that a doctor related to me, a patient was agitated during the terminal stage of his death. The painkiller worked for only ten minutes, after which he began to tremble again. Since he did not know how to do meditation, the doctor offered to guide him in total relaxation. He asked the patient to be aware of each part of his body, starting from the feet and moving to the head. He guided him to be just aware and to relax with the help of light music. After thirty minutes, he became peaceful, both in body and emotion. The doctor also taught his relatives how to help him do this exercise. With this practice, he became more responsive to the medicine, requiring smaller doses to help calm him.

6. Creating a Peaceful Atmosphere

For dying patients to be able to feel at peace and let go of all lingering concerns and attachments in a sustained manner, it is necessary for them to have the support of a peaceful atmosphere around them. If their room is swarming with people coming in and out, and filled with the sounds of people talking all the time or the sounds of the door opening and closing all day, it will naturally be difficult for them to maintain their mind in a wholesome and peaceful state. This includes a peaceful social environment as well as physical one, such as a peaceful family.

The least that family, friends, doctors, and nurses can do is to help create a peaceful atmosphere for them. They should avoid talk that disturbs the patient. Family members should refrain from arguing among themselves or crying. These things would only increase the anxiety and unease of the patient. The states of mind of the people surrounding the dying patient can affect the atmosphere in the room and the person's mind. It is possible even for patients in comas to sense the mental energy of those around them. These findings by our team and our general Thai Buddhist tradition are corroborated by other Buddhist traditions like the Chinese and Tibetan ones described elsewhere in this volume. If family and friends can try to keep their minds in a healthy state—not sad or depressed—this will already be a great help to dying patients.

In addition, family and friends can create a peaceful environment by encouraging dying patients to practice meditation together with them. One style of practicing mindfulness of breathing is as follows: When breathing in, mentally recite "Bud." When breathing out, mentally recite "Dho." When put together, "Buddho" is the recitation of the Buddha's name. Alternatively, with each exhalation, count, "1, 2, 3 . . ." up through the number ten, and then start again. If it is not easy for dying persons to be mindful of the breath, they can focus their awareness on the rising and falling of the abdomen as they breathe in and out by placing both hands on top of the abdomen. On the inhalation, as the abdomen rises, mentally recite, "rising." On the exhalation, as the abdomen falls, mentally recite, "falling."

Encouraging dying patients to do chanting together with family and friends in a room that has been set up to create an aura of serenity and sanctity is another way to bring a peaceful atmosphere to dying patients and incline their mind in a wholesome way. That is why some people choose to die in their homes. For example, my friend Supaporn refused hospitalization and eventually decided to die in her home, at which she had prepared an atmosphere that was conducive to a peaceful death. She had cultivated a beautiful garden that could be appreciated from her bed. In her room, she had a buddha image and pictures of her great teachers like Buddhadasa and Maha Ghosananda. Sometimes she also listened to nice, spiritual music.[3]

I know of another case in which a woman got cancer. She was from a modern, urban Chinese Thai family, and in her last stage also suffered from toxins in her liver. She declined to get further medication and decided to go home for her last period of life. According to the doctor, she was very likely to be unconscious and in pain during her last days. However, on the contrary, she retained her awareness until the last hour, because she tried to keep her mind positive with the help of her relatives. They reminded her of all the good things she had done in her life. In the final hour, her family chanted Amitabha's name in Chinese one thousand times, and she passed away almost unnoticeably, like a candle flickering out. This shows what the family can do without the help of monks, and this is why our network has started to hold workshops for nurses, doctors, and families so they can do this process by themselves.

As important as a peaceful mind is, from the Buddhist viewpoint it is wisdom that is considered the most important thing for a person close to dying. Wisdom means clear knowledge of the truths of life: impermanence (*anicca*), dissatisfaction due to change (*dukkha*), and selflessness (*anatta*). These three truths about all things show us that there is not a single thing to which we can cling. We will find death fearsome if we are still clinging to some things. However, once we fully understand that there is actually nothing we can cling to, death will no longer be fearsome.

7. Saying Goodbye

For those who would like to say what is in their hearts to the dying person, such as saying sorry or goodbye, it is not too late to do so. The important thing to keep in mind is that being able to say goodbye and to guide the dying person's mind to a wholesome state can only be done well if the atmosphere surrounding the person is peaceful and the person is not disturbed by any attempts to perform invasive medical interventions. In most hospitals in Thailand, if patients are in the ICU and their pulse weakens to the point where they are close to dying, doctors and nurses will tend to do whatever it takes to keep them alive, such as defibrillation or using all other available forms of medical technology. The atmosphere around such patients is chaotic, and it is difficult for family and friends to say anything to them. The only exceptions are cases where patients and family members inform hospital personnel in advance of their wish that the patient be allowed to die peacefully, free of any medical interventions.[4]

Even if one has said goodbye to someone when he or she was still conscious, it is still useful to say goodbye again just before the person dies. As a person's pulse weakens progressively and he or she approaches the moment of death, if family and friends wish to say goodbye, they should first establish mindfulness and restrain their grief. Then they can whisper their final words in the ear of the dying person. They should talk of the good feelings they have toward the person, give the person praise and thanks for all the good he or she has done, and ask for forgiveness for any wrongs committed. Then they can guide the person's mind to ever-more wholesome states by advising the person to let go of everything, drop all worries, and recollect the Three Refuges or whatever the person venerates. If the person has some grounding in Buddhist teachings, ask him or her to let go of the "self" and all conditioned things, to incline the mind toward emptiness, and to keep the mind focused on nirvana; then, say goodbye.

CONCLUSION

When death is imminent, nothing is more important than a peaceful death. No success one earns in this life guarantees a peaceful death. Only the appropriate quality of mind can enable one to die peacefully. Influenced by a materialistic worldview, people tend to focus on the physical aspects of illness, while ignoring the emotional or spiritual ones. Such an approach tends to increase the suffering of the dying and diverts them from a peaceful death.

A peaceful death is possible when the dying are embraced by love and relieved of anxiety. It is possible when one lets go of everything or focuses on the goodness either in one's life or as represented by sacred beings. Living a decent life also contributes to a good death. Life and death are actually one and the same matter. As Rev. Mari Sengoku emphasizes in her chapter, we will die in more or less the same fashion as we have lived. If we live in ignorance, our final moment will likely be spent in agony, without any sense of peace and mindfulness. However, if we constantly cultivate merit and self-awareness, we should be able to pass away peacefully, being in a state of mindfulness until our last breath.

Health care systems should be geared to support a peaceful death, instead of prolonging life at all costs. Saving life is important, but when that mission is impossible, no other choice is better than facilitating a peaceful death by promoting an atmosphere conducive to spiritual practice and spiritual assistance to the dying. Hospitals should not be only the theater to fight with death but also the place where one can be at peace with death.

CAMBODIA
Actualizing Understanding: Compassion, AIDS, Death, and Dying among the Poor

Beth Kanji Goldring

In the Maryknoll hospice, Kunthea is dying, of cancer in addition to her AIDS. Souen, our staff member and Kunthea's old friend, has been visiting virtually every day. We have more or less freed her from seeing other patients; she is also going in on her own time.

Today Ramo, my translator, and I have come down to the hospice to talk to the director about something. We stop in to see Kunthea before Souen gets there. Kunthea is crying. Her diaper, terribly loose because her legs and buttocks are sticks, is leaking, and someone has said something unkind to her. We clean her up, saying calming words, and begin to do some reiki. I am working at her swollen feet, Ramo at her back and shoulders. I try to do some reiki with her stomach, hugely swollen from the tumor, but the tissue is utterly unresponsive. Kunthea keeps saying she wants to sleep, but she is restless, not able to stay in one position even for a full minute.

Ramo and I hang in there, doing what we can, until Souen arrives and climbs into bed with Kunthea. Then we go to our meeting. When we are finished, we look in on Kunthea again. Souen has covered her with a blanket and, still sitting by her head, is softly chanting the Buddhist precepts to her. A tremendous peacefulness fills the room and emanates from it. Ramo joins Soeun while I go about other business.

Later, Ramo tells me that it was impossible to know when Kunthea passed from sleep into death. He and Souen, both of them fully attentive to her, became aware that she had gone, but they did not know when she stopped breathing—there is usually some short time between the two events. The transition was seamless.

Later, I reflect that if eleven years of our work had produced nothing more than this one seamless death, it would have been worth every bit of time and effort.

Background of the AIDS Epidemic in Cambodia

Brahmavihara/Cambodia AIDS Project was conceived in 1999 when I was working for the Asian Human Rights Forum, investigating two things: health care for the Cambodian poor, with which I had some experience, and how Buddhism could help the poor. These questions came together around the issue of AIDS.

Cambodia's history over the past forty years has been traumatic and difficult. One of the poorest countries in the world, Cambodia was involved indirectly in the US war in Vietnam during the 1960s, plunged into civil war by the Lon Nol coup in 1970, and then taken over by the Khmer Rouge in 1975. It was liberated in January 1979 from the Khmer Rouge by a government backed by the Vietnamese army. In the resulting state of civil war, Cambodia's reconstruction was also hampered by international isolation. Civil war lasted from 1979 through the Paris peace talks, through the period of the United Nations Transitional Authority in Cambodia, and through the 1993 elections, until the late 1990s, when the surrender of Ieng Sary and the death of Pol Pot effectively ended this opposition.

Although tremendous efforts have gone into rebuilding the country since 1993, they have all too often been hampered by corruption and the impunity of the ruling classes. In 1999, despite increasing wealth in Phnom Penh, this legacy of war, destitution, and corruption was all too apparent. Streets, both in Phnom Penh and connecting major cities, were unpaved; bomb craters dating back to the 1970s still existed; and landmines remained a significant danger in many areas of the country. Schools, hospitals, and other public facilities lacked even the most rudimentary essentials. Salaries for government employees were far below starvation levels. This resulted in what was commonly called "survival corruption": the need for government workers to privately charge patients, students, or other beneficiaries for what should have been free services. "Survival corruption" became compounded by increasing ordinary corruption as people's hopes for improvement diminished.

The AIDS epidemic in Cambodia started relatively late, with the first case being diagnosed in 1991. By 1999, Cambodia had one of the fastest developing AIDS epidemics in Asia, if not the world. AIDS had reached a point where prevalence among sex workers, the military, and the police was in the 30–40 percent range. There were an estimated 175,000–225,000 patients with over 25,000 deaths a year, out of a population of around 12 million; husbands were bringing the disease home to wives and children; time between diagnosis and death was normally less than a year; and the cocktail of available drugs did not include antiretrovirals (ARVs), the life-extending medicines available in the First World. Virtually everyone with AIDS died from it, many as outcasts. The prediction was that by 2010 Cambodia would look like the worst of Africa, with general prevalence rates around 40 percent throughout the country and hundreds of thousands of AIDS orphans being raised by destitute grandparents.

The National AIDS Hospital at the Khmer-Soviet Friendship Hospital, known as Roussey, supported by Medecins sans Frontieres (MSF)[1] since 1997, was working to establish programs but with very few resources. The program had thirty beds, which later increased to sixty. MSF staff worked hard to train doctors and nurses and provided social workers, general cleaning, and food for patients and families, along with diagnoses, testing of family members—mostly wives at the time—and some medicines. The organization employed one person, later two, to do essential caregiving for patients without family.[2] It provided mats for bare beds and one diaper a day for patients with uncontrolled diarrhea.

MSF could not provide even such protective equipment as masks and gloves for medical staff. They could not provide blankets, pillows, mosquito nets, or many medicines, including smaller needles for IV fluid for patients. MSF could not supplement the medical staff's salaries, except by paying for attendance when holding workshops and trainings. They could also not control the corruption endemic to a system of such privation and need.

Mother Theresa's Missionaries of Charity had a hospice outside of town where people could go to die. Medical care was scant, but it was clean and people were not lonely. The two wards, for men and women, each held eight beds.

Maryknoll, the America Catholic mission, was pioneering home care—visiting patients twice a week to give them simple medicines and some support money. They were also running a clinic that did testing. There was no general free testing at the time; in many areas of the country, testing was discouraged, because there was no treatment available. Maryknoll was also providing tuberculosis drugs, doing educational programs and outreach, and providing a little money toward funerals. Most Maryknoll staff members were AIDS patients; very few of them lived through this phase of the epidemic. In 2000, Maryknoll turned the home care work over to a number of small organizations and opened a small hospice, while also keeping its clinic and continuing to test people and care for them as outpatients. The head of their programs, Father Jim Noonan, also acted as my unofficial supervisor for many years. The generous support, guidance, and care he gave me were characteristic of the love his programs gave everyone they touched.

There were also several organizations working to train Buddhist monks in counseling and nondiscrimination[3] toward AIDS patients. Salvation Centre of Cambodia, Partners in Compassion—a combined Christian-Buddhist effort—and the Tean Thor organization in Battambang were all trying to educate Buddhist monks to have a compassionate effect on the epidemic. Later, UNICEF would also try to educate Buddhist monks and nuns in effectively addressing AIDS. However, Buddhism in Cambodia was working to recover from destruction under the Khmer Rouge and the complexities and limitations of its restoration. These included political control by and lack of training under the Vietnamese-backed Communist government, which imposed severe limitations on who could be monks, nuns, and *achars*.[4] The restoration under UN intervention and the establishment of the current government has, unfortunately, been marred by the corruption endemic in other areas of Cambodian public life. In addition, most monks are young and do not have the depth of experience to be emotional and spiritual resources for people with AIDS.

Although over the next ten years conditions within the AIDS epidemic in Cambodia would improve tremendously—Cambodia would become a success story; instead of becoming like the worst of Africa, we became like the best of Thailand—when I first encountered the situation in 1999 and began working in 2000, conditions were uniformly terrible. Many people making decisions about allocations of resources did not believe that the problem of care could effectively be addressed; stress was placed on education and prevention instead.

The problem was huge, and I had no idea of where to ground myself in the ongoing suffering. As part of my research, I began visiting with Maryknoll home care teams and was tremendously impressed with their humanity and kindness to patients. One day I happened to chant silently with a dying patient. The next day, when I visited, his mother said, "He was so relieved by your chanting. He believes he has AIDS because of his karma. Because we have no money for monks (to make merit), he is terrified that his next life will be even worse."

Brahmavihara/Cambodia AIDS Project was created in that moment. I was overwhelmed by the sense that in the whole huge, terrible picture of AIDS in Cambodia this was one tiny piece—terror in the face of death because of misunderstood Buddhist teachings— that did not have to happen. I understood that the automatic connection of merit and money inflicted tremendous unnecessary suffering on the poor.[5]

According to the Pali Canon, the Buddha did not have to teach and was, initially, reluctant to do so.[6] After his compassion overcame his reluctance, he taught both the nature of suffering and the path of emergence from it. As I understand the matter, any and all suffering, without discrimination or regard to external conditions, places us at the center of the Buddha's compassion.

However, the Cambodian poor do not know this. They believe that their destitution, filth, isolation, and the neglect and stigmatization they endure as AIDS patients places them outside the Buddha's compassion and care. It is not enough, and often not even possible, for them to understand intellectually that they are, like everyone who suffers, at the heart of the Buddhist system. That understanding has to be actualized in a way that is life giving. Brahmavihara was founded with the sole purpose of helping people realize that the Buddha's compassion is already fully present, even and especially in the midst of their terrible conditions. Over time, I began to appreciate that our own understandings would also become intimately involved in this process of actualization.

Phase I (2000–2002): Being with the Dying

At the beginning of 2000, I started Brahmavihara/Cambodia AIDS Project, working with my translator Ramo. Later that year, we added Lok Yay[7] Coy Srein. She was the mother of a patient with whom we were close, who died in April that year. In the hospital, she had been a resource to me and to many others and had corrected me about many things. We sent her to train as a Buddhist nun, and then we all worked together.

We saw so much death in our first years. Some of it I will carry with me always, like the death of my first close patient, Vuthy. He held on to life until we arrived in the afternoon and then had me hold his hand and chant to him as he moved away, inch by inch by inch, in his eyes. Sixteen-year-old Sinoun clutched a filthy stuffed animal as she died of kidney failure, her mother by her side. Van Da, blinded by the virus, his wife beside him, kept his courtesy and kindness until the end. Srey Mao, whose children, especially her deaf daughter, stole everything they could, died in terror despite all we could do. Twenty-three-year-old Chanthy had a tough front but cried helplessly and unreservedly when the new husband she met in the hospital lay dying; she followed him not long after. Bunthoeun's mother refused to let him die. She had saved his life during the Khmer Rouge period and was determined to save it again, and clung, refusing to let him go, long after he himself was ready. The list is endless.

Roussey averaged three or four deaths a week, sometimes more, usually coming in bunches. On one horrible day, Lok Yay went to the temple where destitutes were cremated and found four bodies there instead of the one she expected. In 2002, the Roussey mortuary attendants estimated that they saw sixty bodies a month.

In addition to visiting and listening to people, we did hands-on work: massage, holding hands, sitting on beds, hugging people, and kissing them. At first, I did not realize fully how important that was, but then I heard that patients would say to Ramo, "My family never comes to visit me. If they do come, they sit all the way across the room. But that foreign nun, she sits on my bed and *kisses* me!"

We tried to teach the patients to meditate. They would cooperate for a day or two, counting their breaths as they sat, and then would be "too busy" or "too tired" to continue. They were sick, exhausted, and dying, and the effort of learning far outweighed any benefit they experienced. When I was in the US that autumn, someone suggested I learn reiki,[8] since our work was hands-on. When I returned we were astonished at how much the patients loved it and how peaceful they became. I have come to understand that reiki allows people to enter a meditative state without their having to make the efforts. Reiki, and later Healing Touch[9] as well, have become mainstays of our practice.

Our ideas about teaching Buddhism to patients also had to be radically modified. People who are uneducated, poor, and under terrible stress are not in a condition to understand complicated explanations or teachings. Most Cambodians, including many monks, have been taught the Three Refuges and the Five Precepts in Pali by rote and have no idea what they mean. Traditions, originally very similar to those described in Ven. Phaisan's chapter on Thailand, have been lost, and what has replaced them often has not helped to sustain a meaningful relationship with the Buddha's teachings. After some efforts—which are comical in retrospect, except that they failed to offer needed support—we learned that it was important to use particularly familiar forms of Buddhist teachings and to keep explanations simple and clear. Chanting, giving the precepts—which are seen as protection—and using familiar forms and rituals helped to provide a feeling of safety for both patients and families. Safety has significant importance for people with little experience of it who are on the edge of death.

One important intervention we learned had to do with traditional Cambodian beliefs. Traditionally, children believe they owe a debt to their parents for raising them and that they are bound to repay this in reciprocal care. This created tremendous problems on both sides when the elderly were required to care for dying adult children. The elderly, most often mothers, believed that with every act of care they placed additional debt and responsibility on their children; they called this "giving sin to their child."[10] The children, in turn, felt guilty that they were being cared for rather than giving care. On both sides, the beliefs exacerbated the already existing suffering from destitution, disease, and impending death. Without disparaging the traditional view in any way, we did find it possible to help people reinterpret the care in terms of compassion. People were often able to grasp that the compassion in the parents' efforts overrode the danger of sin from the acts themselves. The child, by being the occasion of compassion and merit-making by the parent, received merit, rather than sin, in return. Patients and parents both received comfort by seeing compassionate care in terms of bringing merit to both giver and receiver, despite the reversal of traditional roles involved in the care.

Throughout all this, I was overwhelmingly impressed by Khmer women, especially the wives of patients. These women would come to the hospital with their husbands, be tested, and discover that they, too, were under sentence of almost certain death. Nevertheless, they would remain, tending their husbands with impressive love and care, often exhausting family resources and leaving nothing for themselves.

I have dwelled a long time on the conditions we initially faced working with destitute AIDS patients in Cambodia. This is partly because our conditions and working assumptions appear to me to be very different from those of some other contributors in this volume, although we clearly share deep goals in common. They are working in more viable health care systems and where Buddhist traditions are more intact, albeit with difficulties. This review will show how far we have come in terms of AIDS treatment, both as a country and as an individual organization. These achievements are especially important to remember, because care in Cambodia is now in a major structural crisis.

PHASE II (2003–7): WORKING WITH STEADILY IMPROVING CONDITIONS FOR THE POOR AND ILL

Broad social marketing of condoms helped slow AIDS transmission rates, but the most important change for AIDS treatment came with the introduction of free antiretroviral care (ARVs) through MSF, beginning slowly in mid-2001. This took time to take hold, but by 2003–4 there were many other institutions and organizations providing ARVs. These included Medecins du Monde, HOPE International, CARITAS, Family Health International, Friends/Mitsamlang (an organization working with street children, including those with AIDS in their families), Pharmacists without Borders, and others. Clinics were set up throughout Phnom Penh; some specialized in working with sex workers and transgender people, who were often discriminated against elsewhere. Prevention of mother-to-child transmission (PMCT) programs developed in many organizations. Voluntary counseling and testing centers were set up throughout the country, most commonly at the government health centers. ARVs became available in other cities and provinces; beautiful educational and support materials were developed. HOPE International set up a hospice with First-World care and developed economic support projects. The Dhammayietra, the annual Buddhist peace walk founded by Maha Ghosananda, included AIDS awareness, compassion, and education on its walks. Dhammayietra: People Walking with AIDS, founded in 2001, provided home care to almost two hundred villages in the north of the country. They later branched out, developing groups for emotional, economic, and other practical support. Small nongovernmental organizations (NGOs) proliferated. Maryknoll expanded; in 2008 it had over 2,200 patients, orphans, and families in thirteen different programs.

By 2008 Cambodia was a major success story with official prevalence rates at 0.9–1.9 percent rather than the predicted 30–40 percent. According to Roussey hospital, some 80 percent of patients were able to successfully adapt to ARVs; the death rate from AIDS was somewhere around 3 percent among their patients. Hospitals were renovated. Khmer medical staff became highly skilled AIDS specialists. Trained, skilled social workers were broadly available, as were trained peer counselors. Free treatment for some non-AIDS conditions was broadly available to AIDS patients. In this way, instead of a death sentence, AIDS became a serious, chronic, but largely manageable disease. That this occurred in Cambodia, with all its problems, was seemingly miraculous.

The course of all this, naturally, was hardly as smooth as it seems in retrospect. Those who survived faced tremendous emotional and practical problems. Most of them had lost a spouse and/or child, jobs, housing, and family support and had been repeatedly close to death. Sometimes wives and children were thrown out of a family, without resources, upon the husband's death. During their first months on ARVs, people went through intense emotional and spiritual crises. Patients also, as they began to recover, needed practical help in restoring their lives. Although it took some time for that help to emerge, it eventually did for many people.

Van Ouern lives in what was the Borei Kela slum with his wife and five children. When the slum underwent renovation, he was one of the lucky ones who was rehoused there in better conditions. In 2002–3, Ouern was desperately ill and close to death. I was convinced he would not live. He finally received ARVs. His first months were very difficult, but he persevered, taking the medicines carefully, and began to recover health and strength. By the end of 2003, he had the strength and appearance of a normal healthy person. Ouern works as a peer counselor for other AIDS patients on ARVs and is an inspiration to them.

We have many such stories. Seven out of eleven of my staff members are AIDS patients. All of them have lost people close to them. Several of them were very near death, one repeatedly. They have been able to transform that trauma and loss into compassion for our patients. However, we also know patients who recovered and opened gambling dens, sold ARVs and amphetamines, stole, and otherwise went back to their previous lives. Deeply traumatic events do not often change people for the better. Most often, they simply extend and deepen existing trauma and suffering. When people's inner lives do become better, it is worth celebrating and also worth examining the processes by which it takes place.

Mae Srey Lek, a forty-five-year-old woman, was the mother of a young woman with AIDS who we loved and who died in 2002, aged twenty-three. Her second husband died in 2004. From her second marriage, Mae Srey Lek had three sons. The older two took after their father, who drank and beat her. The second son drank and used drugs. They also mistreated the youngest, Chanthorn, who often stayed away from home and started taking drugs when he was twelve years old. At one point Mae Srey Lek kept Chanthorn chained at home to control him.

In the middle of all this, Mae Srey Lek held everything together as best she could. She would get up at 3 a.m. each day and take a cart around the city to collect recyclables, earning about $2.50/day for twelve hours of work. Although she had AIDS, she remained strong until well into 2006 when her health began to deteriorate. She gave up hope, especially when Chanthorn was having problems, and began drinking and gambling. By the beginning of 2007, she was seriously ill with tuberculosis. In March she was diagnosed with inoperable cervical cancer. Our experience with chemotherapy for Cambodian AIDS patients has been that they die very quickly. Therefore, instead of trying to provide it for her, we tried to make her last months as peaceful and happy as possible.

Mae Srey Lek insisted on staying in her home. Our director, Pheap, who lives not far from her, went to her house every day to make sure she took her tuberculosis medicines. He also insisted that she begin ARVs despite the cancer and made sure she took them. We saw her several times a week for reiki and provided money for rent, food, intravenous fluids, and help when she could not manage on her own. When her pain became severe, we supplemented the codeine she received. With the medicines and without the stress of collecting garbage each day, Mae Srey Lek gained strength. On her own initiative, she found work at home mending shoes and sewing rice sacks together. Emotionally, she was also much better, surrounded by love from her neighbors. Chanthorn was better. He was not living at home, but he had stopped taking drugs and had gone back to school. Her middle son, who had often come home drunk and on drugs, moved out of the house and stopped stealing from her.

In June, Mae Srey Lek told us that she wanted us to ordain her as a Buddhist nun. In Cambodia, ordination for women, unlike that for men, is a very informal procedure. She could not have managed living in a temple, and did not want to, but it was possible for her to be a nun at home. We thought this was wonderful. We shaved her head, bought her nun's clothing, and gave her eight precepts at the Roussey hospital mortuary. She lived her last months as a Khmer nun. Mae Srey Lek died peacefully on September 16, 2007. We provided her with a funeral in which her whole community participated.

Our own work, over those years, developed and changed. When ARVs came into Roussey hospital, we stopped working there exclusively. After some exploration we coordinated with several home care organizations, visiting people at home in various slums. We also began visiting the Maryknoll hospice and their group homes for patients not yet able to support themselves. We visited the various hospitals when our patients were there. By 2003, we were seven people and would go out in teams, covering our areas every week but concentrating where we felt the most needed.

People waiting for ARVs or just beginning to take them needed extensive emotional and other support. During the first month of treatment, patients often saw ghosts. We did ceremonial cleansing in homes, group homes, Roussey hospital, and other places where people were terrified of ghosts they had seen. Crucially, we helped to provide linking services to the various emerging organizations designed to help people rebuild their lives or to care for orphaned children. We took people to hospitals and organizations, got them referrals, and helped to facilitate what we could.

We continued and increased our reiki practice. I had become a reiki master by then and could teach my staff. In the Borei Kela slum, in the center of Phnom Penh, I would often give short treatments to as many as eight patients a day, usually under low tin roofs with as many as fifteen people crowded into a four-by-five meter space with one large bed. In 2006, a Healing Touch teacher instructed everyone on staff, and we all became qualified in both Healing Touch and reiki. We had nine staff members by then, including myself. Although all have become finely capable practitioners, two of my staff are especially gifted. Their styles have become very individual. In 2008, six of my staff became reiki masters, the first Khmer reiki masters in Cambodia.

We continued to see a lot of death but learned more skills to deal with it. My staff began to learn traditional Khmer chanting under Lok Yay, our Buddhist nun. Later, they spent a year formally studying it as well as studying *smot*, the unique form of traditional Khmer chanting that tells stories of the Buddha and is designed to encourage the experiencing, purification, and clarification of deep emotional pain.[11] Although my younger staff members were initially hesitant to chant with living patients, as it is traditionally old people who chant, they gradually grew accustomed to it, especially as the patients themselves wanted it. Lok Yay's retirement at the end of 2009 further encouraged them to take responsibility for chanting.

Often we would accompany destitute patients' bodies to the temple to chant during their cremations. In 2003, we installed a buddha image in the newly built Roussey hospital mortuary and began going there twice a month on major precept days to clean the space, purify it, and chant. When there were bodies in the mortuary, we included them in ceremonies, making sure that they had the traditional incense, candles, and tiny bit of money on their chests to take with them in cremation. We would bring them to lie behind us in front of the buddha image for chanting. Then we would uncover their faces; give them Tibetan *amrita* pills, blessing pills made from healing herbs as thousands of mantras are chanted; and sprinkle them with the *amrita* liquid we use along with reiki signs to purify the space. Finally, we would chant separately for each of them, giving them precepts, before the general chanting. This continued until 2011, when the mortuary was sold to a private company. We can no longer chant there and now celebrate precept days in our own meditation hall.

In 2007, thanks to Firefly Mission, a Singaporean Buddhist charitable organization, we renovated the mortuary at Chea Chum Neas hospital south of the city. That mortuary had not been cleaned in scores of years and was surrounded by an area overgrown with weeds, trash, and used needles. Its rear area was commonly used as an outhouse. We rebuilt it, cleaned the area, put potted plants and flowers in various areas, provided it with incense and candles, and had painted a meditating buddha image in the vestibule and a reclining buddha image in the room for bodies. It became a lovely and peaceful space. We clean and chant there regularly. In addition, we provide cremation for destitutes at Chea Chum Neas. Previously, they had been buried without ceremony or marker in a field behind the hospital. These kinds of ongoing memorial services, akin to those in Japanese Buddhism, we see as an integral part of our own spiritual practice as caregivers and as an offering to those having gone through such suffering.

PHASE III (2008–10): EXPANDING MATERIAL AID WITHIN A VIABLE SYSTEM OF CARE

By 2008 we took many things for granted that would have been unimaginable earlier. Within Phnom Penh and in varying degrees throughout the whole country, patients were diagnosed, received free treatment, received ARVs early enough that their lives had not disintegrated, and recovered if not to full strength then enough strength to live their lives. People remarried and had children safely with PMCT care; women who became pregnant had enough supplementary food support and vitamins that they did not become exhausted and die shortly after giving birth, and their children received free infant formula for at least six months. Doctors at the hospitals were truly skilled in knowing what was necessary for patients. While corruption existed, it was kept in check. The vast majority of destitute AIDS patients, including sex workers, transgender people, and other pariah groups, were able to receive timely, free, skilled care.

People continued to die, of course, and new problems, like cancer, began to emerge in significant numbers. Although we continued to center our efforts on the very ill and dying, there was space for attention to other problems. Thanks largely to the generosity of one Australian couple, we became able to intervene with material aid in areas where other programs left serious gaps.

We were never designed as a material aid program. From the beginning, we left the problems of food, money, and medicine to larger organizations and concentrated on emotional and spiritual support. However, we had long violated this policy, secretly supplying mosquito nets to patients at Roussey hospital and money for transportation home. For several years, we provided housing support in the Borei Kela slum where we worked. We also had some individual cases, like that of Mae Srey Lek, where we provided fairly complex support, depending on conditions. We were able to do this only in situations where supporting one patient more fully would not create jealousy or resentment among others.

This changed in 2005 when the government moved some two thousand families of slum dwellers away from what had become extremely desirable riverfront property to a site in Phum Andong that had no water, electricity, or infrastructure of any sort. Roads leading there were unmaintained dirt. The twenty-two kilometers from my house to there took over an hour by motorcycle. People had poles to support the blue tarps protecting them from rain and whatever they had managed to salvage from their former houses. Visiting with the medical team of one human rights organization, who saw about one hundred people each day, I became aware that the AIDS patients among this group had no way to reach their doctors. Medicines were free but transportation was unaffordable, and several people had already died from the lack. We began what I thought would be a short-term project: finding AIDS patients, keeping track of their appointments, and providing them money for transportation. As of mid-2011, we still have some seventy-six patients at this site and almost one hundred patients coming from the provinces whom we meet at their hospitals. For several years, we funded another seventy patients, whose conditions have improved. In addition to paying all medical transportation, we provide these groups with rice and fish sauce twice a year on major holidays, along with a little money for those in resettlement sites.

In 2005, we began visiting the main men's prison because of a patient we had there. MSF had begun a program to provide AIDS patients in this prison and in the main women and children's prison with medicines. Later, they began to test all prisoners for both AIDS and tuberculosis. In 2008, the prison director asked us to cover all the prisoners; he said that by seeing only a few we created jealousies. At the beginning of 2009, we began providing all diagnosed men and adolescents with monthly packages of supplementary food and a little money (another organization takes excellent care of women with AIDS). In 2010, at the request of the prison doctors, we added tuberculosis patients, but we have had to limit ourselves to a total of 125 patients in both prisons. We see all AIDS patients, all multidrug-resistant tuberculosis (MDR-TB) patients, and all regular tuberculosis patients in their first two months of treatment. We also support some fifty patients in the Cambodian Heath Committee's MDR-TB program with monthly money for food.

Within the development of this vastly increased range of activities, the question of what it means to us that we are a Buddhist organization has also undergone radical change and development. In some ways, what it means to be Buddhist is straightforward. With some exceptions, we work as closely as possible within the Khmer Buddhist tradition. My staff is trained in the Khmer and Pali chanting done in the temples, as well as in smot. We study meditation in the *vipassana* tradition of Sayadaw Mahasi from Burma, the same general Theravada tradition of Cambodia and Southeast Asia. We chant and meditate every day before going out to see patients. We chant on major precept days and several times a month in the Chea Chum Neas Mortuary. We give precepts and chant for patients who are dying and give eight-precept ordination when appropriate. We conduct funeral chanting for the dead and sometimes join in funeral services for families that cannot afford to bring in monks. We continue to give precepts and chant for people for forty-nine days following patient deaths. We sometimes provide small statues of the Buddha for patients. We provide a little money for families to go to the temples seven days after a death, along with urns for the bones of the dead. We continue to conduct ghost ceremonies when asked.

For our own development, we study Buddhist teachings and do extended meditation on Wednesdays. At least once a year, we hold a ten-day staff vipassana retreat. We train in the precepts, the perfections (*paramitas*), and the Four Noble Truths, as well as in other aspects of the Buddha's teaching. The training in the precepts and paramitas is vital. First, the precepts help provide inner safety by preventing us from doing harm. Second, the paramitas not only help us develop the necessary qualities of character for the development of insight, they are also profoundly important in allowing us to continue what is sometimes extraordinarily difficult and painful work over time and to be strengthened rather than weakened by it.

When I began this work, my unofficial supervisor and the head of the Maryknoll project used to say to me, "If it is not life affirming for you, it will not be life affirming for the patients." I used to respond, "Just because it is hard, doesn't mean it isn't life affirming." He would agree. After some years, there was a kind of sea change, and I began to experience a deep intimacy and peacefulness with patients, even under the most difficult and terrible circumstances. Even later, I began to trust and expect this intimacy to emerge. All of us currently on staff have long, deep familiarity with times—sometimes moments, sometimes longer—when both we and the patients (and families) are being held in something profound, wordless, intimate, and deep, when we are as much the recipients as the agents of sustaining compassion.

It is this experience of time and compassion that sustains the work and sustains us within it. All our training, our work on the development of character and insight, and our religious practices have both their testing ground and their fulfillment in this intimacy.

This intimacy is not restricted to our work with patients; it is the supporting fabric of every aspect of our lives. However, it is most fully tested in the work with patients. It is here that we not only experience intimacy but experience, see, and explore the barriers that keep us from it. The more fully we become capable of experiencing intimacy, the more aware we become of the many times when we are preoccupied, annoyed, resistant, distracted, and unable fully to be present. "The patients are our teachers," is a favorite saying of one of my oldest staff members. The longer we work, the more fully we realize how deeply it is we who are in the patients' debt.

Our formal study and practice of Buddhism provides us with both a container to hold this experience and a means of understanding it. Without the container, we would quickly reach and exhaust the limits of our own strength in the work. Without the understanding, we would not know what to do with the experience as it occurs. Because we work in extreme situations, directly in contact with life and death, and often under terrible conditions, we fail often. However, because we study the Buddha's teachings, not only formally but with our whole hearts, we live continually in the possibility of transcending our failures, and sometimes in the experience of that transcendence.

The Buddha often said to place nothing before one's own highest welfare. The Dalai Lama calls compassion "enlightened selfishness." Our work gives us the daily practice in learning the meaning of these teachings and of testing our limits by putting our compassion into practice again and again. As we continue to work in this way, over time our life becomes very ordinary to us. As Suzuki Roshi wrote about Zen practice, "If you continue this simple practice every day, you will obtain some wonderful power. Before you attain it, it is something wonderful, but after you attain it, it is nothing special."[12] This ordinariness is one of the greatest gifts we receive.

CONCLUSION: FACING A NEW CRISIS

In 2010 the Cambodian government took over the major AIDS programs from the NGOs who founded and ran them. MSF left Roussey hospital as well as the regional hospitals they supervised. They have kept their prison program, at least through 2011. Douleurs sans Frontieres left Preah Ket Melea hospital, where they had run a palliative care program. Sharing Experience for Adapted Development (SEAD), an NGO set-up by the staff of Médecins du Monde Cambodia, left Kossamak hospital. Family Health International left altogether. HOPE International, which runs their own hospital rather than working within the government system, was influenced by all this but remains effective. The Cambodian government also decided that NGOs could no longer give supplementary salary payments to government workers, creating economic crisis for medical staff, who remain desperately underpaid.

Overnight, it seemed, the carefully built AIDS health care system collapsed almost entirely. Food, cleaning, social services, health care workers, caregivers, medicines, equipment, and even sheets disappeared from the hospitals. Services and materials that had been free now cost money, both formally and informally through bribes to hospital staff. While the poor received cards theoretically entitling them to health care, the funding for these cards' costs failed to materialize. ARVs remain available for those already on them—some 40,000 people—but few programs have space for new patients. Prevention of mother-to-child transmission programs have ceased to provide infant formula; medicines have become scarce; death rates are soaring. In December 2010, Maryknoll closed its hospice. This hospice, actually a small hospital, had been a major refuge for those who could not find assistance elsewhere. As of mid-2011, we face continuing deterioration. Perhaps conditions will improve again, but because our mandate is for the poor and dispossessed, it is essential that we prepare to work with whatever conditions we find.

Ven. Maha Ghosananda, the great Cambodian Buddhist peace activist used to say, "Truthfulness, forbearance, and gratitude are the three pillars that hold up the world. If one of them is lost, the world collapses." Over the years, we have studied truthfulness and forbearance in our practice. Now we are exploring gratitude, especially its role in providing energy for compassion when conditions become terrible. We understand that it is an enormous privilege to do the work we have been given. We look to gratitude for this privilege to help us face with integrity, strength, compassion, and simplicity whatever awaits us and our patients.

UNITED KINGDOM
The Birth of a New Culture of Active Dying: The Role of Buddhism in Practices and Attitudes Toward Death

Caroline Prasada Brazier

Societies vary greatly in their attitudes toward death and bereavement. Attitudes in turn affect behavior and the practices associated with the care of the dying, the disposal of the body, and the mourning that follows.

In part, societies' practices around death are expedient—reactions to the circumstances of their times. For example, in times of war or epidemic disease, the disposal of the dead may need to be speedy and the accompanying ceremony perfunctory. At other times when life is less pressured, more elaborate rituals prevail. Mostly, though, the reactions to death and the dying process mirror the attitudes and beliefs prevalent in the culture: attitudes that manifest in other areas of life as well.

The quality and character of a culture is reflected in its care and concern for its weakest members. The dying and the bereaved hold a particularly significant place among the most vulnerable; since the dying process challenges humans' longing for omnipotence, it pushes societies and individuals to find meaning in the face of uncertainty and comfort in the face of the irreducible loss of bereavement. The Buddhist tradition arose from the Buddha's struggles with questions of life and death and loss. In their attitudes to death, Buddhists reflect this origin and discover opportunities for spiritual growth in meeting the reality of dying.

DEATH IN VICTORIAN ENGLAND AND BEFORE

When we examine attitudes to death and dying in Britain today, it is impossible to disregard the changing social picture that has emerged over the last century and a half. The historical context reveals a number of layers in this drama of ideas, which can still be traced in current thinking. Let us spend a little time exploring these.

In Britain today one is conscious of a legacy of ideas about death that span many different ages and perspectives. From medieval times one finds graphic imagery that evokes a situation where sudden, early death was commonplace. Skulls and crossed bones, or even representations of wasted corpses, decorate ancient tombs or paintings. Accounts of plagues and massacres abound in the literature. This imagery is overlaid by later styles; baroque churchyards with weeping angels or austere tombstones inscribed with simple messages still testify to attitudes of earlier times in our cities and countryside.

Most influential, however, for our current times, is the Victorian age, the nineteenth century, which seemed particularly preoccupied with matters related to death. This was a time in which large families, a rising urban class, and high infant and maternal mortality rates combined to make death a common visitor in every home, rich or poor. Hardly a family had not lost a child or two, as the highly decorated tombs in Victorian graveyards testify. Diseases of high-density living, such as tuberculosis, typhus, or cholera, swept through populations relatively unhindered by what medical care was available at the time. Average life expectancy was only forty-two years.[1]

In such circumstances, the presence of death was difficult to avoid, and its prominent social acknowledgment seemed inevitable. Queen Victoria's own adoption of deep mourning after the death of her husband Albert in 1861 added to the country's fascination with all that surrounded death. Grief and its expression became not only recognized but also regulated by social norms that dictated minimum periods for mourning, strict dress codes, and curtailment of social activity[2] for close family members of the deceased. These practices, together with elaborate funeral rites and flamboyant memorials, showed that grief was in vogue. There was a good trade in funerary mementos, such as condolence cards and mourning jewelry. Sentimental literature, poetry, and art, recounting stories of tragic and often premature deaths, were popular in the homes of ordinary families.

Interestingly, this highly ritualized culture of death appears not so different from the traditional Japanese Buddhist one, as detailed in the earlier chapters of this volume. The death rituals of nineteenth-century Britain were, however, embedded in the Christian ethos of the times and often accompanied by the Christian metaphysic: images of a salvation in heaven surrounded by angels, cherubs, and other heavenly beings.

People looked for reunification with loved ones. Death was not the ultimate separation. The Victorian glorification of death also, perhaps, echoed the mood of empire with its tales of heroism and youthful sacrifice in the greater cause. Death was romantic, emotive, and sometimes patriotic.

Stoic Views of Death in the War Era

The legacy of these Victorian attitudes persisted into the twentieth century as a continuing but diminishing preoccupation until the time of the First World War. The Great War's carnage swept away the last vestiges of sentimentality and heralded a new era in which attitudes to death changed from the open and even flamboyant mourning to a more curtailed, private expression of loss, and often to psychological denial and distraction. The First World War poets expressed the mood of a generation. Their uncompromisingly harsh accounts of conditions in the trenches challenged the glorification of warfare. The heroic impulse to give one's life in the service of one's country soon looked hollow against the terrible reality of death on the muddy battlefield.

In the grim years that followed, the Victorian romanticization of death seemed excessive and lacking in taste. A new generation, the youth of the war and interwar years, took a more pragmatic approach to life, and, as far as possible, avoided discussion of death—as evidenced by Freud's admonishment to "forget the dead," highlighted in Carl Becker's and Rev. Yozo Taniyama's chapters. This avoidance manifested in the frenetic escapism of the twenties and persisted in the cultivation of respectability through the suppression of emotionality that characterized the following decades: the British "stiff upper lip." It was "work as usual" despite whatever secret pain of bereavement was carried.

Interestingly, both the Victorian and the postwar views of death have left their mark on the popular culture of death in Britain today. The stoicism of the generation that grew up devastated by the effects of World War I remains a characteristic of the elderly. Born in or before the 1920s, they grew up believing that some things, such as death, were to be expected in life and that one should not make too much of a fuss over them.

Until relatively recently, people regarded the Victorian preoccupation with the paraphernalia of death with suspicion and distaste. I recall from my own childhood that many adults saw Victorian attitudes to death as vulgar and morbid, or a subject for ridicule and parody. Death was rarely spoken of, and then, only in hushed, brief conversations. Children did not go to funerals, and many people of my generation were excluded even from the funerals of very close relatives, such as a parent or sibling.

At the same time, the sentimentality of Victorian grieving never completely disappeared from British culture. It met an emotional need for some—not everyone had been taught to regard it as tasteless. Card shops still offered a range of condolence cards, some of which have verses and images of a style that might be drawn directly from Victorian times. Tastes change in society as a whole but, even when the main trend alters, older styles often persist.

Both the Victorians and those bereaved by the First World War knew death intimately. Their responses, though opposite in form, can both be seen as attempts to create psychological containment for the high level of emotion that so many deaths evoked. Containment came either through the emotional but somewhat stylized expression of mourning or through downplaying grief and putting energy into everyday work. It did, nevertheless, allow people to get on with living.

MANAGED DEATH IN THE POSTWAR ERA

Further changes in attitudes to death came with advances in medical practice. The aftermath of the Second World War ushered in the welfare state. Building on advances in medicine in the 1930s and '40s, the new National Health Service promised health for all. The state took on the authority to heal. People had already come to trust the family doctor, a long-standing pillar of the community, to know what was best. Now the doctor's power was nationalized.

With postwar optimism came a belief in the infinite capacity of science to push back the horizons of human limits. The medical practitioner was hailed as the new guru of science. Postwar baby-boom families learned not to question the word of the doctor, which was assumed to rest on a mysterious knowledge transmitted within the profession and guarded from public view. This was a time of social change. The war had disrupted family structures. Over the following decades, people became more mobile, no longer supported by extended families. Welfare provision and social isolation created greater dependence on the state to meet personal needs, and this trend has continued to grow. The age of the expert and the professional was upon us.

In fact, improvements in health have been shown to come far more from advances in public health than from increases in medical knowledge, but the myth persisted that doctors were the ultimate guardians of health. Throughout the 1950s and '60s, the sanctity of science remained paramount in the public imagination.

Against this background, attitudes to death and dying continued to be muted, and the emphasis was still on putting grief behind one and living for the future. It was a time of optimism, encouraged by government propaganda. The focus was on youth and the nuclear family. Medicine reflected this "can do" mentality and set about achieving cures. Science would provide infinite sources of innovation and people looked forward to an indefinite extension of life through medical intervention.

This mythology reached its height in the space-age 1960s. Medical advances aimed at prolonging life almost irrespective of quality of life. The heroes of this age were practitioners who achieved remarkable new feats extending medical knowledge. Dr. Christiaan Barnard, who performed the first human heart transplant in 1967, became a celebrity, more akin to a film star than a surgeon—an icon of his time.

For the gravely sick, the emphasis on medical intervention made it increasingly common for people to die in the hospital. New technologies, drugs, life-extending monitoring instruments, and more sophisticated resuscitation equipment meant that death was now commonly managed by professionals. Relatives, and the dying person her- or himself, were mostly excluded from decision-making. Death was considered to be a medical failure, an embarrassing anomaly in the pristine routines of this medicalized world. The dying were consequently often abandoned in their latter days to minimal care in side wards. New faith in the medical expert thus compounded the notion that death was not to be discussed. It is more than ironic to note the way that we can see so many of these trends replicated in Japan and other developing Asian countries.

By the 1980s, however, new attitudes started to be expressed in the West. Faith in the expert, in medical as well as other areas of professional life, began to be questioned. Now death was described as "the last taboo." Interest in the care of the dying was growing. The 1960s, it was said, had broken the taboos on talking about sexuality, but the taboo on talking about death remained. Slowly, over the following decades, people gained confidence in discussing matters connected with dying, breaking the mold of more than half a century.

REAWAKENING TO DEATH SINCE THE 1960S

The move away from medically managed death began in the late '60s. Elisabeth Kübler-Ross's groundbreaking book *On Death and Dying* was first published in 1969. The Swiss-born psychiatrist, who studied and developed her work in the United States, proposed a model of the psychological stages through which dying people progressed—from denial to acceptance of their situation.

The hospice movement also dated from the '60s. In 1967, Dame Cicely Saunders[3] set up the first hospice, St. Christopher's, at Sydenham. This movement, supporting the dying in practical ways, caught the public imagination and grew steadily through donations and volunteerism. Saunders' biggest contribution, still central to hospice work, was to develop effective pain control. She emphasized establishing a level of analgesia, sufficient to make pain bearable while maintaining good levels of consciousness—a practice clearly of importance to many Buddhists. This was the birth of modern palliative care medicine. Hospices became positive places that offered more personal care than was possible in hospitals.

The hospice movement still has a huge presence in Britain. It has grown steadily, offering both inpatient and outpatient care, and is widely seen as a source of expertise in the care of the dying. Hospital-based palliative care has also improved, modeling itself on methods learned from hospices' experience and offering more patient-centered programs in which care is discussed and planned individually. Pain control is central and, in theory, no one is expected to endure serious pain, though in practice levels of care vary. Complimentary or alternative therapies—such as traditional medicine, folk knowledge, and spiritual beliefs—are used widely, even in mainstream settings, and are often advocated by medical professionals, who are acceptant of the critiques of earlier decades.

Interest in the work initiated by Saunders and Kübler-Ross grew throughout the 1970s, but the advent of the holistic health movement of the 1980s popularized alternative approaches to illness and death. Some holistic approaches were not concerned with dying but rather with offering alternative treatments and cures. Writers like Lawrence Le Shan, for example, advocated an approach to health grounded as much in psychological well-being as in physical treatments. His book *You Can Fight for Your Life* promised healing through personal psychological growth and lifestyle change. Self-help became popular in approaches to terminal illness as well as other fields such as childbirth. Holistic approaches incorporated alternative or complimentary therapies, counseling, and other psychological support; in 1980 the Bristol Cancer Clinic was established to provide such services to cancer sufferers. These holistic approaches are still popular in Britain today. Alongside these changes, medical practitioners were adjusting their roles. No longer god-like figures whose words went unchallenged, doctors began to be seen at best as partners in a cooperative venture, and, at worst, as barriers to the achievement of real health.

The optimism of some self-help and psychologically based approaches to cancer and other serious diseases has not been without its critics. In particular, there has been concern that emphasizing the role of psychological factors in diseases can lead some patients and their carers to feel guilty. They may feel that they should be able to cure themselves. Once again, the sense that a cure must always be possible crept into attitudes to terminal illness. The inevitability of death in some circumstances seemed to have been forgotten. In earlier decades, science and technology offered by the medical profession were seen as the potential sources of the cure. Now, psychology and personal effort became the key.

In addition to the holistic health movement, by the 1970s, the consumer movement was growing, championing people's rights in many fields of merchandising and service provision. It sought regulation and protection as well as choice and availability. By encouraging people to demand quality, it sought to democratize services and make them answerable to their users. In this context, people sought choice in medical care, and particularly in matters of life and death, just as they did in other arenas, such as education or retail. The consumer movement gave impetus to the already significant ability of health services to command political power. Health choice bought votes. With increasing demand for better health services, concern about provision for death and dying also came to the fore.

The movement toward patient empowerment challenged attitudes within the health services themselves and reflected wider changes of attitude in society. Disillusioned with the rational, mechanistic approaches of the modernist world, earlier "belief in the expert" gave way to skepticism. Professional positions relying on certainty gave way to a plurality of approaches that was characteristic of postmodernism. People were now viewed as complex, interconnected systems of mind and body rather than as physical mechanisms. Personal experience and preference was trusted over received knowledge.

Although some gurus of the holistic health movement promised survival against the odds, others saw achieving a good death, once dying became inevitable, as just as important as living well. Following the lead of Saunders and Kübler-Ross, they saw the quality of the dying process as a positive life choice. No longer bound by social norms of silence and stoicism or by deference to professional opinion, people began to take charge of their deaths.

A pioneer of this new active approach has been the Natural Death Centre, established in 1991. It produced Josefine Speyer's *Natural Death Handbook*, which offers practical advice on all aspects of death for both the dying person and for the carer. The book includes information on the later stages of terminal illness and the dying process. It discusses making arrangements for personalized funerals, care of the body after death, different forms of burial and cremation, and environmentally friendly resources. The ultimate in self-help, it invites active participation at all stages of the end of life.

Such resources have elicited growing interest and enthusiasm. More people are now planning ahead for their own deaths. It can be an emotional but satisfying process. Living wills inform carers and relatives of treatment wishes for the end of life, though these are not legally binding on the medical profession. Funerals are becoming increasingly varied, as ordinary people make ceremonies personally meaningful instead of using standard forms. Magazines advertise the video recording of last messages; traditionally run family funeral homes offer eco-friendly coffins, woodland burials, and ceremonials on a made-to-measure basis.

As a Pure Land Buddhist, I find myself interested by the rising influence of self-help methods in health and, particularly, in the care of the dying. These seem to echo our culture's indefatigable belief in the human capacity to control our circumstances, even, it seems, to the point of escaping the inevitable ending of our lives. Similar self-power attitudes can be seen in the way that many Western therapies have embraced teachings of Buddhism, borrowing techniques and ideas with an aim of helping people achieve physical and spiritual wholeness. Belief in the primacy of autonomy, personal choice, and effort is, however, at some remove from Pure Land values of faith, dependence, refuge, and gratitude. The reality is that death is unpredictable, unaesthetic, and not amenable to control of the will. In our deaths, we are in other hands.

The natural death movement is in some ways the ultimate self-help approach to death, but it also recognizes that in the face of death, other powers take over. In this way, it reflects a reverent attitude to life and death and expresses more spiritually based values. We can see this attitude in the opening chapter of the *Natural Death Handbook*:

> Granted that no one can be certain what happens after death, could it be that preparation matters, as the Tibetans argue, to enable the soul at the point of death to merge fearlessly with that bright light reported by many who have recovered from Near-Death Experiences? I remembered how a friend's mother insisted on being given her traveling rug to die with; could the process of dying be the labour pains of the soul, with sometimes the same feeling of expectation and transition as at birth?[4]

This new attitude to death is accompanied by a more open attitude to grief. The extraordinary outpouring of emotion that followed the death of Princess Diana in 1997 reflected this new mood and, in some ways, echoed the public mourning common in Victorian England. It seemed as if, in this collective act, thousands of people expressed the unwept tears of earlier years. In the 2006 film *The Queen* we see the old and the new side by side. Queen Elizabeth, played by Helen Mirren, struggles to understand the public mood in the context of her own more traditional stance of dignity and private grief. Her stoical reaction to news of the death of Diana, reflecting behavior that had been more common several decades earlier, is seen as outdated and in contrast to the expressive emotion of the crowds.

THE MARGINALIZED EXPERIENCE OF DEATH IN BRITAIN

In offering this historic perspective I have demonstrated some of the different forces at work in British society over the past century and have shown how these influences have shaped attitudes and procedures around death. Shifts of attitude cannot be divorced from the social contexts of their times. Rather, they present a microcosm of wider social trends. Events and ideologies shape people's lives. War and the diseases of urban expansion had their effect, as did advances in science and medicine. Authoritarian decision-making gave way to democratic devolvement, as the human potential movement arose in the 1960s out of the Esalen Institute in California and inspired moves toward self-help and personal actualization.

These trends, however, often defined cutting-edge thinking, and, as with many innovations, tended to affect most strongly the better-off members of society—the wealthy and the intellectually engaged. Poverty and deprivation also impacted social attitudes to death. The divide between rich and poor has increased in recent times, and with it, life expectancy and levels of health for some have declined. Choice is limited for the disadvantaged and inarticulate. It is easy to judge a society by its most vocal elements, but the real measure of its worth is the experience of its poor and disenfranchised.

British society today is complex and influenced not only by its historical process but also by the waves of immigration that have brought people with different histories, cultures, and needs to this country. Those who care for the dying now need to learn the ways of other faiths and communities to avoid giving offense. At the same time, financial pressures within the system reduce the quality of services in fields less likely to gain media attention. Those who lack confidence or knowledge to speak up for themselves—and money to pay for extras—are forgotten. Many elderly, for example, die in poorly resourced care homes, where physical needs are met but there is little human warmth. They are unlikely to be concerned with planning a good death or hoping for any more than a basic state-funded funeral.

Old attitudes persist. Despite the fact that most people would prefer to die at home or in a hospice, the majority still die in hospitals. In the West Midlands, for example, in 2005, 55 percent of all deaths occurred in hospitals, 21 percent at home, 14 percent in care homes, and only 9 percent in hospices. Given that many home deaths are not planned, this shows an overwhelming predominance of hospital deaths. On the other hand, some of the trends to self-determination outlined earlier are having effect. With cancer deaths, which might be expected to be more predictable, 25 percent occur at home and 13 percent in hospices, showing a trend toward choice in this area.[5] These latter figures probably reflect a younger group of people who are of a generation educated to demand choice.

For some, the process of dying is planned. Informed consent and family involvement create the conditions whereby terminally ill patients make choices relating to the care they receive at the time of death. This takes foresight, however, and requires the patient or relatives to be assertive. For the majority, the picture is more patchy, dependent on arbitrary factors such as particular staffing patterns or ward availability. With the majority of deaths still occurring in hospitals, limited resources and poor organization can lead to bad experiences for some.

BUDDHIST CHAPLAINCY IN BRITAIN

It is symptomatic of our age that so far in this chapter my main concern has been with the social and medical aspects of the dying process rather than with the spiritual needs of the terminally ill. Modern, science-based medicine has, until recently, put little value on the role of clergy in the care team, though there is some indication that change may be on its way. The hospital chaplain has, nevertheless, been a member of the medical team since the establishment of the National

Health Service (NHS) in 1946. At the time of its creation, the role of the chaplain was written into the original legislation. The chaplaincy that was originally established in the NHS was Christian, reflecting the religious profile of postwar Britain. Since that time, with high levels of immigration, population profiles have changed substantially, and in response to this, a recent government-led initiative has allowed developments in multifaith chaplaincy.

With this in mind, the Multi-Faith Group for Healthcare Chaplaincy was established in 2003 with the aim of supporting the faith communities to develop their own processes for training and approving health care chaplains. In this matter, recent emphasis on patient choice in health care decision making has served the Buddhist community well as a minority religious group. The Buddhist Healthcare Chaplaincy Group was established in 2005 with the support of the Multi-Faith Group for Healthcare Chaplaincy. In 2009 this group was accepted as the body recognized by the Multi-Faith Group as representative of Buddhists in the UK for these purposes. I am currently part of this national team, which has members drawn from a number of Buddhist traditions and which seeks to involve all Buddhists working in health-related settings. The group is involved in establishing standards and methods for approving suitable people from all Buddhist denominations for hospital chaplaincy work.

The processes established by the Buddhist Healthcare Chaplaincy Group will formalize the informal involvement of Buddhists in many hospitals. Currently there are Buddhist volunteers in a number of UK hospitals who are ministering to Buddhists and, sometimes, to people of other faiths or no faith. In a survey of six hundred British hospitals undertaken by the group in 2006,[6] out of eighty-six replies, forty hospitals indicated that they either had a Buddhist chaplain or the details of a Buddhist volunteer on their contacts list. The number has probably increased substantially since 2006 as a result of the group's efforts.

Many Buddhist volunteers have been underused in the past and the new initiative hopes to encourage Buddhist chaplains to become more active. This may open the way for paid chaplaincy work within the

NHS by Buddhists. This year within the Amida Order, a Pure Land Buddhist community in the UK, one of our priests was appointed to a paid health care chaplaincy within the NHS for three hours a week. There is also a paid Buddhist chaplain in London. These small steps mark a great achievement in the establishment of Buddhist chaplaincy in the UK.

The past two years have also seen innovations in chaplaincy training as three Buddhists have gained admission to the master's in theology course in chaplaincy at St. Michael's College, University of Cardiff, a development facilitated by the Buddhist Healthcare Chaplaincy Group. This established Christian course is thus moving toward recognition of the new multifaith setting of chaplaincy within the UK. In addition, the group has started to offer more basic chaplaincy training sessions for potential volunteers in London and other areas of the country.

The role of the chaplain has different aspects. The Buddhist Healthcare Chaplaincy Group has identified a number of levels at which the chaplain needs to function. At the generic level, chaplaincy offers spiritual support to anyone who wants it, regardless of their faith tradition. This requires a facilitative style, listening to the patient's own experience and showing restraint in giving advice or teaching. The chaplain needs the ability to support the patient's spiritual experience without imposing form upon it. Awareness of different faiths is helpful, but so too is an appreciation of the diffuse and diverse experiences of spirituality of different people. We need to be able to nurture faith in whatever form it takes. Such competencies are similar to those general to chaplaincy and specific to Buddhist chaplaincy training in both Asia and the West, as described in other chapters in this volume.

The Buddhist chaplain is a figure to whom people are willing to address questions about spiritual matters, even if they are from a different faith group. It has particularly been our experience that members of the Amida Order, who wear a religious dress, are often stopped when on hospital wards and questioned at length about their beliefs and practices. For Western people who have lost faith in their own religion, Buddhism can be seen as a nonthreatening source of religious advice. For those of faith, our religious experience is often the subject of curiosity and even practical interest. There has been some tendency in Britain for some liberal Christians or Jews to practice Buddhist meditation alongside their own faith, and this intrigues others.

Other Buddhist chaplaincy work requires a breadth of knowledge and experience of different Buddhist traditions. Britain has many different Buddhist communities drawn from different Asian cultures. There are both immigrant and convert Buddhist populations. These groups have different practices and beliefs, and it can be difficult for Buddhist chaplains from one background to understand the needs of Buddhists of other traditions. This can be due to doctrinal differences. Some traditions, for example, as with some Tibetan groups, have specific practices for the time of death. The situation is complicated by ethnic and cultural differences between populations of Asian origin, who are often financially and practically disadvantaged and have a poor grasp of the English language, and more affluent middle-class convert groups. This situation is also evident in the experiences of Buddhist chaplains in the United States, as detailed in a later chapter in this volume. Ideally, the Buddhist chaplain will have a basic grasp of the character of different traditions and of some of the issues practitioners from these different populations may face. However, in practice, it is often appropriate for a number of chaplaincy visitors to be available on call to meet these differing needs.

BUDDHIST CONTRIBUTIONS TO WORKING WITH THE DYING

British society has become increasingly secular over the past half century. Despite being a predominantly Christian country, church attendance in the UK has declined sharply, echoing the experiences of many Buddhist groups in Japan. Many churches struggle to survive with elderly congregations; Christian churches of different denominations often come together for worship and sharing premises in order to strengthen their numbers. Large buildings, built to serve much bigger Victorian-era congregations, are uneconomic, and some are sold off to conserve resources. Of these, many are put to secular uses, but some become places of worship for other faith groups, such as Muslim, Hindu, Sikh, and other Asian religions, that are growing in numbers. On the whole, Buddhist groups are smaller in numbers and do not take on these large premises, but there is a Buddhist group in Birmingham that has bought a former Jewish synagogue. It is in this multifaith context that Buddhist chaplains operate.

Despite relatively low numbers, Buddhists have had considerable influence in the field of caring for the dying. Meditation, visualization, and Eastern philosophical ideas have already been incorporated into programs for cancer sufferers. Since the 1970s, research into the effects of meditation, often as taught in Hindu contexts, established the value of mind-training techniques, making the way for Buddhists to teach meditation techniques in secular settings. More recently, Jon Kabat-Zinn's mindfulness-based programs have gained popularity in mental health services. These techniques are also used by the terminally ill.

Most significantly, though, the popularity of Sogyal Rinpoche's *Tibetan Book of Living and Dying*, which became a best seller in 1992, firmly established the link between Buddhism and the care of the dying in the public consciousness. As a result, Rigpa, the organization established by Sogyal Rinpoche, is generally recognized by Buddhists in the UK as having expertise in this area. It offers training programs and support networks for those who support the dying through its Spiritual Care Programme, which will be described in detail in the following chapter on Germany.

Interest in exploring the relationship between spirituality in its widest sense, health care generally, and the dying process specifically, has grown. Public perception of Buddhism as a nonproselytizing and even nonreligious spirituality has meant that Buddhist thinking and practice has evoked particular interest. The dying person who has no formal religious affiliation but wants to talk to a spiritual person frequently will be supported by a Buddhist chaplain. They may also become involved in conducting funerals for non-Buddhists who are looking for a religious ceremony but do not want a Christian one.

LINGERING ISSUES AND CONTROVERSIES

The time of a death is a time of high emotion. It is also a time when the dying person and his or her relatives are very vulnerable. Customs and beliefs surrounding death are different for different social groups. Personal wishes vary. While there is often a wish to respect the views of the dying person, sometimes respecting others' values raises ethical issues. Medical advances have brought opportunities but have also brought dilemmas that tax medical ethicists. Many emotive issues involve questions of life and death. Embryology research, abortion, IVF treatment, and the use of genetic manipulation raise issues relating to the sanctity of life, debated at all levels both in the popular press and by high-level political and academic think tanks.

At the start of the twenty-first century, Britain is a country with a diverse population. In our cities, people of different cultures and ethnicities live side by side. This diversity is reflected in a government policy that emphasizes multifaith and multicultural approaches. The British government has committed to consulting faith communities on matters that affect them, and, as a result, Buddhists contribute to the debate on a number of ethical and social issues. The Network of Buddhist Organisations, the national body that brings together Buddhists of all traditions in Britain in dialogue, has taken part in a number of such consultations. As the Buddhist population includes nearly as wide a spectrum of opinion as the population at large, reaching consensus is not always easy at these consultations. Often the Buddhist contribution to the debate seems to involve asking pertinent questions and holding an ethical framework within which decisions can be made.

One area discussed at length by the Network of Buddhist Organisations was organ donation. Transplant service organizers requested guidance from the faith communities on how to approach families of particular faiths facing the imminent death of a loved one concerning a potential organ donation. Responses from Buddhist groups were strongly divided. Some were in favor of Buddhists acting as organ donors, believing that the donation was an act of compassion. These groups saw compassion as the central aspect of their Buddhist practice and believed it should override all other considerations. Other groups saw respect for the body during the time immediately following death as vitally important. To this group, the physical body should be left undisturbed for a period of time after death, while the person's consciousness departed. Organ donation requiring intervention during this time was seen as a violation and not something they could advocate. These debates and tensions also exist in contemporary Asia as profiled in other chapters in this volume.

Other concerns for Buddhists in Britain relate to the artificial hastening of death and the level of consciousness at death. In the last days of life, heavy sedation may be used. This can precipitate the death. Other strategies such as the withdrawal of food or even liquids may hasten death. Although such methods are not officially recognized or condoned, in practice, there is often sufficient ambiguity in the situation that a death may be eased. Buddhists may prefer less medication, even if pain relief is compromised, if this enables them to maintain their practice in their last hours. With new technology, the moment of death is also sometimes a matter of choice. Machines may have to be disconnected, or, conversely, new technology creates the possibility for the body to be kept alive after brain function has ceased. Such possibilities raise ethical concerns for many people.

Setting aside such ethical dilemmas, most concerns expressed by Buddhists in Britain about the dying process relate to the basic quality of care and access to spiritual support. The state of mind at the time of death is important; the death will ideally take place where there is sufficient quiet for the dying person to focus on his or her spiritual practice or contemplate the world beyond death. Whether the person is in a hospital or a private room, a quiet space on the ward is important for him or her, as well as access to a chaplain or other senior members of his or her tradition.

These examples illustrate the factors that Buddhist groups consider important. For some, practicing compassion is paramount, while for others the state of mind, whether at point of death or at other times of life, takes precedence. Other groups see the precept on not killing as the preeminent factor. They are concerned with ascertaining that death has really occurred, so are interested in debates on the nature of death and the complexities surrounding it in a technological age where some life functions can be carried on artificially by machines. No group disagrees with the value of compassion, preserving a tranquil mind, or not killing, but groups disagree on the relative importance placed on each. Situations that are the subject of this sort of public debate are relatively rare, and most day-to-day decisions about treatment of the dying are less contentious. Nevertheless, they can illustrate the important issues for Buddhists.

CONCLUSION

This chapter has explored the ways that British society is changing and developing, both in response to the changing attitudes brought about by social trends and as a result of interaction with different ethnic and religious communities now present in the country. These broad trends impact many areas of human activity, but they particularly affect attitudes and practices relating to death and dying.

As a group that has identified itself strongly with the care of the dying, the Buddhist community in Britain has developed an interest in serving the needs of those approaching death and of the bereaved in a number of different ways. Although relatively few in numbers, Buddhists are well represented in public debate on death-related topics. This awareness of the Buddhist role in supporting the dying is timely. With aging membership, many groups of Caucasian Buddhist converts are now supporting their own members as they near the end of life and are also providing support and teaching to a wider population of health professionals and the general public.

Buddhism in Britain continues to develop its involvement with the dying and with funerals and bereavement support. The challenges it faces are mainly in meeting the level of need. Ideally, the Buddhist community would offer its resources across a large number of hospitals and hospices as well as to the community at large. However, in practice, the number of Buddhist practitioners able to fill these roles is limited and often voluntary. With enthusiasm and faith, however, work in this field is growing and being consolidated.

GERMANY
Buddhist Influences on the Scientific, Medical, and Spiritual Cultures of Caring for the Dying

Jonathan S. Watts and Yoshiharu Tomatsu

INTRODUCTION

In our survey of contemporary Asian Buddhist palliative care and hospice activities in this volume, we see the influence of the seminal work of Dame Cicely Saunders, who came from a Christian background. Her pioneering of the modern-day hospice movement has inspired Buddhists in Asia to rediscover and revive their own traditions around death and caring for the terminally ill and the bereaved. In these last chapters, we will examine how Buddhism as a growing force in the West is, in turn, influencing Christian-centered societies to develop new innovative practices toward this vast area of care related to death. In fact, the West is where a fusion of the modern hospice movement and traditional Buddhist approaches to death is creating some of the most innovative work in Buddhist terminal care in the world.

In this specific chapter, we will look at the growth of palliative care and hospice care in Germany, a country which until recently was relatively homogenous, ethnically and religiously. However, over the last twenty years, Germany has been facing major cultural changes with the influx of Muslim immigrants and the growing popularity of Buddhism and other Asian spiritualities. We will look at how Buddhist approaches and practices for caring for the dying and bereaved have had an influence within the medical establishment and how they are also having an effect outside this establishment by bringing forth radically new styles of facing death to the German cultural landscape.

The leading force in this change from the Buddhist side is the Spiritual Care Programme founded in 1993 by Christine Longaker and Sogyal Rinpoche, the founder of the Rigpa Tibetan Buddhist community. Their work in bringing the wisdom and practices of Tibetan Buddhism surrounding death to the United States and Europe over the past twenty years has been seminal. From within the medical establishment, we will look at the pioneering work of the Interdisciplinary Center for Palliative Medicine (IZP) at Munich University Hospital under the leadership of Dr. Gian Borasio and a team of innovative researchers and practitioners. While these organizations have different orientations, they have found important common ground that has led to cooperative initiatives. The innovations that both groups have developed are leading the transformation of care for the dying and bereaved both within and without the medical establishment in Germany.

THE EMERGENCE OF HOSPICE AND PALLIATIVE CARE IN GERMANY

While the modern hospice movement is commonly seen to have begun in Great Britain with the founding of St. Christopher's Hospice by Cicely Saunders in 1967, this movement did not really begin to have influence in Germany until the late 1980s. We have seen in this volume that many conservative Asian cultures, especially Japan, have a tradition of the family and doctor not confronting the patient with a terminal prognosis. German medical professionals report that through the 1970s the same custom held true in Germany and continues on among many of its immigrant communities from Eastern Europe. A more nuanced evaluation of these customs, which we have seen in the chapters by Becker and Brazier, reveals that an intensified fear of death and the need to remove it from conversation, even in times of impending death, is a development that has taken place in both East and West as modern scientific and materialist world views have replaced traditional, religious ones in which death was viewed as a natural part of life.

As in many other countries, the hospice movement in Germany began not within the medical system but at the grassroots level, carried out by volunteers through the popular demand of patients. Even today, the medical system does not encourage institutional hospice care; the average publicly funded hospice stay is only twelve days. One of the key reasons for this is that hospice care is not cost effective in terms of the overall financial management of a hospital, which makes its profits off surgery and other types of specialized medical interventions. Another reason is that official hospices in Germany face a tremendous number of restrictions. For example, if a patient's condition improves—if the patient doesn't die in due time—he or she will be forced to leave the hospice. Such regulations create major barriers in places that have a wider, holistic definition of hospice care, such as the Rigpa Spiritual Care Programme. In this way, most hospice care in Germany has been performed as home care and also on a small scale.[1]

Yet within the German medical system there has been growth in the importance of palliative care, which is a key component of hospice care. While palliative care is a medical specialty focused on the relief of pain and other symptoms, it shares with the concept of hospice care a holistic definition of pain and care for that pain, which covers the four areas of physical, social, psychological, and spiritual, as mainstreamed by the World Health Organization. However, according to Almut Göppert, a former doctor of radio-oncology and palliative medicine at University Hospital Schleswig-Holstein in Kiel and now manager of Rigpa Germany's Spiritual Care Programme, the fourth spiritual component of palliative care has yet to be systematically implemented into the German medical system. Palliative care is often assigned to regular doctors as an additional competency, which must be performed on top of all their other duties. Without a specific doctor who specializes in palliative care and a ward with a support staff for this work, regular doctors are often unable to take the intensive time that certain cases demand when a patient's suffering goes beyond the physical to existential and family-related suffering. This problem is found in the 2007 national insurance system, which has begun to cover palliative care service in the home. While providing coverage for specialized nurses and doctors, it does not cover specialists in spiritual care.

Thus, while there is mandated palliative care in name, it often lacks comprehensiveness unless there is an engaged chaplain active in the hospital. There is a system of professional chaplaincy in the German medical system, but the degree of care can vary; for example, some hospitals with five hundred or more beds may have only one or two chaplains on call. The chaplaincy system in hospitals also varies with the particular region; for example, more Catholic areas of Germany tend to have more highly developed chaplain systems than Lutheran areas. In Germany, there is no system yet for developing chaplains who are not Christian to work in public hospitals. The Interdisciplinary Center for Palliative Medicine (IZP) at Munich University Hospital is trying to foster a more open environment and at present has one Jewish chaplain in training. According to Rev. Traugott Roser, a Lutheran chaplain and professor of spiritual care at Munich University Hospital, a few Muslim mosques in Germany have begun chaplain training. However, the main barrier to working in the public health system or other public institutions like schools is that a religious body must be registered within the German government's representative system. At this point, German Muslims do not have such a single representative body.

While Christian chaplaincy and pastoral care has become relatively mainstream in the German medical system, it still has not evolved to the point where chaplains are fully accepted or integrated as part of a comprehensive team-care system, except in specialized palliative care wards. Unless doctors are particularly open to the concept of team care and are perhaps spiritual themselves, there is usually little connection with the chaplains and the rest of the care system. As opposed to the Clinical Pastoral Education (CPE) system of chaplaincy in the United States, where chaplains are paid employees of the hospital and, as such, are integrated as equal members in a team-care system, chaplains in Germany are remunerated by the churches themselves. In this way, they may sometimes have more evangelical agendas that conflict with the nondenominational competency that a chaplain must develop in the American CPE system.

While the system has yet to fully mature, Dr. Göppert has noticed a major shift since 2007 with the German government earmarking significant new funding for palliative care. Much of these funds will be put into home services rather than into existing medical facilities, such as new medical insurance legislation that pays for home palliative care with a mandate for comprehensive team care that includes spiritual care. This area of home care is where she feels the development of spiritual care will have the strongest growth in the near future.

ORIGINS OF THE BUDDHIST INFLUENCE IN GERMANY AND THE RIGPA SPIRITUAL CARE PROGRAMME

The Rigpa Spiritual Care Programme was established in 1993 at a time when the broader palliative and hospice care movement was just beginning to have an influence in Germany. The program evolved out of the work of Sogyal Rinpoche to bring the wisdom of Tibetan Buddhism to the West through his organization Rigpa, a term meaning "primordial nondual awareness," founded around 1979. Sogyal Rinpoche is a Tibetan Buddhist lama who studied under some of the greatest Tibetan masters of the past century. He collected this learning and practice in *The Tibetan Book of Living and Dying*, which achieved wide acclaim and has now sold over two million copies and been translated into thirty languages. The Spiritual Care Programme has been an attempt to bring the teachings and practices of the book into practical application in the modern world through educating and training health care professionals in the field of dying.

While Sogyal Rinpoche has been the force behind the core teaching, his longtime student Christine Longaker, a professional hospice worker, developed the teaching and training components within Western professional contexts. Her own story and her adaptations of Sogyal Rinpoche's teachings are found in her book, *Facing Death and Finding Hope: A Guide to the Emotional and Spiritual Care of the Dying*. Longaker got involved in this work after her husband died of leukemia in 1977 at the age of twenty-four. She went on to become the director and staff trainer of the Hospice of Santa Cruz County in California. Besides the numerous training seminars she has helped to establish all over Western Europe, she has also helped to create an institutionalized model for the program called the Contemplative End-of-Life Care Program at Naropa University in Boulder, Colorado. The Spiritual Care Programme claims to have trained more than 30,000 health care professionals and volunteers worldwide in all areas of health care and social services, while supporting many people facing serious illness, death, or bereavement, and their families.[2] The program's most conspicuous new initiative has been the Dechen Shying care center for the dying and their families, located in a scenic area of western Ireland as an attached facility to Rigpa's longtime retreat center Dzogchen Beara.

Rigpa, as a Buddhist organization transmitting the teachings of Sogyal Rinpoche, was established in Germany in 1986 with the Munich center. Through the Munich center's ongoing activities and the growing influence of Buddhism in Germany, Rigpa members found that a variety of professionals and individuals in the field of dying began to come to them expressing interest in the Tibetan Buddhist approach to death, especially as outlined in Sogyal Rinpoche's book. In this way, the Rigpa Spiritual Care Programme in Germany has not sought to formally enter the medical and hospice systems in Germany but has worked more at the grassroots level. John Baugher, an associate professor of sociology at the University of Southern Maine, notes in his study of the Rigpa Spiritual Care Programme that the program has not sought to create a specific type of organizational structure or champion any particular policy initiative. He quotes one senior educator in the program:

> We're not trying to move into health care policies saying, "You need to change and do it this way." But it's more this organic growth, and this is what people are asking for from health care professionals to people who are ill and dying, they want this kind of care and training. That's what they're

asking us for in a certain way and so the need is already well established.[3]

In 2000, Christine Longaker held the first training in Germany—called "Wisdom and Loving Kindness in Terminal Care"—at the department for medical psychology at the University of Heidelberg. It was an intensive sixteen-day training broken into four separate four-day modules spaced over a two-year period from December 2000 until February 2002, so that long-term results could be monitored. The course focused on training medical professionals to communicate compassionately and effectively with patients and relatives and to use meditation for self-care and to prevent burn out. Of the total seventy participants who took part in at least one of the modules (fifty-seven completed at least three), 36 percent were hospice caregivers, 29 percent were nursing staff, and 20 percent were doctors.

Dr. Eva Saalfrank, a cultural anthropologist and psycho-oncologist, and the project leader for this program at the University of Heidelberg, wrote in her research report on the training of its remarkable results. She notes that after the first and second modules, the most common reflection by the participants, over 40 percent both times, was the value of learning meditation and "the motivation to deepen one's own practice." Yet, interestingly, after the third module, these reflections "diminished in favor of the description of an inner process of development and self-awareness, which directed to a change of attitude." In the end, participants learned not only the value and importance of self-care as medical professionals, but also how spiritual work with oneself builds a basis for engagement and loving empathy for others.[4] The evidence of the effects of such types of training for care professionals have also been well documented in the United States as described in the chapter by Rev. Joan Halifax.

The publication of Saalfrank's report has had an influence on the palliative care community in Germany, as seen in the several follow-up sessions and the major training conducted at IZP in 2002 by Christine Longaker. Some trainings were also conducted by the local German group. However, Almut Göppert, who assisted Longaker at this first training, notes that the students of these trainings have not gone on to become teachers of these methods. They have mostly sought to learn the methods for themselves in their own work. In 2011, Rigpa Germany revitalized its local program with major training seminars by Kirsten Deleo and Rosamund Oliver, both international training managers of Rigpa's Spiritual Care Education Programme, as well as Christine Longaker. In addition, Frank Ostaseski, the founder of the Zen Hospice Project in San Francisco who has taught in Germany in the past, ran an in-depth seminar with former students in 2010. The spiritual care training expanded beyond private work with health care professionals to offer courses for the general public. It also began to focus more intently on training the Rigpa community proper in the Tibetan Buddhist way of death and dying, such as the new training course "Are you Ready? Understanding and Preparing for Death."

INSIDE THE SYSTEM: THE INTERDISCIPLINARY CENTER FOR PALLIATIVE MEDICINE (IZP) AT MUNICH UNIVERSITY HOSPITAL

A second major training course was held by Longaker in southern Germany in Munich from October 7–10, 2002. As opposed to the program's largely grassroots and informal sector work outlined above, this course was coordinated and run with IZP. It yielded some fascinating results in terms of influencing the formal sector of palliative care in the German medical system. Longaker was invited by IZP and its cofounder Dr. Gian Borasio, a neurologist and palliative care specialist, to conduct a three and a half–day training for sixty-three participants called "Wisdom and Compassion in Care for the Dying." The participants were "working as professionals or volunteers in medical or social support fields from diverse cultural and religious backgrounds."[5] According to Maria Wasner,[6] a researcher at IZP who wrote the report on the training, many people in the IZP community working in palliative care had been struggling with different issues and challenges in the work. They sensed that they were missing something in their approach, so they became open to some of the ideas and teachings of Buddhism. Most of the participants were not doctors but rather nurses, social workers, and other related professionals. She notes that the doctors who did participate tended to have more difficulties with the content, inquiring about the esoteric nature of certain Tibetan teachings and the concrete benefits of them. However, interestingly, many of the other participants had had some previous contact with Buddhism, so they could more easily digest what the training was offering.

Wasner's report says that the aim of the training was to enable the participants to recognize the different facets of the suffering of dying persons and their relatives and to respond effectively. A precondition for engaging in this work was an in-depth reflection on their own fear of death so as to learn firsthand both the needs and hopes of the dying. Christine Longaker taught techniques of active and compassionate listening, and how to recognize and address the causes of emotional and spiritual suffering. Practical exercises were presented to enable the participants to connect with disturbed or cognitively impaired patients, to learn how to deal with unfinished business, and to be able to support the bereaved. Furthermore, nondenominational spiritual practices, such as contemplation and meditation, were introduced to help the participants apply and experience the benefits of spiritual care for themselves, and learn how to integrate these techniques for calming the mind and deepening compassion in their professional work.[7]

Besides supporting these professionals in their work, IZP as a research institute also sought to monitor the training in terms of its concrete impact on the participants and potential use for the development of professionals in the medical system. The study evaluated whether professional caregivers could gain sustained benefits from such training in terms of positive changes of attitude, better spiritual well-being, and lower levels of work-related stress. Changes were evaluated using three different instruments:

- FACIT-Sp (Functional Assessment of Chronic Illness Therapy—Spiritual Well-Being): This was designed to measure important aspects of spirituality, such as a sense of meaning in one's life, harmony, peacefulness, and a sense of strength and comfort from one's beliefs. This measure was found to increase significantly from the training.

- STS (Self-Transcendence Scale): Self-transcendence is defined here as the expansion of one's conceptual boundaries inwardly through introspective activities, outwardly through concerns about others' welfare, and temporally by integrating perceptions of one's past and future to enhance the present. This measure also increased after the course but did not sustain after six months.

- IIR (Idler Index of Religiosity): This contains two scales: one that evaluates public religiousness in terms of connection to religious organizations, like churches and their members; another that evaluates private religiousness in terms of how much one is personally aided by religious teachings and practices. In this measure, no change was noted.[8]

The report concludes by stating that the "spiritual care training had a positive influence on the participating palliative care professionals which was preserved over a six-month period. There were significant improvements in self-perceived compassion for the dying, but also in compassion for oneself. Furthermore, the attitude toward one's family and the attitude toward colleagues improved, satisfaction with the work increased due to the training, and work-related stress decreased."[9] The report does note that this positive effect was not preserved over six months and surmised that this was due to the routine effect of everyday working conditions. It also noted that some of the participants inquired about holding regular meetings or a refresher training every six months.

Another training with Longaker was held from November 14–16, 2005, during a symposium on spirituality and palliative care in which most participants were Catholic and Protestant priests. However, the evaluation of it was not as positive, because the priests had greater difficulty in absorbing and accepting the Buddhist approach. By

2010, this experimental training had not been mainstreamed into the training programs at IZP, and no one at IZP had the competencies to conduct such a training on their own. Still, Borasio notes that this is probably the first experiment in Western medical literature to show the long-term efficacy of spiritual training based on Buddhist traditions but not done for Buddhists themselves. Borasio has also expressed the hope that Longaker will be invited back to IZP to develop a regular training system for spiritual care.

While on the surface the Rigpa training conducted by Longaker seems to have had minimal impact on IZP and the culture of spiritual care in Germany, the training itself shows some important, deeper influences within IZP in particular and the Western medical world in general. The first is the growing interest among scientists and medical researchers in the influence of spirituality and spiritual care on the well-being of patients, especially terminally ill ones. Jon Kabat-Zinn, professor emeritus of medicine at the University of Massachusetts Medical School and founding executive director of the Center for Mindfulness in Medicine, Health Care, and Society, is one of the most renowned examples of this movement and has developed close ties with Rigpa. Borasio himself became interested in these issues through his work as head of the Motor Neuron Disease Research Group at the department of neurology, University of Munich. Borasio notes that one famous case in this field was of Philip Simmons, an ALS patient who wrote *Learning to Fall: The Blessings of an Imperfect Life*. As part of the therapy for his condition, Simmons learned meditation. This skill in tandem with his growing mortality had a transformational effect upon him in which his quality of life actually increased. This was contrary to what all scientific studies say, that death only brings up afflictive emotions. At first, the medical team labeled him as "pathological," though he had no legitimate symptoms. However, he eventually became a guide to his caregivers, turning the notion of caring for the dying on its head as the dying cared for the living.[10]

Under Borasio, IZP engaged in a series of studies to scientifically examine spirituality in dying, especially area of values and meaning. Martin Fegg, who coauthored the report on the Rigpa training and is a psychologist at IZP, developed an index called SMiLE (Schedule for Meaning in Life Evaluation) that showed that meaning in life can actually increase as one enters the latter stages of life—a conclusion that parallels the emphasis by Buddhist groups in Taiwan and Thailand in previous chapters that the mind can still develop in the body's terminal stage. They found that while people do experience diminished health, if one examines other areas, like values, there can be an increase in meaning and hence well-being. As people age, they tend to become less attached to the self-enhancement goals of career and increasingly drawn to the self-transcendence goals of altruism, spirituality, and nature.[11] In this way, Borasio notes that, "although religion and spirituality may not offer a cure, they may ease a patient to accept their diagnosis and the transitions of life that occur in the process of dying." Their studies, which included the Longaker training, have also reached the conclusion that the medical establishment can save money by applying spiritual care to not only patients and their families but also the medical care team.[12]

In sum, research like that being done at IZP is having a huge impact on medical systems in Europe, the United States, and now Asia by *proving* to recalcitrant and secularized bureaucrats that spiritual care is a legitimate and integral intervention in the overall care of all participants in the medical system. The Longaker training at IZP also indicates a very significant overall shift in attention paid to the spiritual well-being and maintenance of not only the receiver of care (the patient) but also the giver of care. We have seen this focus on supporting and developing the spiritual well-being of caregivers and medical professionals in other chapters in this volume, and it marks the full maturation of a comprehensive and holistic care system, which in Buddhist terms sees all participants as an interconnected whole.

A second deeper issue behind the Longaker training is the influence of Buddhism among the staff of IZP. Maria Wasner, for example, describes herself as Catholic yet also notes that she regularly attends a local Tibetan temple in the Karma Kagyu tradition founded by a Danish teacher named Ole Nydahl. Wasner feels that for her Buddhism is not a religion but rather a view and attitude for looking at the world. She also notes that it is quite helpful for working with dying people. Coming from what she calls "an old fashioned Catholic region which emphasized guilt," she sees many dying patients struggling with the guilt of not having lived up to God's teachings. In this way, she finds the Buddhist teachings of karma and rebirth help her approach people with a different image of death and afterlife. She also finds that the practices emphasized by Sogyal Rinpoche and Christine Longaker, such as the *tonglen* practice of breathing in another's suffering and breathing out loving kindness, is very helpful before entering a room of a patient with which she has been having difficulties.

Such Buddhist mind practices are found among other staff at IZP. Martin Fegg practices at a local Zen temple based in the Japanese Sambo Kyodan Zen lineage. At IZP, he has developed a psychotherapeutic group intervention using Buddhist-based mindfulness practices for relatives of palliative patients facing the imminent or recent loss of a loved one. In this project, ten groups have participated over the last three years, each led by a trained psychotherapist. The intervention was comprised of six meetings, two successive half-days at the beginning followed by four weekly evening sessions. Basic information on mindfulness was given at the first two meetings. At every meeting, formal mindfulness training was included. Participants were instructed to follow their breathing for ten minutes and to notice and then let go of their thoughts, feelings, and various perceptions. They were encouraged to practice two times for at least five to ten minutes every day at home, and they were given CD recordings to help with practicing. Additional informal practice was introduced, such as doing simple activities mindfully, e.g. brushing teeth. A first analysis of the data was taken in 2010, and it was found that participants improved significantly in quality of life and decreased psychosocial burden after participating in the intervention.

Finally, Dr. Borasio has very important Buddhist influences. Firstly, his wife, a self-described Catholic, is also a devout Rigpa follower who exposed Borasio to Sogyal Rinpoche and Christine Longaker's work, thus leading to the eventual training at IZP. Borasio, who also says he is Catholic, is at the same time, like Fegg, a committed practitioner of the Sambo Kyodan Zen lineage and very well versed in Buddhist teachings. As an Italian national, Borasio has had a seminal influence on the German medical system. First, in 2003, under Borasio's and IZP's influence, Munich University was the first medical university in Germany to include palliative care as a mandatory course and an examination subject for medical students. Pushing to spread this system to other medical universities, Borasio was a central part of the successful movement in 2009 to make palliative care a mandatory subject in all medical universities in Germany. Finally, Borasio and the IZP team have established the first fully endowed spiritual care professorships in Germany at the University of Munich, currently held by Rev. Traugott Roser and Rev. Eckhard Frick.

The important point to be drawn from the experience at IZP is the way Buddhism is being adapted into the system—not as a replacement for the existing spirituality, which is grounded in the local culture, but as a complement to the existing culture. As we have seen, it has never been Rigpa's intention in the Spiritual Care Programme to convert others to Buddhism or to push its programs on unreceptive audiences in the medical establishment. Rather, Rigpa has made personal connections with those inside the system who are keen to expand and improve their competencies. Borasio, Wasner, Fegg, and other staff members at IZP, especially Rev. Roser, show an impressive ability and keenness to accommodate multiple competencies in medical science and a variety of spiritualities, which until recently have been compartmentalized at best or seen as antagonistic at worst, whether it be Catholic vs. Buddhist or Medical Scientist vs. Religionist. For the future of Buddhist-inspired spiritual care in the public sector of non-Buddhist and multicultural societies, this is a model case in multiple disciplines enhancing themselves.

OUTSIDE THE SYSTEM: RIGPA'S NEW SPIRITUAL CARE PROGRAMME AND CENTRE

Despite the above conclusions for the public sector in Germany, there is still a place for (1) extended care by private groups, and (2) intensive spiritualized care by religious-based organizations like Rigpa.

Concerning the first point, as we have noted, home-based care is still the norm for hospice care in Germany, while recently the German government has mandated an extension of palliative care beyond hospitals and into home care. For all its strengths, IZP and Munich University Hospital still have a limited scope in terms of extended, holistic care.

While IZP has its research staff and holds trainings on the first floor of its complex, the second floor houses a fully staffed palliative care unit with ten rooms (almost always for private use). The ward staff consists of fourteen nurses, two assistant doctors, one attending doctor, a social worker, and on a part-time level, a physical therapist, a respiratory therapist, a psychologist, two spiritual care workers-*cum*-chaplains, and an art therapist. However, because it is a palliative care unit, the average stay is only ten days, while in Germany a formal hospice can accept patients with a prognosis of up to six months. In this way, although half of their patients do die on the ward, the focus is on symptom control and empowering patients to leave the hospital so they can die elsewhere: either at home, a hospice, or a nursing home. IZP has begun a home care program but only doctors and nurses are funded, so they do not do much home spiritual care.

Furthermore, IZP's postmortem grief care activities are also limited. The aforementioned grief care program run by Martin Fegg for families using mindfulness meditation was only a research-based one and not an institutionalized, regular program. Rev. Roser notes that because the average time spent at IZP is short, neither families nor patients have developed close, extended ties with the staff or the place. Thus, most families do not come back for extended postmortem consultation. He explains that grief care in the ward is mostly done as anticipatory grief in the closing days of a patient's life. Still, IZP has a psychotherapist who continues to offer informal support to families afterward, and IZP does hold three memorial services per year, to which families are invited, for all who have died on the ward. Rev. Roser admits that this support is not enough and needs to be followed up. However, at present, there are financial and human resource limitations to extending this work.

It is in these gaps in institutional care where the wide variety of private-based home hospice care plays an important role in Germany. As of 2010, there were four such Buddhist-based hospices in Germany, which provided only volunteer care and not specialized medical care: (1) Bodhicharya Hospice, a Tibetan-based group founded by Ringu Tulku Rinpoche in Berlin; (2) Mandala Hospice, located in western Germany, near Dortmund, (3) Buddha House Hospice in Munich, and (4) Da-Sein ("to be there for someone"), a Theravada-based group out of Munich that has shed most of its outward Buddhist character. Rigpa's Spiritual Care Programme is a different kind of Buddhist initiative. It does not operate a home care hospice program. It rather extends itself further to envision and develop a totally comprehensive form of spiritual care, one that goes beyond care in the period before death and immediate grief care in the postmortem period. Sogyal Rinpoche has emphasized, along with many of the writers in this volume, that developing one's spirituality to face the great matter of death is a life-long project that begins today. This is the vision that has been enacted at Rigpa's retreat center, Dzogchen Beara in western Ireland, with the addition of the Dechen Shying spiritual care center to the facility. Dechen Shying offers specialized care to those living with illness or facing death and to their family and carers amid a regular community of Buddhist practitioners in an atmosphere where life and death blend together.

Baugher comments about this facility in his study:

> Equally important is that the scope of after-death care will be much broader than that provided by hospice organizations. Hospices typically offer bereavement services to survivors during the first year of their loss, sometimes in the form of one-on-one grief counseling with hospice social workers. . . . In contrast, bereavement services at Dechen Shying will be life-long trainings and spiritual retreats offered to bereaved persons at various points following their loss (e.g., within the first year, five years later, ten years later) in the view that grief is an ongoing opportunity for profound spiritual practice rather than a problem that must be "resolved."

The understanding of bereavement that informs the Spiritual Care Programme is consistent with new models of grief that focus on "continuing bonds" between the living and the dead, rather than seeking "resolution" through detachment from the loss.[13]

There is significant connection here between Rigpa's vision and practice and the traditional practice of ancestor veneration through Buddhism in Japan as outlined by Carl Becker in his chapter. Traditional Japanese Buddhists, as well as most East Asian Buddhists, have long understood the importance of revisiting grief as a way of keeping alive the wisdom and the bonds of previous and present generations.

Through the direct influence of the opening of Dechen Shying in 2007, German Rigpa members and donors have come forward to propose such a center in Germany. According to Heinz Siepmann, chairman of the board of the Spiritual Care Center and the Tertön Sogyal Foundation, they have envisioned three interconnected centers on a lake in the small town of Bad Saarow outside of Berlin, slated to open in 2013. The first is a living community of Buddhist practitioners committed to regular practice who can also perform dedication practices on behalf of the care center patients and even practice together with them. The second is a care center that aims to support and care for people at moments of transition or crisis in their life, such as when diagnosed with a serious illness or when mourning the passing of a loved one. The third is a seminary where the Spiritual Care Programme will continue the training work developed by Christine Longaker in a sustained and long-term manner.

Conclusion

In this study, we have come across some innovative approaches not encountered elsewhere in our research. One is the combining of a research and training center in spiritual and holistic care with an actual place of practice. The IZP facility in Munich was specifically designed for this integration; the first floor is built for research and training facilities and the second floor for a fully staffed and equipped palliative care ward. In this way, the researchers at IZP are not merely academics but engaged practitioners whose projects seek to support patients, families, and care workers while investigating practical methods for improving methods and systems of care. The Rigpa Spiritual Care Programme center in Ireland and the proposed one in Germany seek a similar integration. These centers not only are a place for care workers to train and practice but also offer direct connection to an intensive spiritual practice environment. This is different from the initiatives we have seen in the United States. American CPE chaplains practice in medical environments separate from both their educational seminaries and their places of religious training. In the Zen-based projects in the United States as well as in Buddhist-based hospices we have researched in Malaysia and Singapore, the training of spiritual care workers and their continued spiritual development is usually conducted off site from the medical environment in which they work.

Indeed, the distinctive aspect of the Rigpa vision that has evolved from the Dzogchen Beara and Dechen Shying center is the intensity of spiritual practice offered to the patients and their families. In the other Buddhist terminal care programs that we have researched, conscious efforts have been made to not only scale down and simplify distinctly Buddhist practices for the benefit of a non-Buddhist general public but also to address spirituality with patients in a more passive manner. These projects do extremely important work in using Buddhist principles and practices in a nondenominational way to support the general public. Furthermore, their emphasis on listening over preaching and addressing a patient's spirituality from where they are rather than where they could or should be is highly commendable. However, with the growth of Buddhism as an active spirituality in the West and the need for its revitalization in the East, there could be spaces for intensive spiritual practice environments combined with ones for holistic care for the sick and terminally ill. This is a sentiment that may also apply to people from other religious backgrounds, who may in fact desire a more active form of spiritual practice in such times of critical illness. In this way, while the Dechen Shying care center does not push Buddhism on its patients and their families and is open to other forms of spirituality, it does provide a much more spiritualized environment. With the Dzogchen Beara practice center next door, it encourages its patients and families to actively pursue their spiritual path. This is in contrast to many of the hospitals and hospices we have researched in this volume, which contain only small places of worship that are little used by resident patients. Rigpa envisions that its spiritual care centers will bring the ancient traditions of active and mindful dying (and living) into numerous contemporary societies suffering from human alienation and spiritual disconnection.

USA
Being with Dying: The Upaya Institute Contemplative End-of-Life Training Program

Joan Jiko Halifax

I have worked in the area of contemplative care of the dying for forty years, beginning my professional work in 1970 at the University of Miami School of Medicine as a medical anthropologist. There was a significant amount of cultural diversity in the hospital, so it was important to have an anthropologist on hand to help be a bridge between cultural and medical perspectives. There, I realized that the most marginalized people in the hospital system were those who were dying. My interest in the work with dying people, however, opened for me with the death of my grandmother, who took care of dying people. There were other factors that led me to this work, like becoming a Buddhist practitioner in the mid 1960s.

After I left medical school in 1972, I worked with psychiatrist Stanislav Grof, who was involved with a major project using LSD as an adjunct to psychotherapy with people dying of cancer. This work was profound, as most of our dying patients had the opportunity through the therapy to go through a contemporary rite of passage. This changed their experience of dying, benefited their quality of life and relationships, and transformed their view of death as they lived their final days.[1]

After this work with Grof, I received the Buddhist precepts in 1975, became a teacher in the Kwan Um Korean Zen School in 1980, and subsequently took Japanese Zen ordination from Rev. Bernie Tetsugen Glassman. This deeper step into the practice of Buddhism brought me in touch with the profound perspective that Buddhism offers to those who are dying, a perspective that normalizes death and sanctifies it as well. These three forces opened me to the work with the dying: my grandmother, my experiences with Grof, and Buddhist practice.

CLINICIAN BURNOUT AND TRAUMA IN THE UNITED STATES

The hallmark of compassionate and contemplative-based end-of-life care is relationship-centered care of people living and dying with life-threatening conditions and their families. A number of curricula using different teaching methods have been developed to give health care professionals the knowledge and skills to care for dying people. Despite the development of these curricula, health care professionals report a lack of skills in psychosocial and spiritual care of dying people. They also report difficulties in caring for the dying, with high levels of moral distress, grief, and burnout.

There is increasing research on the deficit of empathy and compassion among health care professionals. This compassion deficit often begins during the medical and nursing training experience. This suggests that health care professionals need more than technical skills to care compassionately for others and to sustain themselves in their caregiving roles. Clinicians are typically not given the tools to address their stress.

There are five "syndromes" that clinicians suffer from, in terms of encountering the challenge of their vocation.

(1) Burnout: cumulative work demands and stress.
(2) Secondary trauma: dysfunction that arises from prolonged exposure to the suffering of others.
(3) Moral distress: moral conflicts when the clinician knows what is right to do but cannot do it.
(4) Horizontal hostility: disrespect among members of a peer group.
(5) Structural violence: violence in the system.

Burnout

There are specific symptoms and signs of burnout on the individual level. These are the kinds of things that we see often in clinicians here in the United States:

- complete emotional and physical exhaustion
- cynicism and being very detached from the job
- deep inadequacy about lack of effectiveness in being able to do the job
- overidentification or involvement, and an almost addictive relationship to the job
- hypervigilance and neurotic alertness that lead to a state of chronic irritability
- increasing social withdrawal from family and social relationships
- poor judgment and personal and professional boundary violations
- perfectionism and rigidity
- existential crisis in which the meaning of life and spiritual and religious beliefs are questioned
- increase in interpersonal conflicts
- avoidance of emotionally difficult situations
- issues with addiction, detachment, and an increasing sense of numbness
- difficulties in concentrating and various psychosomatic ill-nesses like headaches and immune system impairments

Secondary Trauma

This is very close to posttraumatic stress syndrome and involves hyper-arousal, burnout, disturbed sleep patterns, irritability and anger out-bursts, hypervigilance, avoidance, and reliving disturbing encounters. On the team level, when there is a diminution of morale because of burnout, secondary trauma, moral distress, horizontal hostility in the institution, or structural violence, you see the morale of the institution drop. The result is impaired job performance, increased absenteeism, staff conflict, and high job turnover. It is a pretty dramatic situation that clinicians are facing in the United States. I am not saying that everyone is in this dilemma, but many clinicians are. A statistic that demonstrates this situation is the suicide rate among clinicians. A male clinician is 1.41 times more likely to commit suicide than the average American male, and the female clinician is 2.27 times more likely to commit suicide. The incidences of depression, addiction, and so forth because of stress are also very high among clinicians.

Moral Distress

These stresses are actions, dimensions, and experiences that we find common in many different clinical settings in the United States.

- Resources: There are a number of small hospitals that simply do not have the resources for patients to be supported in specialized intensive care situations. There can also be a shortage of nurses to take care of patients. As a result, the few nurses can easily burn out. This inadequate access to resources can thus cause the nurses serious ethical challenges, when they see their patients suffering and can do little to help.
- Informed consent: Another stress is a lack of adequate informed consent. For example, a patient may arrive at a hospital who is comatose, but there is no paperwork indicating an agreement with regards to resuscitation or nonresuscitation, intubation, and so forth. In other words, the advance directives have not been articulated.
- Conflicts in care: In other situations, the clinician, patient, and patient's family often have different goals in terms of care. The patient wants to live as long as possible; the family is running out of patience or economic resources and feels like nothing should be done, or that everything should be done; the hospital mandates that it can only keep the patient in the hospital for a certain amount of time.

- Causing pain and feeling guilt: Clinicians often experience a tremendous amount of stress when engaging in interventions that cause pain and suffering. It is also not uncommon for a clinician to make a mistake, so clinical errors cause a feeling of guilt among clinicians.
- Futility: Clinicians also encounter a sense of futility with, for example, patients' demands, clinical errors they have committed, feelings of inadequacy of not being able to really help a patient adequately, seeing that many interventions do not really benefit the patient, and demands made by the institution.
- Death and quality of life: Often clinicians encounter deep disputes about life-sustaining therapies related to hastening death. What is the merciful thing to do with someone who is in a persistent vegetative state—keep the body alive or help death happen? What does a patient need to have quality of life? Is another intervention going to compromise the quality of life—will it make patients more miserable or hurt them physically? What if the patient's family insists that the patient wants to be kept alive no matter what? There is also the issue that a small increase in the morphine dosage will both make the patient more comfortable and help him or her die more easily and more quickly. However, is this legal or right? How does the family feel about it? How does the nurse feel carrying out the doctor's orders? Does she feel like she's engaging in homicide? There are quite a number of issues that come up.
- Denial of death: These issues are compounded by Western clinicians' training to save lives at any cost. This leads them to a kind of denial of death. Clinicians may feel angst being in the presence of someone who is suffering from intractable pain, is in a state of extreme mental suffering, or is terribly afraid of death.
- Relational inabilities: Another issue is that many clinicians simply do not have the ability to discuss interventions with patients and families concerning death and dying. They may also not have the capacity or interest to discuss stresses at

work. In this way, they do not have the opportunity to work out issues, such as ones related to workaholism, perfectionism, or self-neglect.

Horizontal Hostility

This issue was brought to my attention by a nurse and student of mine, Jan Jahner, who has done a powerful presentation on this challenge in the medical setting. She has defined horizontal hostility as disrespectful behavior among peers, bullying between clinicians, and hazing that frequently occurs in medical training. Lateral violence or horizontal hostility is the consistent and often hidden patterns of behavior designed to control, diminish, or devalue another peer or group that creates a risk to health and/or safety. Horizontal hostility shares three elements common to racial and sexual harassments laws: (1) it is defined in terms of the effect on the recipient; (2) it must have a negative effect on the recipient; and (3) the bullying behavior must be consistent. Signs include two domains: (1) overt—name-calling, sarcasm, bickering, fault-finding, back-stabbing, criticism, intimidation, gossip, shouting, blaming, put-downs, raising eyebrows, etc.; and (2) covert—unfair assignments, eye-rolling, ignoring, making faces behind someone's back, refusal to help, sighing, whining, sarcasm, refusal to work with someone, sabotage, isolation, exclusion, fabrication, etc.

The prevalence of horizontal hostility in the United States has been documented: 33 percent of nurses leave their jobs due to horizontal hostility; 44 percent report bullying; 33 percent intend to leave because of verbal abuse. Bullied staff members have lower job satisfaction and higher stress, depression, and anxiety and higher intent to leave. In the United States, 90–97 percent of nurses experience verbal abuse from physicians, 60 percent of newly registered nurses leave their first position within six months because of some form of horizontal hostility, and verbal abuse is often cited as the reason nurses leave their jobs.[2]

Structural Violence

This is the discrimination against groups within an institutional set-ting causing suffering. The term "structural violence," first used in the 1960s, has been attributed to Johan Galtung and his book *Peace by Peaceful Means: Peace and Conflict, Development and Civilization.* It is a type of violence that corresponds to the systematic ways in which a social structure or institution discriminates and causes suf-fering to others by preventing them from meeting their basic needs. Structural violence is attributed to the specific organizations of soci-ety that injure or harm individuals or masses of individuals. In medi-cine, structural violence occurs in relation to the uninsured, ethnic minorities or people of color, women, people with AIDS, and so forth. It involves not only the denial of medical services to marginal-ized groups but also the use of interventions that are suppressive or harmful. Structural violence is also meted out toward those employed by the medical system who are perceived to be lower in status.

BEING WITH DYING: PROFESSIONAL TRAINING PROGRAM IN CONTEMPLATIVE END-OF-LIFE CARE

To address the concerns explained in detail above, the "Being with Dying: Professional Training Program in Contemplative End-of-Life Care" (BWD) course was created in 1996. The premise of BWD is that in order for clinicians to provide compassionate end-of-life care, it is necessary for them to (1) become self-aware and recognize their own suffering, (2) make a commitment to addressing their own suffering, and (3) develop receptivity, compassion, and resilience through nur-turing physical, emotional, mental, spiritual, and social dimensions in their own lives and in relationships with others.

We feel that cultivating stability of mind and emotions enables cli-nicians to respond to others and themselves with compassion. BWD provides an opportunity for participants to discover wisdom and insight from their peers and an interdisciplinary team of facilitators that includes contemplative practitioners, clinicians, and educators. BWD is for clinicians who have been through extensive medical training. These include physicians, nurses, and the interdisciplinary team of social workers, psychologists, and chaplains.

We establish a fixed quota in the program to ensure that one quarter of the participants are doctors, one quarter are nurses, and the other half are individuals from the interdisciplinary team. The eight-day residential program uses many learning modalities (e.g. didactic teaching, self-directed learning, inquiry, and creative processes) to enhance awareness of the importance of the inner life and professional responsibility.

The training has four components that center respectively on the transformation of the clinician, the patient, the community, and the institution.

Transformation of the Clinician

(1) Worldview
Our first step in this work is to identify and clarify the worldviews, values, priorities, and knowledge of the clinicians. This gives the clinician a functional base from which he or she can work. The worldview of clinicians actually influences how they deliver care. The worldview includes their values, which influence their priorities, which influence their knowledge—so we sequence it in that way.

(2) Contemplative Interventions
The second area we work with in exploring how we can transform the clinician is related to contemplative interventions—in other words, we teach them meditation. We call them "contemplative interventions" as a skillful means, because when you say "meditation," it produces resistance in most medical settings. Our focus in these reflective practices or contemplative interventions is on the cultivation of insight, mental stability, and compassion. We work with a number of different contemplative interventions during the eight-day training program.

Let's look at what we mean by "contemplative" dimensions since we use that term to precede the term "end-of-life care." This work has come out of my relationship with the formation of the Mind and Life Institute, which sponsors neuroscience research and dialogues with His Holiness the Dalai Lama. For many years, we needed the neuroscientific evidence to prove that these interventions were trackable and traceable and that the benefits could be clearly mapped. As mentioned in previous chapters in this volume, Jon Kabat-Zinn is one of the pioneers in this field and is also a board member of the Institute. The work in this area has increased exponentially over the past decade in large part due to the work that the Mind and Life Institute has done—much of which has been published.

When we say "contemplative," we mean traditions that encompass moral and ethical virtues and values and that also engage in reflective practices that cultivate the mind. We are now learning from contemporary neuroscience that these practices provide deep benefits in emotional regulation and improved skills of attention. Meditation, specifically, assists with creating greater resiliency for individuals, inducing greater calm, reducing stress, and enhancing coping skills. These practices also cultivate prosocial mental qualities, like empathy, compassion, and so forth. We have also learned that these practices have a profound effect on the well-being of health care providers. This in turn has an effect on how the clinician interacts with the patient and how the patient perceives his or her own experience of dying.

In this context, we feel it is very important to teach clinicians how to develop a metacognitive perspective, which is the capacity to be self-aware, to be resilient or pliant, to develop intentional balance, to be compassionate, and to discover meaning in their work. We endeavor to help clinicians understand that there are beneficial outcomes to these contemplative strategies, including attentional and emotional balance, cognitive control, and resilience. Attentional balance, for example, means having an attention that is sustained, vivid, stable, effortless, and nonjudgmental. We also explore emotional balance and the psychosocial impact and neural substrates of empathy, compassion, and altruism. We point out the benefits of cognitive control and how you can guide your thoughts and behavior according to your intention. We teach how to override habitual responses and down-regulate aroused emotional reactivity. Through these contemplative interventions, one can develop mental flexibility, insight, and metacognition, which means you are able to reframe experiences in ways that are prosocial. There has also been important work in the area of resilience, which involves not only stress reduction and relaxation but also enhanced immune response and other health benefits.

- Physiological practices: We employ a number of different contemplative interventions to help people learn the very basic mental state of focused attention: learning how to have a narrow attention aimed at an object. For example, practices include mindfulness on the breath, body-scan meditation, and walking meditation. We also use yoga and chi-gong as a means for enhancing embodied concentration. Through these concentration practices, people begin to stabilize the mental continuum.

- Compassion practices: Connected to these basic physiological practices, I would like to also address the relationship between the clinician's ability to be aware of his or her visceral processes, which is called interoceptivity, and its relation to compassion. This interoceptivity involves experiencing one's digestive processes or cardiovascular or respiratory systems. It is basically mindfulness of the body, which is one of the Four Foundations of Mindfulness taught by the Buddha in the Satipattana Sutta of the Pali Canon. What we have learned is that people who are numbed out or autistic do not have the ability to be interoceptive and to track their internal visceral processes. If you do not have this capacity, you will lack the capacity to actually sense into the feelings of another. Your capacity to be interoceptive is a building block in the experience of empathy. Without empathy, which is the ability to recognize and feel the suffering of another, there is no capacity for compassion.

In this way, compassion is comprised of a number of different features. The first is its progression in stages from the ability to recognize suffering, then to feel suffering, then to develop the aspiration to transform it (either directly or indirectly), and finally to not be attached to the outcome. There are also two basic forms of compassion: biased or referential compassion and unbiased or nonreferential compassion. Referential compassion has an object, and nonreferential compassion has no object; it is universal compassion. We ultimately train clinicians in nonreferential compassion, but we begin by using referential compassion as a base. Finally, it is important that clinicians learn that compassion along with empathy and presence are not a one-way street. They are bidirectional; that is, experiences of mutuality. This means that in the moment, the individual is present, attuned, sincere, and well boundaried so that he/she does not go into a state of "empathic overarousal." Authenticity is very important in such a situation.

In this way, we teach the four brahmaviharas ("boundless abodes") of loving kindness, compassion, sympathetic joy, and equanimity, as well as a very long teaching on the Tibetan practice of *tonglen* ("giving and receiving") in which one visualizes taking on the suffering of others and giving back to them well-being—a practice that we have seen the Rigpa Spiritual Care Programme develop highly elsewhere in this volume.

- Investigative practices: The next domain in mental training that we feel is important to address is the investigative faculty. We have set practices that develop insight, focusing on values, altruism, pain, suffering, death, and violence. These are existential dimensions. We do this through the practice of classical vipassana insight meditation from the Theravada Buddhist tradition, the Nine Contemplations of Atisha that come from the Tibetan Buddhist tradition, and the Contemplation of Priorities developed by Lama Yeshe.

    For the subjective familiarization of the experience of the moment of death, we teach the meditation on the dissolution of the body after death, as also explained in the Satipattana Sutta, and also the dissolution of the elements from the Tibetan tradition. We also do writing meditation that explores death and lead a process called "sandtray" that uses symbols based in Jungian psychology.

In addition, we address how to be present with pain and suffering without consoling or personalizing. One meditation we use for this is an adapatation from the Lotus Sutra. First, we do an exercise called "Seeing Purely," which is to perceive an individual from his or her most unconditioned self. Then we do a complimentary practice called "Bearing Witness" in which people learn how to be simply present with the truth of individual suffering. Another practice that we teach is comeditation practice. This is a breath and visualization practice done with a caregiver and a dying person. We also train people in Council Process in which people sit in a circle and speak of their experience while not seeking consensus. This process helps one to learn to bear witness to an individual's experience as it is.

- Nondual Practices: The final area that we teach is called Open Presence, which is the developing of panoramic, receptive, nonjudgmental attention. This is basically a reflective practice of choiceless awareness.

(3) Moral Character

The third area that we address has to do with the development of moral character. We explore the moral and ethical basis of what it is to not only cure but to care. We look at how one of the biggest challenges that clinicians encounter is moral distress. Thus, we teach people how to deal with moral dilemmas and moral conflicts.

We also have developed contemplative interventions to support relationship-centered care. When one has emotional balance, for example, one can be in better relationship with people, have better interpersonal communication, be emotionally intelligent, have an easier time communicating difficult news, be more sensitive on the social and cultural level, and be a better facilitator of community. We find that having intentional and emotional balance and a metacognitive perspective assist with insight into ethical reasoning.

In this regard, we use the work of James Rest in terms of moral development. We think his ideas help develop increased moral sensitivity with which one is better able to empathize with another person's distress. Because of intentional balance, you are better able to (1) discern the most ethical action; (2) have a deeper moral motivation, which means putting moral values ahead of other values; (3) develop moral character, which is to become a person who manifests strength in their convictions; and finally (4) engage in moral actions.[3] To learn how to take action that is consistent with an ethical perspective is a big piece of training that we do.

As important as the development of compassion is, we feel becoming a wise clinician is equally important. In this area of training, we use the work of Thomas Meeks on the neurobiology of wisdom. Meeks looks at how wisdom is comprised of a number of different features including what we have already addressed in prosocial states of mind and behaviors; in other words, how do you actually value the promotion of the common good? We see how one rises above self-interest and engages in empathy, compassion, social cooperation, and altruism as a function of wisdom.

When the mind is truly stable and deep, one's capacity to engage in wise decision-making is heightened. Such decision-making takes place on the social level based on having lived a life in which one has been self-aware and not just operating out of an automatic perspective. This means one is able to learn from one's own life experience. This capacity is very important in the domain of wisdom.

Meeks also talks about how emotional balance and stability are essential in terms of the cultivation of wisdom and in the capacity to be self-reflective, to have self-understanding, and to not only be tolerant but to value altruism. From the point of view of tolerance, this means that one is able to see things from multiple perspectives and to be in a situation where there is an absence of projections. Meeks sees having a metacognitive perspective as essential in terms of the domain of wisdom, because it enables you to more easily deal with ambiguity. He talks about the capacity of the wise person to be open to new experiences and to act in the face of uncertainty.[4]

(4) Self-Care

The fourth and last area for clinicians that we feel is very important is to train them in strategies for self-care and how they can actually support their well-being in a high-stress profession. Many professional caregivers experience burnout because the system—particularly conventional medical institutions or hospices that are fiscally driven—pushes them so hard. It may even be that these institutions benefit little from caregivers' taking care of themselves. Often professional caregivers are financially rewarded for working overtime or taking on the night shift, and the overwork can produce stress that results in numbness. Numbness makes it difficult for a caregiver to feel what is really going on. It may make it difficult for him/her to perceive dysfunctional work patterns that the institution is perhaps encouraging. In the meantime, it is easy to become weary and gray with despair, sick from overwork and stress. We ask caregivers to assess nine areas of self-care: physical, emotional, intellectual, social, spiritual, cultural, relational, fun, and vocational.

These are four very large areas, but it basically comes down to the fundamentals of Buddhism;[5] that is, how can we assist clinicians to be wise and compassionate? The training from many different perspectives opens up the values of wisdom and compassion, which are fundamental qualities to be developed for a sane and good person in the world today. We look at wisdom and compassion not only from the point of view of the individual but also in terms of helping institutions become wise and compassionate.

Transformation of the Patient

This focus on the clinician personally is not separate from the clinician's work in an area that we call transformation of the patient.

Here we again have four major areas with a large curriculum behind each one.

(1) Patient Issues

We train the clinician to use various interventions to ascertain the social, cultural, and psycho-spiritual issues from which patients suffer. Cultural issues could be, for example, if they are from Japan or certain other Asian countries where denial of death is common and speaking about death actually induces fear within the patient. This is the kind of thing—that it is actually not appropriate to speak about death in front of the patient—that is important for a clinician, especially a Western doctor, to identify and understand.

(2) Pain and Suffering

We address the distinction between pain and suffering by looking at physiological and psychological changes. Pain is acute physical stress, and suffering is the story around it, the perception of pain. If a clinician asks patients whether they are more afraid of pain or death, many will say pain and the issues around pain control that interfere with physiological or mental function. This is something that has to be worked with. In the program, we feel that humans have enough pain just being in their bodies and that there is nothing redemptive about pain. Thus, we feel it is important to relieve pain in the most skillful way possible and to try to make that relief spiritually relevant.

(3) The Moment of Death

We deal with peri-death phenomena, which are all the processes around the moment of death. This includes what we call "active dying" (the final stage of the dying process), the actual moment of death, what happens for and around the patient at the moment of death, and then care of the body after death.

(4) Grief

We then focus on grief, in which we address issues related to anticipatory grief. This part also relates to clinicians and family members, because anticipating the death of a person affects people deeply and leads to grief. The anticipation of one's own death and the loss of capacity is also often accompanied by feelings of deep grief. Finally, there is, of course, the grieving experience for the patient's family and for the clinical team. One of the questions we ask our clinicians is, "How do you mark the death of a patient?" Many clinicians do not mark it, and, of course, there are consequences to this.

Transformation of the Community

We have a deep emphasis on the profound value of relationship, relationship-centered care, and the development of the interdisciplinary team. The relational dimension could be clinician-patient, clinician-family, clinician-community, clinician-institution; patient-clinician, patient-family, patient-community, patient-institution; and so forth. In these terms, we try to teach clinicians about presence, how to not personalize, and how to not devalue the relationships of other people who are offering care within the wider community system. We also have a deep emphasis on the development of respect. This leads us into techniques in community development and cultural sensitivity. This work helps clinicians to ascertain the culture of the community and become sensitive to the cultural dimensions within the community in their caregiving process. In terms of our training process, we frequently use role-playing, particularly for culturally complex situations. Another issue that we work with in terms of community development is interprofessional relationships, such as respecting other members on the interdisciplinary team and teaching doctors to listen to chaplains. Here we address issues related to horizontal hostility and the profound importance of respect.

Transformation of the Institution

This area addresses the ethical issues that arise in an end-of-life care situation and the way that the institution responds to them. This area deals with everything from having patient advocates, to advance directives, to how patients are communicating with family members about do-not-resuscitate orders, and so forth. There is also increasing inquiry into the spirituality of clinicians, which asks, "Where does our sense of meaning come from?" The contemplative dimension looks at what practices actually open up our capacity. The challenge is how to input this content in clinician training and then how to actually apply it to clinical settings. In this way, we are strongly advocating increased research initiatives in the medical field, such as with the Fetzer Institute in Kalamazoo, Michigan. Due to the diminishment of empathy and compassion in the clinical setting, Fetzer is very interested in us developing compassion-based training for clinicians. For our training to be effective, it very much depends on the clinician learning how to value well-being, insight, and compassion—and to basically have self-respect.

There is more and more interest today in spiritual care that is being mandated in very important ways in conventional medicine. For example, the Mayo Clinic in Rochester, New York, one of the most renowned medical institutions in the United States, says spirituality is an integral dimension of compassionate care and an important aid to healing for patients, their families, and their caregivers. The University of Virginia Medical School, where an academic chair in contemplative end-of-life care is now funded, says the good practice of medicine depends upon physicians' awareness of both their patients' and their own spirituality.

This major shift by many medical institutions in the United States to embrace the complete care of patients, their families, clinicians, and their communities has come about from the increasing suffering on the part of patients and clinicians. It has also come about because the efforts of some people in the field have begun to influence medical policy in this country. For instance, Christina Puchalski's commitment to introducing spiritual inquiry into medicine by taking spiritual histories has sparked change; policy now mandates that, during the intake of the patient, there must be a spiritual interview.[6]

THE BUDDHIST CHAPLAINCY PROGRAM AND TOTAL SYSTEM CHANGE

In our Buddhist Chaplaincy Program, not only do we address suffering on a person-to-person level but, like the BWD program, we also look at whole systems that are suffering. Many clinicians have gone into medicine because of a calling. What is fascinating is that many clinicians are coming into our Buddhist Chaplaincy Program because their calling is not being fulfilled in medicine. All they want to do is what a chaplain does: address the spiritual dimensions in health care. We also have lawyers in our chaplaincy program who in a similar way changed fields because their desire for justice was not being realized in a dysfunctional legal system. We have people who are doing specializations in environmental chaplaincy, youth chaplaincy, and chaplaincy in businesses and government, in addition to prison and hospital chaplaincy. We have people now who are engaged in projects related to gender minorities, working with people who have gender identities that are not the two most common ones. We have people in human rights organizations and legal organizations that have become chaplains, because they are trying to understand justice in terms of compassion.

Our training program does not provide certification from the Association of Professional Chaplains, but you do not need this to sit with dying people or work in a legal institution. As a religious person, I think the kind of certification that is required in this country is useful, but I do not think it is necessary at all. If you are a minister, then you go and minister—but if you are a good person, then you step in and you care. We have a chaplaincy program that is very powerful. However, I really think this is about the human heart and about compassion, not certification. In those environments and countries where there is resistance to compassion, you have to be skillful; certification alone is not going to help get you into a system that is not interested in caring for people. As seen in the following chapter on Buddhist hospice care in San Francisco, hospice volunteers do tremendous work in this country, and they do not have psychological credentials. They do a brief hospice training, have good supervision, and serve dying people. Ultimately, I think the idea of certification makes it harder for people to do something that is only human. We would not even need a system of certification if our communities were inspired to take care of the dying.

I feel that there is not much that separates the trained from the untrained, that aspiration is really the key. If you truly care, you can do the work. If this is not your work to do, then you won't do the work. You won't do the service. You won't be engaged in compassionate care. It is not everybody's job. I think it is fine that people want to create systems and standards, but I think it can prevent more good from happening and does not stop so much of the bad. For example, I know many people who are certified at the highest level as religious personages, professional psychologists, and psychiatrists but who are unsympathetic and unable to do this work. They have spent so much time getting certification that their own hearts have not awakened. You can try to train people in presence, but this is not how it works. Meditation is helpful in this regard. There are all kinds of games and techniques, but it is in a way a natural gift. Moreover, one's aspiration really matters in this kind of vocation.

Our vision of chaplaincy operates on many different levels. Because you cannot separate the patient from the clinician, the clinician from the community, or beings from the institutions themselves, we have used a systems-theory[7] approach for both our Buddhist Chaplaincy Training and Being with Dying training programs. Joanna Macy, the well-known Buddhism-and-systems theorist, is a teacher for us. Merle Lefkoff, who worked with Jimmy Carter in his White House administration as a diplomat and is a systems theorist, is on our faculty. We feel that a systems perspective is the only viable one. Individual clinicians can go through a deep change in how they approach their work, but the institutional demands create a moral conflict within them and within how they can approach their work. Therefore, you cannot look at things in isolation. Everything is interconnected—as Buddhism teaches. We also have a very strong emphasis on neuroscience, direct and structural violence, and ethics, relationship, and communication. In this way, our training, especially the chaplaincy program, is basically on socially engaged Buddhism.

After participants leave the chaplaincy training, they are supported by a cohort system of around twelve to twenty-four people. These cohorts are broken into smaller groups that are mentored by students from the preceding cohort. Students who have already been through the program mentor four to five people. They form a mindful community, a mini-cohort. They use email, the phone, and the Ning social networking website. They are a complete support and learning group. It has been a powerful process, overseeing these micro-communities as they have developed. We also have another network based on the participant's chosen discipline; many people who come into the program are very interested and committed to end-of-life care, so there is a learning group on end-of-life care.

We do not use this cohort model with the Being with Dying program; it's not necessary because BWD program attracts people from the same institution. For example, we have a large group of people from the University of Virginia who train every year, as well as clinicians from Duke University and San Diego Hospice, which is the largest hospice in the US. These are regional groups who then ask our faculty to continue the training process in those venues. This is necessary because isolated individual training does not work. You cannot sustain it.

I think that our model is a powerful one, because it has Buddhism, systems theory, neuroscience, and finally community development, all sitting on a contemplative base. I think we have been successful in introducing this work into the culture, because we see more and more of our curriculum appearing out there in the landscape. We are not proprietary about our curriculum or about our faculty, so people have a chance to develop the curriculum in their own terms and make it appropriate to who they are and the institution that they serve. Our work at Upaya is a model of a possibility in bringing Buddhism into Western culture in a very pragmatic way. As time passes, we have seen more programs around the country that are following our model. This bodes well for an engaged and applied Buddhism that is not only national but global.

USA
Zen Approaches to Terminal Care and Buddhist Chaplaincy Training

Jonathan S. Watts and Yoshiharu Tomatsu

The San Francisco Bay Area of the United States has had two significant factors that have made it a major center for the development of Buddhist-based spiritual care for the terminally ill and the bereaved.

The first factor is that San Francisco has been a center for the counterculture and alternative-culture movements in the United States since the 1950s. Buddhism has been part of this movement from the beginning, and the Bay Area has developed an incredible variety of different Buddhist communities (a high number of indigenous Asian ones as well as convert ones), major Buddhist retreat centers and temples, and Buddhist groups involved in all sorts of social engagement (such as peace advocacy, prison chaplaincy, and terminal care).

The second key factor emerging out of this first one is that San Francisco as a center of gay culture in America became one of the major flashpoints in the beginning of the AIDS crisis in the late 1980s. With people falling ill, declining rapidly, and dying suddenly without the support of the advanced therapies we have today, there was an urgent need for hospice care. As seen in the pioneering hospice work among AIDS patients in Thailand and Cambodia profiled in other chapters in this volume, many of these sufferers were extremely exposed, having been ostracized by their families and society and lacking the financial means to combat their illness.

Since this time, Buddhist care for the terminally ill has expanded to include other at-need groups in the area. In San Francisco, there are three basic options for the poor and terminally ill: (1) Laguna Honda Hospital, (2) Maitri Hospice, which specializes in AIDS patients, and (3) using insurance if you want to stay at home. However, if you are poor, one's home may be less than ideal, with challenging physical and emotional environments. A patient may also have a double or triple diagnosis, mental illness, and so forth, so staying at home may not really be an option. Fortunately, because of these three different resources and a growing interest in studying and training as a volunteer or chaplain in such care, there is ideally only a need for another twenty hospice beds in the city.[1] The situation has become much more manageable than at the peak of the AIDS crisis in the 1980s. Both individual Buddhists and Buddhist communities have been in the center of this movement for spiritual care, and in this chapter, we will provide an overview of some of the key individuals and groups involved.

Maitri Hospice for AIDS

Maitri was founded in 1987 by Issan Dorsey, the abbot of the Hartford Street Zen Center. Dorsey was a gay Soto Zen priest and former prostitute, drag queen, and drug addict who died of AIDS complications in 1990. Before he himself fell ill, he responded to the AIDS epidemic of the late 1980s by taking in destitute and homeless AIDS victims. He eventually opened an eight-bed hospice in the Castro district, the heart of San Francisco's gay community, called Maitri Hospice—the first Buddhist hospice of its kind in the United States. In 1997, Maitri moved into a custom-made building with fifteen private rooms. Its executive director from 2001–10, Tim Patriarca, who refers to himself as a Lutheran Zen Buddhist with Italian background, describes the environment of Maitri:

> AIDS is a great equalizer because after twenty years of being positive [for HIV] and going through various illnesses, all of our patients are poor by the end. We have doctors and lawyers next to people who are streetwalkers and drug addicts. They all have no money. And the system works

because one of the best aspects of any hospice is the support created among each of the residents. They come together, share experiences, and are at each other's bedsides. And this gives them complete comfort.[2]

In this way, Maitri in addition to being focused on AIDS is also specifically aimed at the poor. In 2008, patients had to have an annual income of less than $31,950. Other basic criteria are having an AIDS diagnosis or disabling HIV; being a San Francisco resident; being 18 years or older; needing twenty-four-hour care, skilled care, or hospice care; and having had a chest x-ray for tuberculosis within one month prior to admission. Maitri's fifteen rooms are always full, and they have a waiting list of between six and fifteen people. The average length of stay is three and a half months (a traditional hospice in the United States is around thirty days), so there are a total of fifty to sixty patients per year who go through Maitri.

Maitri has one nurse on duty twenty-four hours a day, a role shared by three different nurses—some of whom come to train from the University of San Francisco. They have three certified nursing assistants on duty during the day and two on duty at night. These assistants help patients with activities like going to the bathroom or taking a bath. In this way, the ratio of patients to attendants is 1:3 whereas the national ratio is 1:15. Because of the support of an expansive care team, hospice attendants at Maitri have an average employment period of seven to nine years, as opposed to sixteen to eighteen months in typical hospices where they bear a heavier load of the work and thus suffer from burnout more quickly. Maitri also has two social workers, each of whom work half time helping to make the residents feel more at home through decorating their individual rooms, ordering food, going shopping, etc. Finally, Maitri has twenty-five to thirty-five medical professionals on budget who address the variety of medical needs of the patients.

In order to provide such a high level of care for the poor, Maitri actually does not take insurance and does not receive payments from any insurance systems. Since insurance coverage and government assistance for the poor is very inadequate in the United States, Maitri decided to create its own financial base in order to make its work more secure and reliable. They receive funding from four different government sources within the city, state, and federal systems, which subsequently bars them from taking insurance. They further augment this by raising significant funding from private sources as well as conducting major fundraising events. Finally, they designed their new building to pay for itself by putting in a commercial unit on the first floor and also established a foundation in 1993. In order to handle all this work, they have two full-time fundraisers.

Maitri also makes active use of the aforementioned growing interest in studying and training as a hospice volunteer or chaplain. Maitri has a base of over sixty volunteers who work every week for at least four to six hours visiting residents; assisting them with meals, walks, and activities; picking up prescriptions; helping with shopping; taking residents to physician visits; hosting regular activities for residents; and assisting kitchen staff. Their training involves an initial four-day course held twice in the spring or fall in which they study the following: updates on AIDS research and treatment; body mechanics; cultural competency; working with multiple-diagnosis residents; boundaries, limit setting, and confidentiality; touch and music therapy; dealing with grief and multiple loss; and spirituality.

Spiritual Preparation for Death

At Maitri, some patients stabilize and are thus reevaluated every six months. Some do get better and move out. For example, one man was told repeatedly by doctors that he had one month to live but he ended up living two years. He moved out of Maitri but after six months returned as he got worse. Patriarca notes that traditional hospices force you to leave if you are getting better—as seen in the chapter on Germany as well—but Maitri is more flexible and reserves space for people to come back. He explains that the prevalent model for receiving hospice care is that the patient has to completely abandon curative care and just take on palliative care. Maitri rejects this model. He admits that while they want everyone to have a mindful and peaceful death, it just does not happen for everyone. Some people want to pursue curative treatment even up to the last month although they know they are dying. In this way, he recalls Issan Dorsey's admonition that "You need to meet people where there are and not where you want them to be." Patriarca thus emphasizes that at Maitri they do not force on a patient their own view of what is a "good death."

In turn, social workers at Maitri do not force family reconciliation and other end-of-life matters, but they do try to get patients to take care of basic business like funeral arrangements. The fact that many of their patients are gay presents a special challenge in that they have frequently been rejected by their religious traditions as well as their families. They often have very difficult deaths and need extra attention and support; Patriarca notes that those with some spiritual background seem to have easier deaths—a point emphasized by Rev. Mari Sengoku in her chapter on hospice care in Hawaii and Japan. Only about 10 percent of Maitri's patients are connected to religious groups like the nearby Hartford Street and San Francisco Zen Centers, yet about 60–70 percent do have active religious belief.

In this way, Maitri is ecumenical in philosophy, though the majority of volunteers come from Tibetan and Zen Buddhist backgrounds. Maitri does not have any chaplains on payroll, because they have access to a number of chaplains who come to do such work for free. A Lutheran minister comes in every Tuesday, and a Zen priest also comes in often. Further, many neighborhood people also stop by from places like the Hartford Street Zen Center, connecting Maitri to both the area and to the city. Patriarca comments that:

> It's not only about creating community here within the walls but making sure we are part of the greater community and the neighborhood. AIDS has facilitated this, because death has become so much more a part of life. Someone who is twenty now has to think of a friend who is dying, rather than when they are sixty. Death has become part of the neighborhood.[3]

In this way, Maitri is an ideal care community, because the average person is religious and spiritual. Many patients have their own local spiritual communities come in and guide them; for example, many Christian patients have created their own group prayer at Maitri; African Americans often have used singing; and numerous Native American patients have brought in shamans.

Maitri has a shrine or altar with a strong Buddhist element where the large number of Buddhist volunteers and staff hold group meditation practice. In this way, they will suggest patients try meditation and have used it to help patients deal with addictions to pain medications developed while staying in hospitals. Many have used meditation for other issues like their death experience. However, only a very small percentage of patients—those who were serious Buddhists—have used meditation as an alternative pain-control therapy.

At the time of death of a patient, there is always someone in the room with him or her. A candle is lit and put in the front parlor to inform everyone else in the hospice of the death. The body is left at the hospice for a few days. The residents gather flowers from the outdoor garden. The body is bathed and dressed, and the room is prepared. Patriarca notes that they encourage residents to be active in this preparation so that they know exactly what will happen to their body when they die. Such a practice ultimately gives them a sense of comfort about their own death.

Maitri has a formal grief-care program in which for six months they send cards and make calls to family members and loved ones as well as offering referral to other support groups. Maitri will continue to work with a family until they think they are well enough; they also will refer the family to a group called Hospice by the Bay, which has more developed home-care and bereavement-care programs. Maitri will also provide, upon request, individual memorial services at the hospice that the social workers arrange. They hold memorial services for the whole Maitri community every other month with a rotating religious professional that commemorate everyone who has died in that period. Patriarca notes that in certain cases they encounter conflicts between the wishes of the patient and the family concerning

funeral arrangements, yet they endeavor to fulfill the final wishes of
the patient. Family members may often visit Maitri for the first few
weeks after the death of their loved one. After a year or two, they may
show up one more time and that seems to close the cycle for them.

THE ZEN HOSPICE PROJECT AT LAGUNA HONDA HOSPITAL

The Hospice and Palliative Care Ward at Laguna Honda Hospital in
San Francisco was created in 1988 as a collaborative project with the
Zen Hospice Project (ZHP) based out of the San Francisco Zen Center. Like Maitri, it sought to reach out to the community that Zen
practitioners lived in, especially toward people who were homeless
and destitute. They found that many in their community were coming to Laguna Honda, so they created a collaboration with the hospital to provide training, maintenance, and support for volunteers.

Laguna Honda Hospital has a history of serving the poor and indi-
gent. The site of the hospital goes back to the 1800s as a meeting
place of travelers on the gold rush. It later became an almshouse for
widows and orphans at the end of the nineteenth century, and then a
refuge during the Depression. The hospital was built in the 1920s and
many of the facilities are now being rebuilt. The hospital used to have
1,100 beds but has now reduced its size to 780 beds. Laguna Honda,
along with San Francisco General Hospital, is a public hospital serving San Francisco and regions to the south. The hospice receives all
kinds of terminal patients with a wide variety of conditions, some
with multiple diagnoses. Many of these people are poor with little
insurance, so this is one of the few institutions they can access. The
only limitations to admission are on those with psychosocial problems who endanger the well-being of the larger community.

Because Laguna Honda was such an old facility until its major renovation in 2010, the hospice was distinctive in being an open-ward unit
with twenty-six beds and only two private rooms. Florence Nightin-
gale (1820–1910) created this open-ward medical care model, because
the access to open air and light improves health and the shared space

provides a sense of community between residents. The founder of ZHP, Frank Ostaseski,[4] also advocated this kind of model in which residents live in a communal atmosphere.[5] The Dhammarak Niwet Hospice, the first Buddhist hospice established in Thailand that is specialized for AIDS patients, has also used this model effectively: less-critical patients care for the more critical.

Eric Poché is the head of volunteer services and training for ZHP at Laguna Honda and has been with ZHP for thirteen years. He was a volunteer for ten years and on staff for four years with Shanti Project, which was created in nearby Berkeley to offer volunteer emotional and practical support for people dying of cancer in a home environment. Poché notes that at Laguna Honda they have found that patients help each other, support each other, and share things that only the dying know. In this way, patients may find a strong sense of purpose in helping others. They learn how to love and how to accept being loved, which for some of them may be something they have never experienced in their lives. These shared bonds often result in a small group of patients dying in succession within a short time of each other. In this way, Poché feels it is unfortunate that it is no longer legal to build such open wards.

To balance the intimacy of the open ward, a garden was created by the volunteers as a place for residents to have more individual quiet space that they may share with visitors. A butterfly garden was built with plants that attract butterflies by a local business, and they have a special path so that those in wheelchairs can enter into that part of the garden in their chairs. The garden is also a popular place to hold memorial services for those who have died, and some residents have had their cremated remains put in this garden. There is also a hospital chapel accessible to patients and family, but there is not a meditation room. The hospice does have a quiet room with a Lazure Painting method[6] used on the walls, which aids grieving families and patients who are disruptive or who need less stimulation. They also have a solarium where the staff meets and practices meditation. This is another place for family to have private time with a resident or to stay overnight.

The hospice's care team consists of one attending physician, three nurses on call in the day and one at night; four to five certified nursing assistants who do all the bedside care (bathing, changing, etc.) on call in the day and two at night, one social worker, and one activity therapist. There was one chaplain on the care team but the position was terminated in 2008 due to funding cuts. Almost none of the residents are Buddhists. Most are Christian, some Jewish or Muslim, and some "undeclared." However, they still have spiritual needs for which the chaplains can provide, so they do provide access to outside chaplains.

The Work and Mission of Zen Volunteers

Like Maitri, the heart of the Zen Hospice Project is in the volunteers. Their training is inspired by Buddhist principles, and one third of the volunteers come from the Zen community—a ratio that was larger in the past. Many now come from the Tibetan Shambhala tradition and also from the Theravadan Insight tradition. Non-Buddhists can become volunteers as well, and some volunteers are Christian or "undeclared." However, candidates are asked at the beginning about their spiritual orientation and whether they have a practice that helps to ground them. There is a fifty-hour training course that is required to become a volunteer.

The commitment to personal spirituality and group practice among volunteers is a distinctive part of the program. The volunteers have a monthly community meeting at which teachers from a variety of Buddhist backgrounds are invited to speak. They also come together before every shift to meditate and check in with each other so that these ideals are constantly being reinforced. Poché remarks that this helps keep people focused and ensure longevity with their commitment. As a result, they have volunteers that have been with them for as many as fifteen years—much longer than other volunteer communities. ZHP also has a program for medical professionals to prevent burnout and help them psychologically. However, Poché notes that there is a prevalent attitude among medical professionals of "We don't burn out," and so they usually do not recognize it until it has become critical.

Out of a pool of eighty people, volunteers work generally four to five at one time in three shifts per day (9 a.m.–2 p.m., 1 p.m.–6 p.m., 5 p.m.–10 p.m.) with overlapping shifts to ensure they are caught up properly on events since they tend to work only once per week. Volunteers are required to work for at least five hours per week, and some do more. The average age of volunteers is forty to forty-five years old, the youngest being twenty-two and the oldest seventy-eight. The majority are women. At one point, 80 percent of them were women, but now there is better gender balance. Many are students and many are retirees including retired medical professionals. Some volunteers are focused on beginning careers, especially as chaplains. Poché comments that:

> Patients do not know we are Buddhist, but they do know how we present with compassion, listening, patience, and care. We offer the connection that is hard to get from a busy doctor, nurse, or social worker. We do offer what is essentially a Buddhist perspective, but we don't spell this all out to the dying and their family members, because they don't care. They are here for a few hours, weeks, or months, and their focus is on "How can you help me through this life-changing experience?" I tell the volunteers that this is practice off the cushion. Just as you sit on the cushion and see what arises and be with it, things are going to arise working on the ward, so you use this as an opportunity for practice. It is rich and fulfilling, and the volunteers see it as not only an important part of their lives but as a necessary part of their lives, which is why they stay.[7]

In terms of postmortem grief care, the volunteers follow up with the family for the first year. They check in with a phone call or a card if it seems appropriate, but sometimes it does not because some patients have painful or lost connections with their families.

Every three months they hold a memorial service to which everyone is invited. The memorial garden is also a place where people can grieve and can leave something behind. Families may come back years later to remember them here even if they have been buried somewhere else.

BUDDHIST CHAPLAINS IN THE UNITED STATES

At Maitri and the Zen Hospice Project at Laguna Honda Hospital, volunteers serve as the core means for delivering Buddhist-based spiritual care. However, there is increasing demand for more highly trained, professional Buddhist chaplains in the growing field of spiritual care and counseling, not just in the San Francisco Bay Area but also across the United States. Volunteer chaplains tend to focus more on listening and companionship for patients. Professional chaplains, however, have a wider range of skilled responsibilities, such as ethics work as part of a team of professional clinicians in the hospital, work with the community, and nurturing the spiritual health of the medical organization itself. For Buddhists who wish to become such professionals, this usually involves the need to attain accreditation in one of the two major chaplaincy training systems in the United States: the Association of Professional Chaplains (APC) or the Association for Clinical Pastoral Education (ACPE). Clinical Pastoral Education (CPE) was developed by the Congregationalist minister Rev. Anton T. Boisen in the 1920s following a period when he himself was institutionalized for psychological problems and encountered a priest who could offer him no practical help. When he was discharged, he and Dr. William A. Bryan developed a new training system for priests so that they could be of real benefit to others. CPE offers experiential training in hospitals and health institutions that one does not get in a seminary.

The major stumbling block, however, for many Buddhists in becoming chaplains is the lack of Buddhist seminaries in the United States. Seminary study, especially a master's degree in divinity, is commonly a prerequisite for licensure with the APC and ACPE, which are still trying to figure out ways to provide licensure to Buddhists. There are only two specifically Buddhist graduate programs in the US for such pastoral training and for acquiring a master's in divinity: the Institute of Buddhist Studies (affiliated with the Jodo Shin Japanese Pure Land denomination in Berkeley, CA) and the Naropa Institute (founded by the Tibetan Buddhist teacher Chogyam Trungpa, in Boulder, CO). Outside of these, one has to simply study and train at a Dharma center. As a result, ordination also tends to be a problem; students can get education but often not official ordination from their group, as many American Buddhist communities emphasize lay practice and have not developed programs for full ordination. For Buddhists in the San Francisco Bay Area, there has been some leniency regarding these criteria so as to encourage diversity in the care community. Some people are allowed to enter CPE programs with lower criteria, and then later on may backtrack and finish up studies that might have been required before. Carlyle Coash, former bereavement coordinator at the Zen Hospice Project, reviews the qualifications and can grant equivalency for such CPE candidates who do not come from the aforementioned Buddhist divinity programs.

An example of this situation is Eileen Phillips, practicing in the Theravada tradition, who received her CPE training under Rev. Thomas Kilts, a Tibetan Buddhist chaplain formerly at the John Muir Medical Center in Concord, California. The orthodox Theravada Buddhist tradition of Sri Lanka and Southeast Asia has very strict ordination requirements and, further, has not recognized women's full ordination for a millennium. In the United States in particular, there is no specific graduate school run by this tradition. In order to get her master's equivalency, she underwent the Spirit Rock Meditation Center's two-and-a-half-year training as a community Dharma leader in community ministry and teaching meditation in groups. Phillips also gained further credits by undergoing personal practice with various teachers and taking chaplaincy training at the Sati Center with Rev. Jennifer Block, a Zen Buddhist chaplain and bereavement manager at the Zen Hospice Project. She then entered the one-year, full-time CPE training program at the John Muir Medical Center and had an additional year of work as a chaplain before gaining certification. During this additional year, Phillips also finished a number of essays and other procedures before gaining final certification in front of a board of six accreditors. Having completed the entire process in 2009, Phillips began working for Kaiser Hospice in Vallejo, California, where she visits patients' homes in the quite expansive area of Napa and Solano counties.

After seminary or equivalent training, CPE requires one intense year of internship at a hospital or health institution. However, to become a CPE supervisor qualified to train others is even harder; it takes four to six years of further training. As of 2009, there were only three CPE supervisors in the United States who are Buddhist, though others around the United States were in the process of gaining their accreditation. These three are Thomas Kilts, formerly of the John Muir Medical Center, Trudi Jinpu Hirsch, a Zen nun at the Beth Israel Medical Center in New York, and Julie Hanada, a Jodo Shin minister at the Harborview Medical Center in Seattle. Although Rev. Jennifer Block does run chaplaincy training courses through the Sati Center for Buddhist Studies, she does not yet have full accreditation as a CPE supervisor.

Introductory and Informal Training for Chaplaincy

Jennifer Block helps to run CPE preparation courses at the chaplaincy-training program at the Sati Center. The program has developed since 2000 from people interested in combining their Buddhist practice with a livelihood. It is an introductory course similar to what one might take in pastoral care at a seminary. The Institute of Buddhist Studies (IBS) is now designing a specific chaplain-training curriculum, so for the time being their students can take classes with the Sati Center for credit. IBS has also developed a relationship with the Zen Hospice Project through Block where their students can receive credit for courses taken at ZHP. Besides a wide variety of programs and events for educating family caregivers and bereaved family members, ZHP also runs courses in how to care for the dying.

Block, in both her experience in gaining certification and in teaching others at the Sati Center and ZHP, relates that through CPE training prospective chaplains must go deeper into their own tradition and find out what it says about death. Since your CPE instructor may not be of the same tradition as you, he or she may not be able to guide this investigation but will encourage you on the path. For example, while doing her internship in a Catholic hospital, Block felt compelled to go back to ZHP for more study and training. Most candidates already have significant intellectual learning when they enter CPE internship work, but the training is about bringing that learning down into the heart. She remarks that the training is like water wearing a stone down, as one experiences death after death. Some people cannot or will not do the work, and so they drop out. In the CPE training she leads, she emphasizes her relationship to the bodhisattva vow to save all beings:

> So I sit with you in your suffering to fulfill my vow. My intention is to alleviate suffering, so I come back to the teachings, to what I believe inspires me or keeps me in my seat when I want to run. If I forget my vow, I need to go back to my temple, sangha, or teacher to be inspired to then go back to the hospital.[8]

There is a maturation process for a chaplain from starting as a basic member of a sangha, to becoming a leader in that sangha, to then going to seminary and gaining ordination as a minister, to ultimately entering chaplaincy training. Block feels this is "a natural progression, a development over time of wisdom, compassion, maturity, and real skill" in areas that are not just religious but also psychological and sociological.

Block says that meditation practice is an essential activity to develop the skill of presence. She notes that:

> In chaplaincy or in any work being with people who are sick, the hardest thing is to be present, to really be there

with suffering, and not to try too hard to fix it. For Buddhist chaplains, the Dharma and this sense that we all suffer becomes a common ground. However, it is really the meditation training that helps us to be present. Even when I train Buddhist chaplains, they need to already have experience, because I cannot teach people to be present. That is the hardest thing to teach. I can teach how to do a prayer, to find a priest, to resolve conflict, but teaching you to be present is very difficult.[9]

Block further elaborates on the importance of such presence; in group work with the bereaved, if just one person can be mindful, be quiet, breathe, and *make observations rather than interventions,* others start to pick up on that, which has a collective effect. Thus, they have found that they must model such presence themselves rather trying to "teach" it.

Formal CPE Training and Internship

Rev. Thomas Kilts is the former director of spiritual care at the John Muir Medical Center in Concord, California, about forty minutes outside of San Francisco. Having been raised as a Buddhist, he planned to become a monk at a young age. However, encountering various difficulties in this course, he chose instead to train as a chaplain as a way to realize the Buddhist teachings in a practical and engaged manner. In this process, he began training under a number of different Tibetan Buddhist teachers and received ordination in the Nyingma lineage, which allows for marriage and certain other lay forms of comportment. He received his master's in divinity from the Naropa Institute and then did CPE training in Massachusetts at a Catholic hospital.

In 2008, the spiritual-care department at John Muir Medical Center consisted of one CPE supervisor (Rev. Kilts), one CPE supervisor-in-training (SIT), and four full-time CPE residents. These residents do the complete four-part training in one year while receiving a stipend from the program for living wages. The department also provides a one-part summer program, which requires tuition. John Muir Medical Center also offers CPE supervisor training, which is extremely arduous, and also the two levels of base CPE training, CPE I and CPE II. Today, the once relatively small program has expanded from four to twelve residents, requiring one more supervisor and two more supervisors-in-training. 2008 was the first year that none of the residents were Christian; they had a Theravada Buddhist (Eileen Phillips), an interfaith minister, a Unitarian, and a SIT who was Unitarian as well. In 2009, they had an Episcopal SIT, a Zen nun resident, and Presbyterian, Seventh-Day Adventist, and Methodist residents as well.

The spiritual-care department works with doctors, nurses, three medical social workers, and a psychiatric nurse liaison who connects them with the psychiatrists who work at the behavioral health center next door. The CPE residents also work in the behavioral health center, which has spiritual-care groups and a staff chaplain who is Baptist but with Quaker leanings. The John Muir Medical Center has no hospice and only just started a palliative care team. They do have a grief letter program that is a series of twelve letters over the year, a program that families can refuse. They also have Grief Support Facilitators who are locals that run a retreat for the grieving and also run a free open support group twice a month.

However, grief support services are separate from the CPE program. The CPE training is not focused on death but on a wide range of issues and problems; residents cover the whole hospital. CPE residents are assigned to each floor for eleven weeks at a time, so within in a year they experience the whole hospital. They have on-call rotations with one intern on call every day and on weekends, who are required to live within a thirty-minute drive of the hospital. Chaplains, even the interns, are one of the few personnel allowed in a patient's room without prior approval of a doctor.

The spiritual-care department does have a meditation room but patients usually do not use it; it's mainly for family and medical staff. There are no specific religious icons in the room. Within the local area, the largest denomination is Roman Catholic. There are a few Buddhists, some convert Westerners but mostly Asian American from a variety of backgrounds, such as Japanese Pure Land Jodo Shin, Chinese, Southeast Asian Mahayana Buddhists from Vietnam, and Theravadan Buddhist Cambodians.

In this way, Rev. Kilts has had to focus on clinical chaplaincy, because there is not very much need for specifically Buddhist chaplains in the United States. He remarks that "No one is going to hire you as a Buddhist chaplain, so most Buddhist chaplains must work as interfaith clinical chaplains." Although Buddhist chaplains are becoming more popular in the San Francisco Bay Area because of religious diversity, most Buddhist patients are Asian American and are sometimes surprised or disappointed when a Caucasian Buddhist chaplain enters their room instead of an Asian Buddhist monk. The department also has had to do a significant amount of education in the hospital among patients and also staff that the role of chaplains is not just people who deal with last rites.

Rev. Kilts notes that chaplaincy is about dealing with relationships and crises and that one has to learn that while out in the world with people, not in a temple. One also has to learn when it's appropriate to use Buddhism and when it's not. Similarly, supervisors have to train residents to know their place and not engage in turf wars with other professionals in the care environment. Still, conflicts do arise with some doctors and psychiatrists who prefer pharmaceutical interventions for psychological problems or persistently pursue treatment when palliation and hospice are in order. The hospital, however, has a board of ethics on which Rev. Kilts sits that mediates conflicts among the care team.

CPE training and chaplain work in general involves not only working with the problems of patients but also serving as a support for the entire hospital community. The work is thus extremely intense. Students may complain about different things that are really just covering the deeper anxiety about their own issues around death. At the same time, they must continue to act as comforters and caregivers. Rev. Kilts recalls that his first CPE mentor was an Episcopal priest who noticed him struggling during long night shifts. He suggested that Kilts visualize the hospital as a monastery. Kilts recalls that the priest taught him "to start your day in prayer, take time out in the middle of your day to do prayer, and at the end of the day do prayer. The day is regimented that way and that's how I do it in our department— starting every week with a ritual and ending every week with a ritual. We function in a monastic way. We begin group sessions with three rings of a bell."[10] Kilts further comments that:

> Personally, I could not do this work without my own spiritual practice and my own connection to community. I tell my students all the time that you cannot be an effective clinical chaplain unless you are rooted in your tradition. I am not a big advocate of the wishy-washy "I can take care of everyone" thing. You have to be rooted and have a strong foundation in your own tradition in order to be able to work with everyone, which is the opposite of what some people think. This is what we train people here in, to claim their own tradition.[11]

CONCLUSION

The three facilities and programs that we have looked at in this chapter offer a fascinating spectrum of caring for the critically ill, dying, and bereaved. In Maitri Hospice, we see the least-formalized form of engagement in terms of Buddhist practice. Chaplains are replaced by a group of volunteers who, while receiving some training, do not partake in organized Buddhist practice facilitated by Maitri. As a small private institution, Maitri focuses on creating a spiritual support network through integration into the local community and its especially strong Buddhist resources. Zen Hospice Project's program at Laguna Honda Hospital, while also relying on volunteers rather than chaplains, has a more intensive training and a regular system for developing and maintaining strong spiritual practice and culture among its volunteers. Operating within a large public health institution, it uses this more-disciplined form of volunteer care to replace the local community support system that Maitri Hospice employs. Finally, the John Muir Medical Center, in part as a center for training chaplains, uses the most formalized system of spiritual care, replacing volunteers with highly trained religious professionals. Using the interdisciplinary team-care system, a group of highly trained professionals create a care community, like ZHP, in lieu of a localized community, like Maitri. Each, as we have seen, has its strong points and weak points. Yet this variety of styles and options make care for the dying and bereaved, especially Buddhist-grounded care, in the San Francisco area very rich.

The remarkable point that they all share is that emphasis on Buddhist practice is put on the caregiver as an essential competency to, as Issan Dorsey said, "meeting people where they are." While none of the groups would deny the potential benefits of patients developing a strong spiritual practice, the essential Buddhist teaching here appears to be more about manifesting Buddhism through one's own behavior rather than on working to change others'.

USA
"Listening to the Dharma": Integrating Buddhism into a Multifaith Health Care Environment

Julie Chijo Hanada

INTRODUCTION

> Though in the morning we may have radiant health, in the evening we may return to white ashes.
>
> —Rennyo Shonin

Even when religion does not seem important to people, when life surprises them and events occur, and they find themselves or someone they love admitted into a hospital, feelings they may have never known they have about religion surface, or feelings they already have get amplified.

Wearing a variety of hats is the life and ministry for a priest. As a temple priest, I was the Dharma teacher, officiant of ritual, representative to the broader community, consoler, and cheerleader. My education and academic foundation was focused on doctrine. Since 2001, I have integrated "listening to the Dharma" (*monpo*) in my professional work in the health care industry as a chaplain, clinical educator, and spiritual-care department director.

In this chapter, I will share my perspectives about how health care is transformed by the practice of "listening to the Dharma," and how I use Buddhist teachings to help heal and transform people's religious and spiritual lives. I will present vignettes that highlight seemingly different experiences yet continue to support this theme. The first vignette highlights the differences between the role of a chaplain in a multifaith environment and the role of the temple priest, and what priests can learn from the training that chaplains receive. The second vignette shows how medical staff members are supported to handle challenging situations when they engage chaplains. The third vignette highlights how Buddhism informs me as an educator who develops programs and journeys with individuals in ministry formation and/ or professional chaplaincy. The fourth vignette presents a situation of the impact of chaplains as part of the medical ethics team.

These vignettes are gathered from across my ten years of working within five health care systems and from being a chaplain student to department director and clinical educator. In all the examples below specific details have been altered or eliminated to protect the privacy of the individual(s).

1: Chaplain and Priest

She cries. I sit silently with her until she's ready to start talking again. Jane has just told me how she wants to know and have faith and hope but feels none of it. The emptiness is overwhelming and so she weeps. She looks back at me deeply. "Do you see me? Can you see my pain? If you can, will you leave or stay?" These are the unspoken words I hear. I look at her and try to convey, "Yes, I see your pain and am holding it with loving kindness (metta)." However, to say so at this point would be premature as it provides a way out of her pain by giving it over to me. Instead, we hold eye contact for a few minutes, and I say to her, "I see years of pain"; I acknowledge the pain, but do not own it. Jane nods and sighs deeply, and she begins speaking again. She tells me that as a child her parents took her to the temple for religious services, and she was taught to recite the childrens' sayings. She learned right from wrong and how to properly behave and act in society. "That's the Golden Rule, isn't it?" she says in an exasperated voice. She thought that would be enough to ensure things would always work out. However, it wasn't enough and isn't enough to support her through this spiritual crisis. She needs something more, now that she feels her life has fallen apart. I hear anger in her voice, so I ask, "You sound angry; are you?" "Perhaps," she says quietly looking down. Oops, I realize my comments triggered feelings of shame by even hinting about being angry with her parents, which is not culturally or socially acceptable in the Asian community in which she was raised. "It just sounds like what you were taught as a child isn't working for you now," I say, trying to normalize her experience so she won't completely check out of the conversation. Jane questions her parent's religion, wondering if they have any faith themselves, not even claiming it to be her own. "I think the temple is just a cultural and social experience for them. Seems like other religions have more to offer," she says. I cringe inside.

Role of Chaplain and Priest

I have had many encounters like this as a chaplain with patients, but few as a priest with temple members. Frequently, patients tell me that they would not be able to tell their pastors what they are telling me: "It's my parent's religion, but it never became mine"; "I'd be too embarrassed to tell them that I don't have faith or hope." Even a pastor's wife said it was hard for her to have visitors, because as she said, "How would it be if they saw the pastor's wife was scared in the hospital? They would not only question my faith but my husband's effectiveness as the pastor."

Ministers, priests, and/or clergy serve the religious and spiritual needs in a defined religious community. As a Buddhist priest, I am academically grounded in my Japanese Buddhist Jodo Shin Pure Land tradition. I accepted my responsibility to teach and share the Buddha-dharma. Over a twelve-year span, I served at two Jodo Shin temples: the Los Angeles Honpa Hongwanji and the Oregon Buddhist Temple. It was important in this role that I clarified and explained the teachings. A major focus of my ministry was preparing for the many Dharma talks I would present at memorial or funeral services, Sunday adult and Dharma School services, as well as developing curriculum for adults and children. In essence, my focus was educational. In my preparation for ministry, education was also central. Accurate or not, I understood that education equated to knowledge, and the more one had of both the better prepared one would be as a minister.

A chaplain serves in a multifaith environment, such as in hospitals, colleges, and in the military. Depending on the arrangement with the institution, the chaplain generally serves anyone in that environment regardless of religious or no religious affiliation.[1] In the hospitals where I am the director, we have fifteen chaplains from a wide range of faith traditions who visit all patients. In addition, we have more than twenty denominational chaplains who only see people from their faith tradition. Who the chaplain visits is based on the chaplain's training and focus of ministry.

> Each patient carries his own doctor inside him. They come to us not knowing that truth. We are at our best when we give the doctor who resides within each patient a chance to work.
>
> —Albert Schweitzer, M.D.

Multifaith chaplains do not bring the patient religion, faith, the sacred, or the holy. Rather they help patients articulate their religious and/or spiritual crisis, conflict, dilemma, or despair. Chaplains are professional listeners who listen deeply and reflect back what they hear so patients discover more about themselves, their thoughts, and feelings. In this process, chaplains assist patients to find the sacred that already exists inside themselves.

In Jane's situation, my role was to provide her with an environment to share openly her fears, anger, and loneliness; to journey alongside her so she could explore the depth of her experience; and when she was ready, to also hear her explore her options and possibilities. I shared my observations of areas where I heard tension, gaps, conflicts, and dilemmas, as well when I saw her strength and spirit come forward. As I heard more of her story, I wondered if she wasn't more religiously connected with her grandparents than her parents, since she had expressed strong feelings of contentment sitting with them in front of the Buddhist shrine in the multigenerational family home, even though she did not understand what they were doing.

I am less concerned about whether Jane's understanding of Buddhism is incorrect or inaccurate. This is her understanding, her belief. I am more curious how she learned that information and if it is helpful for her in this situation. This is a clear departure from my ministry with temple members. Yet I find this especially helpful working with the multitude of different religions in the hospital. It matters less what I know about the religion than how I am learning about how patients use their religion and spirituality. I am less likely to make assumptions of their faith and am more open to listening and engaging them around their experience and use of it.

As with all patients who express this type of spiritual crisis, my work is not to give answers, teach, or provide religious instruction. Rather, it is to listen carefully and deeply, so that the points of truth that they share can be brought forward and become a place for patients to lean into. Jane found it helpful to lean into her grandparents' religious life. I supported her to recreate a Buddhist shrine for her hospital room and to perform the rituals that she realized she longed for. This cultivated her inner peace and strength, since that was where she was most happy growing up. Working with her feelings for her parents and their faith would be an issue to explore in a more therapeutic relationship, if she decided to do that at a later date.

Talking with Buddhist patients is a rare treat. I neither see only the Buddhist patients nor all the Buddhist patients. Board-certified chaplains are trained to work with people of all faith traditions and people who have no faith tradition. This is true for the publicly owned county hospital where I am currently employed and was equally true when I worked in Catholic-owned hospital systems. Medical organizations now acknowledge the connection between patients' physical or medical condition and their emotional and religious or spiritual needs.

The Joint Commission (TJC), an independent not-for-profit, is one of the most important organizations that accredits and certifies many of the health care organizations in the United States. Formerly known as the Joint Commission of Accreditation of Healthcare

Organizations, its standards outline and evaluate an organization's performance for safe and effective quality of care. One such standard outlines that the hospital respect the rights of patients; "Each patient has a right to have his or her cultural, psychosocial, spiritual, and personal values, beliefs, and preferences respected." Specifically related to religious preferences, it states, "The hospital accommodates the right to pastoral and other spiritual services for patients." TJC acknowledges, "Patients deserve care, treatment, and services that safeguard their personal dignity and respect their cultural, psychosocial, and spiritual values. These values often influence the patient's perceptions and needs. By understanding and respecting these values, providers can meet care, treatment, and service needs and preferences."[2]

In the hospital, chaplains can serve an important role when the patient's clergy is unavailable. Later in this chapter, I will discuss how chaplains can also help patients receive better care from their doctors and nurses by being a part of the interdisciplinary team. Chaplains can help shorten length of stay in the hospital, communicate with the medical team, and help patients and families feel heard—all of which can reduce complaints and lawsuits, and facilitate end-of-life and medical ethical discussions.

Differences and Overlaps

Jane's story is the most common spiritual crisis that I see in the hospital. Since I am no longer an assigned temple minister, when I meet Buddhists who grew up attending Dharma School on Sundays, they seem to feel safe to express their thoughts to me. What I frequently hear are similar sentiments as to why and how they have become disconnected from the temple. In the same way, people of other faith traditions seem to find it easier to speak to someone not connected with the religion of their youth.

I find that patients frequently rely on the knowledge, understanding, and experience of "faith" that they had in their childhood, which cannot support their adult crisis. Relying on their childhood understanding of religion during an adult crisis can lead to a spiritual crisis. Some have not needed to reflect on what it means for them to be an adult and a Buddhist or Christian or any other religion in which they were raised. They realize they do not have enough of a religious foundation to cultivate their childhood faith into an adult one. They express anger, frustration, cynicism, loss of respect for, and even betrayal by, the religious institutions of their parents. The result is commonly like Jane's: a growing interest in seeking out other religions. Internally, I cringe when I hear patients say that they are considering leaving their family's religious tradition. I know that providing her information about other religions will not resolve her crisis.

Because Jane expressed sadness, loneliness, isolation, anger, and frustration with her disconnect as a Buddhist, I assessed that as her spiritual distress. My plan of care was to support her in ways to feel understood and to focus on her experiences where she felt spiritually content. From that point, we could begin to discuss Buddhism from an adult perspective. The Buddhist shrine she created in the hospital room was a blending of her memories from her youth with adult perspectives. I would have been willing to support her to explore other faiths, if we decided that was a next step. However, by the end of our visits she was more comfortable with her Buddhist identity and was no longer curious about exploring other religions.

As a chaplain, I often think that there would be less need for chaplains if temple priests, church pastors, and religious community clergy were able to do what we do in visits with patients; that is, to be more of a companion on their spiritual journey than a teacher of doctrine. This is because what I essentially do is to help patients lean into their faith during their medical, emotional, and ultimately spiritual crisis.

Ideally, the temple is the heart of the sangha. Jodo Shin temples were established in Japan in the cities and towns by lay priests, not by celibate monks. However, where priests are teachers, the tendency is to focus on the head, to focus on academia. Responding to Jane's question about the nature and cultivation of faith with, "Just say the *nenbutsu* and entrust in Amida Buddha's Vow," or reminding her to be grateful for this life would not be sensitive to her weeping heart. Later, after she shared what brought on her dilemma, we could explore the meaning of *nenbutsu*.

When appropriate and with the agreement of the patient, chaplains integrate the patient's religious leader or clergy into the patient's ongoing care plan or in discussions for when the patient leaves the hospital. Patients are in the hospital for a limited amount of time, so the core clergy in patients' religious life needs to be their minister, not the chaplain. Patients benefit more deeply when they connect back to their religious community. It is unfortunate when patients say they are not comfortable talking with that person, because they feel religiously isolated. It is then that they often seek other religions and spiritual practices.

Patients are not the only ones who experience spiritual crisis in the health care environment. Care providers, doctors, nurses, and staff also struggle with understanding and resolving their head and heart. Chaplains support them as well.

2: CHAPLAIN AND STAFF—A DOCTOR'S DILEMMA

"You're the chaplain. I have a question for you. I have a patient I know who experiences pain because of the medical treatment I prescribe," said the physician from Japan over dinner. A group had come to visit our hospital, and the dinner gave us a chance to talk casually after a day of lectures and presentations. "Is it wrong for me to encourage him and say *ganbatte*, 'hang in there'? I did it once and he looked sad afterward. I feel like I am causing him more pain, but it seems wrong to not encourage him. Do I encourage or not?" The physician had furrows in his brow and looked at me for an answer. "What a challenging dilemma!" I replied. "It is! So do I or don't I encourage him?" he said with resolve.

My automatic reaction is to want to answer his question with a response that will have him feel more at ease. Yet I knew little about the patient, doctor, or situation, so providing a yes or no response might not have been helpful and could actually have been harmful. What I did know is that the physician had not worked with a board-certified multifaith chaplain. He had just heard an introductory presentation of our role with patients and staff. More importantly, I was hearing anxiety and frustration in the physician's voice, so I hoped that by being *his* chaplain in the moment, I could be more helpful to him and his patient, and deepen his understanding of the role chaplains have in the health care environment.

"Hum, that sure is a tough situation. Sounds like you don't want to cause more pain than he already is experiencing," I said slowly, offering empathy to the emotions I was hearing.

"I can't tell him he can give up, because he doesn't have that many options. But I'm not sure encouraging is right either. I just see him looking distressed, and I don't want him to be sad. He's already got cancer." The physician's voice had less revolve, more uncertainty and sadness.

"Sounds like you're sad for him," I said, reflecting back the tone I was hearing.

"He's a very kind man," the physician replied, and I noticed he again avoided confirming the "feeling" words. "I don't like his prognosis. We're not confident that treatment will work, and then he would have just suffered. There's no guarantee for a cure," he says, sticking with the medical facts.

Acknowledging the challenges of this situation, I reply, "No, probably not with cancer. How disheartening for you both."

"I guess that's why I feel I must remain hopeful, optimistic. I don't want him to lose his courage." I notice that the young doctor sounds like he's trying to be strong.

"Sounds like this is a tough part of the work you do. You sound very kind," I say, without trying to be too encouraging, which would be doing to the doctor what he has been uncomfortable doing with the patient.

"My friends say I am too soft. It is challenging at times," he says, and I notice he's willing to stay connected to my observation of him.

"Sounds like it. Physicians are supposed to heal, not harm," I reply in a thinking-to-myself tone of voice. Our conversation slows down as we both reflect on the challenges of his work. He looks up at me, and I ask, "It wouldn't help if I said *ganbatte*, would it?"

"No, it wouldn't," he says thoughtfully. Then he looks at me in surprise and cries out, "I want my own chaplain!" as he makes the connection.

Using the Four Noble Truths to Be a Chaplain

As a Jodo Shin Buddhist, in every spiritual care encounter, whether with a patient, staff member, or student, I rely on the Buddhadharma and the teachings of Shinran Shonin (1173–1262) to guide my plan of care. While I do not teach Buddhism in the health care environment, the Buddhadharma is the structural foundation that informs my interventions and allows me to lean into support so I can remain engaged. In essence, being a chaplain and supervisor is a deeply profound spiritual and religious practice.

The historical Buddha's teaching of the Four Noble Truths is a foundation stone in Buddhism and is a central formula for outlining my chaplaincy encounters. The wording I use for the Four Noble Truths is as follows:

1. Identify the nature of the dis-ease, or suffering
2. Explore the cause or causes of the dis-ease
3. Imagine possibilities for the cessation of the dis-ease
4. Outline action plans for the cessation of the dis-ease

As the physician described above approached me, I saw his furrowed brow and heard impatience in his voice, which I identified as anxiety (the nature of his dis-ease). Responding empathetically and affirming that this was a challenging situation gave the physician a way to also identify his dis-ease, which was essential if we were going to be able to mutually determine what would be the best way to respond to his question. Being conscious of and acknowledging his internal conflict opened space for him to explore the causes of his dis-ease, which he did when he talked about the patient being kind, that he did not like the prognosis, and that he struggles with his soft side.

Where my use of the Buddha's Four Noble Truths shifts from conventional presentations is in the third noble truth. My own experience is that awareness of being in the midst of dis-ease and understanding its cause does not necessarily provide relief or extinguish the dis-ease. What is necessary for me to do is to shift, tweak, correct, expand my thinking process. While I might be able to temporarily experience relief in the moment as I explore ways of addressing my dis-ease, my life is a samsaric existence, a continual cycle of experiencing suffering and dis-ease. I have no doubt that dis-ease will arise again, probably in similar encounters. Being an intelligent and caring young doctor, the physician described above will attract many patients, and be faced with this situation again.

I supported the physician to imagine possibilities when I held open options beyond the physician's dilemma of "Should I or shouldn't I tell him?" Either/or discussions are limited by their nature and thwart expansive thinking. While we did not outline an action plan for when he saw the patient next, the doctor developed a deeper understanding and ability to be able to hold his own dis-ease of the tension between encouraging and discouraging.

Monpo: *Listening to Others as a Religious Practice*

The previous example outlines how I use the Four Noble Truths in being a chaplain to others. However, in order to support those for whom I am caring, I must simultaneously walk myself through the Four Noble Truths. This is what I find so satisfying as a chaplain and supervisor of chaplains—working and living so intentionally with the Buddhadharma as a focus of my life. To listen to others requires me to be aware of my own dis-ease, my ego-self, and follow the outline of the Four Noble Truths. Only then can I listen to others talk about their dis-ease, and then be of assistance to them.

When the physician asked me what he should do, I had to identify my own dis-ease. Initially, I did not have a sense of my anxiety. I felt honored that he wanted to engage with me. Then, I started to feel nervous and asked myself what this was about; I identified my dis-ease and began to explore its cause. Perhaps it was because we were at a dinner with several other doctors and professors that I respected and admired. My ego had started talking to my brain,

"Wouldn't you look so smart and wise if you could gave him a quick and witty response? But what if I screw up?" Fortunately, I heard my ego-voice and was able to take a deep breath, which usually settles down my nervousness and ego-mind and is usually at the top of my list of methods to open up space and imagine possibilities. I acknowledged my anxiety and realized I wanted to "fix" both of our insecurities. I began to wonder, "What does he really want to know?" and "What would be the best way to support this man?" It was not my intention to avoid answering his question, but to try and understand him, the patient, and the situation more clearly before determining what intervention would be most helpful. Throughout the conversation, I reflected back to him the feelings I heard and empathized with his struggles, his discomfort, and dis-ease. Answering his question or asking him questions would not help him, as that would shift him back to his head and out of his dis-ease. It would be a quick fix for the moment, but his dis-ease would return when he saw the patient next. Attempts to resolve emotional experience with an intellectual response only result in resistance or passive acceptance. Intellectual responses come about not because we are intelligent, but more often because we are anxious, uncomfortable, and want to fix the situation so we feel more comfortable. Responding with empathy allowed the physician to explore his dis-ease so that its cause could be more clearly understood by both of us. To be empathetic requires us to be willing to sit alongside someone in the midst of their dis-ease.

In the Jodo Shin Buddhist tradition with which I am affiliated, "listening to the Buddhadharma," or *monpo*, is a practice that many assume means to listen to the temple priest and/or learn about the teachings. While those are methods of listening to the Buddha's teaching, if practiced alone they allow a person to remain on a merely intellectual level. I see the uniqueness and value of Shinran's teaching is in addressing the emotional, personal, and relational aspects of human experiences. For me, "listening to the Buddhadharma" is also listening to the truth-reality of another person and being aware of the truth-reality of my own experiences. My ability to listen to another is limited to my ability to listen to myself. I collude with others to not speak their truth and avoid their dis-ease whenever I sit on my own suffering that I do not want to face. In order to lean into the dis-ease of others and of myself, I rely upon the Buddhadharma, which heals my heart. Dis-ease is not something to be avoided; doing so moves us out of relationship with others. Rather, our experiences with dis-eas can support us to be more compassionate when others are suffering.

During a visit to Seattle in the spring of 2008, His Holiness the Fourteenth Dalai Lama spoke about how society can become more compassionate and empathic. In particular, he focused on starting with children, so they can learn to be empathetic. The Dalai Lama summarized that parents must be comfortable with their own dis-ease in order for them to be able to hear their child's dis-ease. When parents monitor their own anxiety, children can express their anxiety and dis-ease. The result is that the child's dis-ease does not lead to anxiety, but rather, they can learn to turn their life experiences into empathetic responses to others.

Balancing the Intellectual and Emotional, Integrating the Head and Heart

In many ways the chaplain's contribution to the medical environment is to balance the emotional and intellectual reactions for staff. Chaplains work as part of the medical team for the benefit of both patients and staff. They help support the medical team to stay connected, compassionate, and focused, and to provide a balance between the medical and the religious or spiritual. When staff members feel settled, they are more efficient and effective, and this decreases burn out, as in the second vignette. The medical education of doctors and nurses has evolved to include more training in being attentive to the emotional and spiritual needs of the patient and family. They understand the value of offering empathy and compassion but often find the support for themselves lacking.

Currently, I am the director of the department of spiritual care at Harborview Medical Center in Seattle, WA. In addition, I am an educator with the Association of Clinical Pastoral Education program.

Clinical Pastoral Education (CPE) is a graduate-level program with clinical opportunities for students of all faith traditions who are interested in ministry or health care chaplaincy. The educational process bridges their academic theological foundation with ministry situations to people who, because of life's circumstances, are questioning meaning in their lives, their faiths, their spirituality. For example, up to this point in their formation as ministers, they have been studying how their religion understands human suffering; applying this understanding to people who are actually suffering often requires them to translate their intellectual understanding through their heart experience.

CPE is where students integrate the heart and the head, the intellect and emotion, their academic understanding with their emotional stirrings. When students enter into a relationship with a patient and are willing to hear his or her pain and suffering, their own stories surface and things start to get messy for them. The educational experience for certified chaplains is designed to support this parallel process. In order to support them to do the reflective work necessary to grow and change, I have to create an environment that feels safe. I use concepts of play, art, film, and books. I also share my own stories, vulnerabilities, foibles, and idiosyncrasies. They know how human I am. My own personal work is to be willing to enter the chaos and mess. I walk alongside students who are willing to grow and change so they can be of service to others.

3: CHAPLAIN AND SUPERVISOR

"It's just so sad," he says, with an overwhelmed look on his face. Each term there is always one student who seems to get a higher number of death calls or more tragic and challenging situations. This term it was John. On his most recent shift, John ended up with a call to the labor and delivery unit. A baby had just been born and was not expected to survive. John spent some time with the parents and at their request provided a ritual for blessing the baby before she died. It was beautiful, sacred, and horribly tragic.

After he returned home that evening John could not focus on the

other things that needed his attention. He thought about sending a
note to the couple, which was something he had not done following
other deaths he attended. That surprised and bothered him enough
that he decided it would be helpful to talk about it with me, his educational and clinical supervisor. In John's supervisory time with me,
he said he found himself overwhelmed by the amount of sadness he
felt for the parents.

Experiences trigger past memories and can impact our ability to
listen "cleanly" to another's story. In John's case, he quickly identified his dis-ease as feelings of sadness as he ministered to the parents
and coordinated the blessing for the lifeless baby. In his willingness
to explore the cause of his dis-ease, he came to realize that the sadness that was touched in his life was his unfulfilled desire to become
a father. John was a thirty-eight-year-old Catholic layman. While he
had seriously considered entering the priesthood, he also knew that
he desired to have a family. Ultimately, he decided not to enter the
priesthood. He had hoped, and expected, to have found a life partner
by this point in his life. While he claimed to be "very content" with
his life, he acknowledged his loneliness and desire for companionship.
Seeing the tenderness between the parents and connecting with their
feelings of loss pulled at his own desires and sense of emptiness. He
questioned why he had not yet been blessed with the relationship he
so desired and was wondering if he had misunderstood God's plans
for him. After a deep sigh, John wondered aloud if he would ever find
his life partner. John is a lovely human being; kind, compassionate,
faithful, intelligent, fun, funny, and nice looking. While he felt doubt-
ful in the moment, I did not, so I replied, "Sounds like that's how
you feel right now." "Yes, right now," he replied. John has enough
self-awareness to know that he's not a "loser" and has expressed in
the past a self-assurance that his dreams will be fulfilled in the future.
Knowing that these feelings will again return in a future encounter,
my role as his supervisor is to support John to develop a process to
address this the next time these feelings get stirred up. Therefore,
rounding off the session, I wondered aloud how he would feel if he
were assigned to the labor and delivery nursing unit. "I guess I would

have to keep a sign in my cubicle. Maybe something like 'All in good time.'"

Using the Four Noble Truths in Supervision

Just as my patients are usually not Buddhist, neither are my students. The Buddha's Four Noble Truths outline my work in all spiritual care encounters, whether with patients, staff members, or students. When my students see patients in physical, emotional, or spiritual pain, it touches an emotion and can stir up a memory from their own lives. They experience dis-ease and I need to respond empathetically. We identify their dis-ease and begin to explore the cause or causes. When they are ready to move forward, we imagine options and outline a plan for when these same feelings come forward again. This is how they learn the craft of chaplaincy.

In John's case, as he touched on his grief, I shifted into the role of his chaplain, offering empathetic responses so he felt known and companioned. This created a space for him to feel free to identify his dis-ease and explore its causes. He was open to exploring if there might be more to his sadness than his feelings for the parents. He realized that these feelings were on the surface and that there was a deeper sadness that was getting stirred up. He was aware that he wanted to do something more for the couple that was different from his previous other death situations. His real feelings were of grief that his dreams of starting his own family were growing dimmer. Recognizing the deeper grief, John wept. When he was ready, he began to explore again the causes of his dis-ease. He said he was angry at God, at first for the parents' loss. Then he went deeper and said he was mad for his own loss. How, he wondered, could God give a precious baby to this young couple then take it away, and how could God not hear the cries of his own heart? Back and forth we roamed between identifying dis-ease and exploring the causes. When he sighed deeply and wondered if he would ever find his life's partner, I heard him open up to imagining possibility. He was not demanding, angry, or absolute. His tone was not "Will I *EVER* find someone?!" Rather, it was "I *wonder* if I'll find someone." To which my response was that perhaps it was a feeling he had in the moment, implying that this was not a consistent feeling for him. John could imagine that he would feel differently in the future. Possibilities exist for him. In working with students, a key component to their professional development and growth is the ability to reflect on the encounters and integrate their new awareness into the next opportunity. In John's situation, he outlined a plan that included a sign in his cubicle that said, "All in good time." Additionally, the anxiety he felt to do something extra for the couple could be put into context, and he could release his need to overfunction in this situation. In this way, he did not deny feelings of sadness as they arose but rather acknowledged them and soothed them simultaneously. Through the process of compassionately moving into our dis-ease, our suffering has the potential to be transformed. What we experience is an unlimited potential for relating to others and for growth and change in ourselves. In supervision, I facilitate the learning environment where students grow in awareness of dis-ease, within themselves and with patients. I support students to use their own understanding and experiences with the source of compassion from their own faith tradition. By doing this, they are able to explore their potential as spiritual care providers.

4: Ethics—Autonomy and Community

The patient was a wife, mother, and grandmother. She was an immigrant and spoke little English. Her husband understood and spoke English, but often an interpreter was called in to navigate the technical medical terms and conditions. He had accompanied her to every doctor visit and stayed by her side during her hospitalization. There was an atmosphere of affection between the two of them beyond the traits typical of a couple their age and cultural background; he attended to her needs and she deferred to him to make decisions. Their children lived in the city, and staff thought it was odd that they were not coming in to see their mother with this hospitalization, especially since her condition grew graver each day. The husband eventually told the staff that he did not want their children to know their mother was in the hospital. It was then that he also said he did not want his wife to know how ill she had become for fear she would lose hope and die more quickly. His comments were troublesome to her doctors, who wanted to outline a couple of options so the patient could choose her plan of care. One option would require surgery and, if successful, had the potential of extending the patient's life another year. Without surgery, or if it was not successful, the patient probably only had a couple of months before she would die. Because the husband did not want the patient to know these options and was not telling their children, the doctors decided to contact the ethics committee for an ethics consultation.

Independent thinking and choice are values in the US that are not shared around the world. Community and collective decision making is prominent in many cultures and in many countries. The patient's doctors wanted to be sensitive to the cultural and generational preferences of the patient and her husband and, at the same time, realized that the institution in which we provide health care values patient participation in health care decisions. Thus, they sought consultation from the ethics team about how to navigate values they were experiencing as conflicting. They wanted some guidance to find out to what extent the patient would want to participate in this important decision about her care since it impacted her life expectancy.

This ethics consultation was a meeting that consisted of more than ten medical staff members that were caring for the patient, including several physicians from different disciplines, nurses, medical interpreters, and chaplains. Including the ethics committee members that would facilitate and participate in this discussion, there were nearly twenty people in the room. These meetings are called consultations because the ethics team helps the medical team think through issues and only gives recommendations, not mandates. On occasion, patients and family members attend and participate in the dialogue, often adding important perspectives and opinions. Each time I have participated in an ethics consultation, I am touched by the compassionate intention of staff members to provide the best patient care.

In this case, the patient's attending physician outlined the patient's medical information and family information, and the reasons for requesting the consultation. At one point during the consultation, I shared that the husband's decision to not involve his children was contradictory to his cultural background, which valued collective decision making. I thought about his dis-ease and was struck by the loneliness and isolation I heard about the husband. "He sounds so lonely. They sound devoted to each other. It must be scary for him to think that he might lose his life partner," I said. "Absolutely!" the attending physician replied. I wondered aloud how we could support him to connect with his family so that he would be less alone during this difficult time. I added, "And it is clear he needs their support now and will need it even more after the patient dies, whenever that is." Heads nodded. We also discussed our concerns that if the children are not included in the process, there will be a greater risk that they will feel resentment toward their father later and in turn might isolate him, or he might continue to isolate himself from them after his wife's death. As our understanding of the situation grew in complexity, the attending physician let out a deep sigh. "You sound sad, too," I ventured to share. "I am. They are a very sweet couple," she said. I added, "I'm touched by your affection for them and wonder if sharing your observation of his loneliness and your concerns will be helpful for him to reconnect with a supportive community and his children." At the conclusion of the consultation, the committee recommended that the patient's medical team learn more about how she had been making medical decisions up to this point; if she preferred to have her husband make the decisions or if she generally wanted to know the details of her condition. Additionally, they recommended that the team explore ways to support the husband's grief and isolation, including involving chaplains to attend to grief issues for the husband, children, and staff.

Even with a planned surgery, there is a feeling of a loss of control regarding one's medical condition. This becomes acute when unexpected situations arise. What little control a patient and his or her family may feel often rests in making their voices heard. Responding to emotional concerns with an intellectual response exacerbates their sense that they are not being heard or understood. Patients and family members then spend more time and energy trying to get the staff to listen to them; making decisions takes more resources, like multiple family conferences where the medical team discusses with family members together what they understand is happening with the patient and outlining options. Yet all the family wants is to be heard, so they bring in more people. This draws out the decision-making process, as more people weigh in on the decision. Hospitals also have learned that patients and family members who feel heard are less likely to file complaints, even when the results are less than anticipated. In participating on the ethics committee, I try to be mindful that all participants feel heard. In this case, the doctor's feelings dovetailed with the husband's, allowing the two of them to develop a sense of community, which is what the husband needed.

Remembering Buddhist Stories

In working with patients, families, and staff members, I often remember stories from my Buddhist heritage; doing so supports and guides me in making assessments and determining interventions. The story that has informed my understanding of the importance of community during grief and loss is the often-told story of Kisa Gotami, a young woman living at the time of the Buddha whose young child fell ill and died. Grief stricken, she wailed out and pleaded with everyone she met, "Bring me back my child!" Her community sent her to the Buddha, who quietly listened to her story. He said gently that he could help but that she must bring him some mustard seeds from a home that has not known death. Kisa set off on her task, nearly joyful, thinking that she should be able to find the mustard seed. At the first home, she was told they have mustard seed, but that they also have had death in that home. At the next home, she heard the same thing, and again at the next home. This continued until Kisa understood that every home has known death.

When I initially heard this story as a child listening to the priests in the temple, I understood the lesson to be about the impermanence of this life and the reality of death. In recent years, and in this ministry I am now doing, I also see that the Buddha was developing a community of support for Kisa. As she shared her story of her child's death, she also heard the story of the person who had died in that home. People shared their stories with Kisa, and she began to hear and see that she was not alone in her grief and loss.

Grieving alone amplifies the feeling of loss, yet we often feel too ashamed, embarrassed, or scared to reach out to ask for help. The patient's husband in the previous vignette also needed a sangha, a community, to realize he was not alone in his grief. We all need to be companioned when we experience loss. A sangha develops when community members can support each other in their personal, religious, and spiritual life.

Notes

PAGES 1–17

1 The term "hospice" has an original meaning, according to Merriam-Webster, of a place to stay for travelers, youths, or the needy, frequently associated with a religious order, which directly relates to its Latin origins in *hospes*, meaning "to host."

PAGES 19–36

1 One fascinating quality of the Japanese is how they broadcast astrological fortunes in the newspapers, on the trains, and even right after the weather reports.

2 People's choice of more than one method brought the total to 120 percent.

3 This became an indispensable resource for my book *Breaking the Circle*, 1992. For more on this topic see Jacqueline I. Stone and Mariko Namba Walter, *Death and the Afterlife in Japanese Buddhism*.

4 Pim van Lommel, et al., "Near-Death Experience in Survivors of Cardiac Arrest," 2039; Sam Parnia, et al., "Near Death Experiences, Cognitive Functioning, and Psychological Outcomes of Surviving Cardiac Arrest."

5 In Japanese, the term might be *kizuna* or *tsunagari*, meaning intimacy in relationship with people, nature, and the invisible.

PAGES 37–56

1 "In the moment of facing death, which person would you most rely on?" [shi-ni chokumen-shita-toki-no kokoro-no sasae], Japan Hospice Palliative Care Foundation, http://www.hospat.org/research2-12.html.

2 Overall lawsuits remained steady during this period, reflecting an actual decrease of other types of suits. Please see "The Situation and Problem of Medical Malpractice: The Heart of Improving Basic Policy for Medical Malpractice" and the Supreme Court of Japan public data, http://www.courts.go.jp/saikosai/about/iinkai/izikankei/toukei_01.html.

3 Japan has actually halved its average length of stay from 34.4 days in 1994. "OECD Health Data 2010: Frequently Requested Data," http://www.oecd.org/document/16/0,3343,en_2649_34631_2085200_1_1_1_1,00.html.

4 Interview with Thomas Kilts, July 24, 2008.

5 Jon Kabat-Zinn's pioneering work on the tangible benefits of meditation and mindfulness practice for medical patients is one of the earliest examples. For a selection of Kabat-Zinn's more formal research publications, see "Bibliography," Center for Mindfulness in Medicine, Health Care, and Society, http://www.umassmed.edu/Content.aspx?id=42440.

6 This is a marked increase from the 1990s when informed consent toward patients was around 29 percent. Nobuo Konuma, "Research Concerning the Switch to Palliative Care from Active Treatment in Cancer Treatment" (gan iryo-ni okeru sekkyoku-teki iryo-kara kanwa kea-he no tenkanten-ni kansuru kenkyu) Presentation on results from 1993 International Cooperative Research (1993), www.pfizer-zaidan.jp/fo/business/pdf/forum2/fo02_026.pdf.

7 Takanobu Nakajima, "Is There a Path Towards Reviving the Temple?"

8 Yoshiharu Tomatsu. "The Secularization of Japanese Buddhism."

9 Jonathan S. Watts and Masazumi Okano, "Reconstructing Priestly Identity and Roles and the Development of Socially Enaged Buddhism in Contemporary Japan."

10 "Vihara Activities 20 Year Report," http://social.hongwanji.or.jp/html/c11p9_07.html.

11 Although there are fourteen Buddhist denominations with over one million followers respectively [*Diamond Weekly* 97, no. 36 (September 12, 2009): 76.], there are only three major Buddhist-based hospitals in Japan: Kosei Hospital owned by Rissho Kosei-kai, Tohoku Welfare University owned by the Soto Zen denomination, and Asoka Clinic owned by the Jodo Shin Nishi Honganji denomination.

12 For more details on Tanaka's work, see "Welcome to Saimyouji," http://fumon.jp/e-idx.htm.

13 Yoshiharu Tomatsu, "Funeral Buddhism as Engaged Buddhism."

14 The *mu-en shakai* was presented in detail in a NHK documentary on January 31, 2010, showing how over 30,000 Japanese annually are dying alone, usually unnoticed by anyone in their apartments or houses, with no one eventually coming to claim their remains from the police. See "NHK Online," http://www.nhk.or.jp/special/onair/100131.html.

PAGES 57–73

1 Moichiro Hayashi, "Five Years of the Palliative Care Vihara Ward," 24.

2 Ibid., 38–39.

3 Ibid., 49–51.

4 Ibid., 77.

5 Preamble to the Constitution of the World Health Organization, 100.

6 "WHO Definition of Pallitive Care," World Health Organization, http://www.who.int/cancer/palliative/definition/en/

7 For more on this teaching, see Nikkyo Niwano, *Buddhism for Today.*

8 Hayashi, "Five Years," 61.

PAGES 75–93

1 *Funeral Buddhism Never Dies.*
2 In 1955, the number was the opposite with 77 percent dying at home and 12 percent in hospitals. Since 2000, the numbers have remained steady with 78–80 percent dying in hospitals and 12–13 percent dying at home. Japan Ministry of Health, Labor, and Welfare.
3 Masashi Tamiya, "Promotion and Development of Vihara."
4 Yozo Taniyama, "What Is *Vihara?*"
5 Tsugikazu Nishigaki, *Tasks Surrounding Pastoral Counseling*, 83.
6 Maurice Walshe, *The Long Discourses of the Buddha*, 264.
7 Kokan Sasaki, *Buddha's Power*, 201.
8 Dennis Klass, "Grief in an Eastern Culture."
9 Kairyu Shimizu, *Study on the Thought and Development of Buddhist Welfare*, 330–37.

PAGES 95–110

1 Shinran, "Tannisho."
2 Mari Sengoku, "Social Application of Shin Buddhism in Counseling."
3 Kazuko Kikui and Meiko Yamaguchi, "Current Hospice Care."
4 Minoru Kamata, *Healing with Words.*
5 Shigeaki Hinohara and Reiko Yukawa, *The Power of Music.*
6 Haruhiko Dozono, *To Each His Own.*
7 J. Nakazawa, *What Is Person-Centered Care?*
8 Dayoku Murase, "Lecture on the *Life-Extending Ten-Line Avalokiteshvara Sūtra.*"
9 Yujiro Ikemi, *The Department of Psychosomatic Medicine.*
10 Mari Sengoku, "Does Daily Naikan Therapy Maintain the Efficacy of Intensive Naikan Therapy against Depression?"
11 Mari Sengoku, "Religious Education in Family."
12 Tatsuya Konishi, "The Chaplain and Spiritual Care."
13 J. Kakehashi, *Contemplating Life and Death.*

PAGES 111–29

1 *The Lotus Blossom.*
2 Ibid.
3 Ching-Yu Chen, "End of Life Indigenous Spiritual Care in Taiwan."
4 Huimin, "The Cultivation of Buddhist Chaplains Concerning Hospice Care."
5 Chen, "End of Life Indigenous Spiritual Care."
6 Ching-Yu Chen, "Clinical Buddhist Chaplain-based Spiritual Care."
7 *The Lotus Blossom.*
8 Ibid.
9 Rong-Chi Chen, "The Spirit of Humanism in Terminal Care."
10 Chien-An Yao, "Spiritual Care in Palliative Care Team."
11 Ibid.

12 Yutang Lin, "Crossing the Gate of Death in Chinese Buddhist Culture," 94.
13 Ibid., 97.
14 For more on the use of Buddha images and paintings in Pure Land Buddhist deathbed practices, see Jonathan Watts and Yoshiharu Tomatsu's *Never Die Alone*.
15 This view is expressed by the great Tibetan Buddhist master Dilgo Khyentse Rinpoche, in Sogyal Rinpoche's *The Tibetan Book of Living and Dying*, 383–84.
16 *Silent Mentor*.

PAGES 131–48

1 Watts and Tomatsu, *Never Die Alone*.
2 For more details of Supaporn's remarkable death, see Watts and Tomatsu, *Never Die Alone*.
3 Watts and Tomatsu, *Never Die Alone*.
4 The life and death of Buddhadasa Bhikkhu, one of Thailand's most renowned monks of the twentieth century, had a strong influence on Ven. Phaisan's views on this matter. Buddhadasa refused hospitalization in his final days, when he felt his life was coming to a natural end. However, after slipping into a coma, there was a conflict among his caregivers, and he was briefly brought to Bangkok and kept on life support before eventually being able to return and die peacefully in his own temple. See Peter A. Jackson's *Buddhadasa*, 275–82.

PAGES 149–68

1 MSF is known in North America as Doctors without Borders.
2 Most of what Westerners consider nursing functions are normally provided by family members in Cambodia.
3 As also seen in Thailand at the outbreak of its AIDS epidemic, popular Buddhism tended to support notions that those who had contracted AIDS were receiving their karmic reward for immoral behavior, specifically drug use and homosexuality.
4 A function unique to Cambodia, *achars* are responsible for temple maintenance and serve as officiants in many kinds of ceremonies.
5 For more on the problems caused by misconceptions of the nature of karma and merit-making as well as understanding social discrimination and social injustice as karmic rewards for the immoral, see Jonathan S. Watts's *Rethinking Karma*.
6 Bhikkhu Bodhi, *The Connected Discourses of the Buddha*, 231–33.
7 *Lok Yay* is a formal term of address meaning "Reverend Grandmother."
8 *Reiki* is a spiritual practice developed in 1922 by the Japanese Buddhist Mikao Usui. It uses a technique commonly called "palm healing" as a form of complementary and alternative medicine. Through the use of this technique, practitioners claim to transfer healing energy in the form of *ki* through the palms. *Wikipedia*, last modified on July 6, 2011, accessed on January 9, 2011, http://en.wikipedia.org/wiki/Reiki.

9 Also known as Therapeutic Touch (TT), Healing Touch is a method that claims to assist the natural healing process by redirecting and rebalancing the energy fields within the body. A practitioner places his or her hands on or close to the body of the patient and redistributes the patient's energy or transmits his or her own energy as appropriate. This technique is employed as a healing system and claims to be useful for reducing pain and anxiety, promoting relaxation, and stimulating the body's natural healing process. Leonard C. Bruno, *Encyclopedia of Medicine*, April 6, 2001. http://findarticles.com/p/articles/mi_g2601/is_0013/ai_2601001343/

10 "Sin," used here in a Buddhist context, does not mean violations against some kind of god but rather the emotionally and spiritually painful, inherent consequences of wrongdoing, willful or otherwise.

11 This experience is described through the Pali terms *samvega* and *pasada*. Difficult to translate in single terms in English, they indicate the proper emotional comportment of a devoted Buddhist. See Thanissaro Bhikkhu, "Affirming the Truths of the Heart: The Buddhist Teachings on *Samvega* and *Pasada*," http://www.accesstoinsight.org/lib/authors/thanissaro/affirming.html; and Trent Walker, "Quaking and Clarity."

12 Shunryu Suzuki, *Zen Mind, Beginner's Mind*, 46.

PAGES 169–88

1 "Victorian Mourning Customs," http://www.essortment.com/victorian-mourning-customs-63807.html

2 Ibid.

3 For more on Dame Saunders, see her obituary in the *Times*, July 15, 2005, http://www.timesonline.co.uk/tol/comment/obituaries/article544059.ece.

4 Josefine Speyer, *Natural Death Handbook*, 5–6.

5 "Key Health Data for the West Midlands 2005," University of Birmingham, http://medweb4.bham.ac.uk/websites/key_health_data/2005/index.htm.

6 "Buddhist Healthcare Chaplaincy Group: Background to Its Aims and Purposes," The Buddhist Society, http://www.thebuddhistsociety.org/pdf/CHAPnhs_groupBckgnd.pdf.

PAGES 189–207

1 Where Germans die: 50% hospital; 25% nursing home; 20% at home; 2% PCs and hospices; 3% other. *Seelsorge in Palliative Care (Pastoral Care in Palliative Care)*, Diakonie Position Paper (Stuttgart: German Evangelical Church, December, 2009), 10. http://www.diakonie.de/Texte-12_2009_PalliativeCare.pdf.
   Rev. Traugott Roser of IZP notes that there is a need to redefine "nursing home" because they have become full-time homes for many.

2 The homepage of the Spiritual Care Programme, http://www.spcare.org/.

3 John Eric Baugher, "The 'Quiet Revolution' in Care of the Dying."

4 Eva Saalfrank, *Pausing Is Gaining Time*.

5   Maria Wasner, "Effects of Spiritual Care Training for Palliative Care Professionals," 100.
6   Wasner is a professor of social work in palliative care at the Catholic University of Applied Sciences in Munich, which includes doing research at IZP. Her research focus is on psychosocial and spiritual aspects in palliative care.
7   Wasner, "Effects of Spiritual Care Training," 100.
8   Ibid., 101.
9   Ibid., 103.
10   Gian D. Borasio, "Scientific Evidence on Spiritual Care."
11   Martin J. Fegg, "The Schedule for Meaning in Life Evaluation," 4.
12   Borasio, "Scientific Evidence."
13   Baugher, "The 'Quiet Revolution,'" 15.

PAGES 208–28

1   Stanislav Grof and Joan Halifax, *The Human Encounter with Death.*
2   Kathleen Bartholomew, *Ending Nurse-to-Nurse Hostility*, 10.
3   James Rest, *Development in Judging Moral Issues.*
4   Thomas W. Meeks and Dilip V. Jeste, "Neurobiology of Wisdom."
5   In fact, the first three areas mirror the classic Buddhist pedagogy of *sila-samadhi-panna* (moral development–contemplative/meditative practice–wisdom/worldview), which are an encapsulation of the Buddha's Noble Eightfold Path, the way to realize the end of suffering.
6   Christina Puchalski and Betty Ferrell, *Making Health Care Whole.*
7   Systems theory is the interdisciplinary study of systems emerging from Ludwig Von Betalanffy's General System Theory that sought to develop a theory to explain all systems in all fields of science. Joanna Macy did seminal work in linking systems theory to Buddhism in her *Mutual Causality in Buddhism and General Systems Theory.* (Albany, NY: State University of New York Press, 2001.)

PAGES 229–47

1   As estimated by Tim Patriarca, former executive director of Maitri Hospice in San Francisco from 2001 to 2010.
2   Interview with Tim Patriarca, July 23, 2008.
3   Ibid.
4   Ostaseski left Zen Hospice Project in 2003 to create the Metta Institute, which teaches the spiritual dimensions of living, dying, and transformation through professional trainings and educational programs, including the End-of-Life Counselor Program.
5   According to Tim Patriarca at Maitri Hospice, Frank Ostaseski feels this openward model could also allow for patients to pool their insurance and distribute it among everyone equally.
6   Lazure Painting method is a painting technique developed by Rudolf Steiner that uses layers of varied colors to create a light-filled and soothing effect.
7   Interview with Eric Poché, July 23, 2008.

8 Interview with Jennifer Block, July 23, 2008.
9 Ibid.
10 Interview with Thomas Kilts, July 24, 2008.
11 Ibid.

PAGES 249–69

1 In this article, I use the term chaplain for individuals who have completed or are in the process of completing academic requirements and clinical training toward achieving professional certification affiliated with the Association of Professional Chaplains or an organization that is recognized by the Spiritual Care Collaborative. There are other types of chaplains who largely serve as ministers attending to the needs of their specific religious communities and are remunerated by their respective denominations. Within our hospital system we have begun the discussion to shift from using the term chaplain to spiritual care provider and/or specialist.

2 "The Joint Commission 2008 Requirements Related to the Provision of Culturally and Linguistically Appropriate Health Care," *The Joint Commission* (The Joint Commission, 2008), Version 2008-1.

Bibliography

Bartholomew, Kathleen. *Ending Nurse-to-Nurse Hostility: Why Nurses Eat Their Young and Each Other*. Marblehead, MA: HCPro, Inc, 2006. http://www.hcmarketplace.com/supplemental/3994_browse.pdf.

Baugher, John Eric. "The 'Quiet Revolution' in Care of the Dying." In *Inner Peace and Global Vision: The Influence of Tibetan Buddhism on Leadership and Organizations*, edited by Kathryn Goldman Schuyler. Charlotte, NC: Information Age Publishing, 2012.

Becker, Carl B. *Breaking the Circle: Death and the Afterlife in Buddhism*. Carbondale: SIU Press, 1992.

Bhikkhu Bodhi, trans. *The Connected Discourses of the Buddha: A New Translation of the Samyutta Nikaya*. Boston: Wisdom Publications, 2000.

Borasio, Gian D. "Scientific Evidence on Spiritual Care." Lecture presented at the International Spiritual Care Conference, Killarney, Ireland, April 27, 2009.

Chen, Ching-Yu. "Clinical Buddhist Chaplain-based Spiritual Care in Taiwan." Lecture presented at the International Association of Buddhist Studies Conference, Dharma Drum College, Taiwan, June 25, 2011.

———. "End of Life Indigenous Spiritual Care in Taiwan: Foundation for Clinical Buddhology." Lecture presented at National Taiwan University Hospital, Taipei, September 28, 2009.

Chen, Rong-Chi. "The Spirit of Humanism in Terminal Care: Taiwan Experience." *The Open Area Studies Journal* 2 (2009): 7–11.

"Death in Germany" [Sterben in Deutschland]. *Diakonie Texte* (December 2009).

Dozono, Haruhiko. *To Each His Own [Various Outlooks]: People Die as They Lived* [Sorezore-no Fukei: Hito-wa Ikitayoni Shinde-iku]. Tokyo: Nihonkyobunsha, 1998.

Fegg, Martin J., et al. "The Schedule for Meaning in Life Evaluation (SMiLE): Validation of a New Instrument for Meaning-in-Life Research." *Journal of Pain and Symptom Management* 35 (April 2008): 356–64.

Funeral Buddhism Never Dies [Soshiki Bukkyo-wa Shinanai]. Tokyo: The Japan Young Buddhist Association, 2003.

Galtung, Johan. *Peace by Peaceful Means: Peace and Conflict, Development and Civilization*. Thousand Oaks, CA: Sage Publications, 1996.

Grof, Stanislav, and Joan Halifax. *The Human Encounter with Death*. New York: Dutton, 1977.

Hayashi, Moichiro. "Five Years of the Palliative Care Vihara Ward: Making a Place to Journey Together with Patients" [Kanwa-kea Bihara Byoto-no Go-nen-kan: Kanja-san-to tomo-ni Ayumu Genba-zukuri]. In *Religion and End of Life Medicine* (Shukyo-to Shumatsu Iryo), edited by the Chuo Academic Research Institute. Tokyo: Kosei Shuppan, 2009.

Hinohara, Shigeaki, and Reiko Yukawa. *The Power of Music* [Ongakuriki]. Tokyo: Kairyusha, 2004.

Huimin. "The Cultivation of Buddhist Chaplains Concerning Hospice Care: A Case Study of Medical Centers in Taiwan." Lecture presented at Dharma Drum Buddhist College, Taiwan, September 29, 2009. Translated by Jonathan S. Watts.

Ikemi, Yujiro. *The Department of Psychosomatic Medicine* [Shinryo-Naika]. Tokyo: Chuo Kuronsha, 1986.

Jackson, Peter A. *Buddhadasa: Theravada Buddhism and Modernist Reform in Thailand*. Rev. ed. Chiang Mai, Thailand: Silkworm Books, 2003.

Kakehashi, J. *Contemplating Life and Death* [Seitoshi ni Omou]. Compact Disc. Kyoto: Ichihara Eikodo, n.d.

Kamata, Minoru. *Healing with Words* [Kotoba-de Chiryo-suru]. Tokyo: Asahi Shimbun Shuppan, 2009.

Kasulis, Tom. *Intimacy or Integrity: Philosophy and Cultural Difference*. Honolulu: University of Hawaii Press, 2002.

Kikui, Kazuko, and Meiko Yamaguchi. "Current Hospice Care: Visiting a Hospice in Hawaii" [Hospice Kea no Choryu]. *Journal of Kango Kyoiku* 45.6 (June 2004): 496–500.

Klass, Dennis. "Grief in an Eastern Culture: Japanese Ancestor Worship." In *Continuing Bonds: New Understandings of Grief*, edited by D. Klass, P. R. Silverman, and S. L. Nickman. Washington, DC: Taylor & Francis, 1996.

Konishi, Tatsuya. "The Chaplain and Spiritual Care." *Kanwairyogaku* 8.2 (2006): 59–64.

Kübler-Ross, Elisabeth. *On Death and Dying*. London: Routledge, 1973.

LeShan, Lawrence. *You Can Fight for Your Life*. New York: Jove Publications, 1977.

Longaker, Christine. *Facing Death and Finding Hope: A Guide to the Emotional and Spiritual Care of the Dying*. New York: Broadway Books, 1997.

The Lotus Blossom: The Clinical Buddhist Monastics Practicing in Hospital Sites. Taipei, Taiwan: Buddhist Lotus Hospice Care Foundation, August 2009. DVD.

Lin, Yutang. "Crossing the Gate of Death in Chinese Buddhist Culture." In *Living and Dying in Buddhist Cultures*, edited by David W. Chappell and Karma Lekshe Tsomo. Honolulu: School of Hawaiian, Asian, and Pacific Studies, University of Hawaii, 1997.

Meeks, Thomas W., and Dilip V. Jeste, "Neurobiology of Wisdom: A Literature Overview." *Archives of General Psychiatry* 66.4 (2009): 355–65.

Murase, Dayoku. "Lecture on the *Life-Extending Ten-Line Avalokiteshvara Sūtra*" [Enmei Jyuku Kannon-kyo Kogi]. *Daihorin* (April 2009): 173–79.

Nakajima, Takanobu. "Is There a Path Towards Reviving the Temple? Let's Think about the Needs of Citizens Today" [otera saisei-no michi-ha aruka: ima-koso kokumin-no neezu-wo kangae-yo]. Lecture presented at the Japan Buddhist Federation's Special Public Symposium "Performing Funerals Is for Whom? Thinking about the Problem Surrounding Donations" [soshiki-ha dare-no tameni okonau-no-ka? O-fuse-wo meguru mondai-wo kangaeru], Akihabara Convention Hall, Tokyo, September 13, 2010.

Nakazawa, J. *What Is Person-Centered Care?* [Ninchisho kaigo-no kihon—Basic Book for Dementia Treatment]. Tokyo: Chuohoki Shuppan, 2007.

Nishigaki, Tsugikazu. *Tasks Surrounding Pastoral Counseling* [Bokkai Counseling-wo meguru Shomondai]. Tokyo: Christ Shinbun-sha, 2000.

Niwano, Nikkyo. *Buddhism for Today: A Modern Interpretation of the Threefold Lotus Sutra.* Tokyo: Kosei Publishing Co., 1976.

Parnia, Sam, et al. "Near Death Experiences, Cognitive Functioning, and Psychological Outcomes of Surviving Cardiac Arrest." *Resuscitation* 74 (2001): 215–21.

Preamble to the Constitution of the World Health Organization. Official Records of the World Health Organization, no. 2. Adopted by the International Health Conference, New York, June 19–22, 1946; signed on July 22, 1946, by the representatives of sixty-one states and entered into force on April 7, 1948.

Puchalski, Christina, and Betty Ferrell. *Making Health Care Whole: Integrating Spirituality into Patient Care.* West Conshohocken, PA: Templeton Press, 2010.

Rest, James. *Development in Judging Moral Issues.* Minneapolis: University of Minnesota Press, 1979.

Saalfrank, Eva. *Pausing Is Gaining Time: Practical Relief for Developing Awareness in the Culture of Dying* [Innehalten ist Zeitgewinn. Praxishilfe zu einer achtsamen Sterbekultur]. Freiburg: Lambertus-Verlag, 2009.

Sasaki, Kokan. *Buddha's Power* [Butsuriki]. Tokyo: Shunjusha, 2005.

Sengoku, Mari. "Does Daily Naikan Therapy Maintain the Efficacy of Intensive Naikan Therapy against Depression?" *Psychiatry and Clinical Neurosciences* 64 (2010): 44–51.

————. "Religious Education in Family: Hawaii and Japan." *Daihorin* (February 1999): 178–84.

————. "Social Application of Shin Buddhism in Counseling." *The Pure Land* 18–19 (December 2002): 207–14.

Shimizu, Kairyu. *Study on the Thought and Development of Buddhist Welfare* [Bukkyo Fukushi no Shiso to Tenkai ni kansuru Kenkyu]. Tokyo: Daito Shuppansha, 2002.

Shinran, "Tannisho: A Record in Lament of Divergences." In *The Collected Works of Shinran*. Kyoto: Jodo Shinshu Hongwanji-ha, 1997.

Silent Mentor. Hua Lien, Taiwan: Tzu Chi University, 2009. DVD.

Simmons, Philip. *Learning to Fall: The Blessings of an Imperfect Life*. New York: Bantam Books, 2003.

"The Situation and Problem of Medical Malpractice: The Heart of Improving Basic Policy for Medical Malpractice." National Diet Library, issue brief no. 433, December 11, 2003.

Sogyal Rinpoche. *The Tibetan Book of Living and Dying*. San Francisco: HarperSanFrancisco, 1994.

Speyer, Josefine. *Natural Death Handbook*. London: Rider & Co., 2003.

Suzuki, Shunryu. *Zen Mind, Beginner's Mind*. New York: Weatherhill, 1970.

Stone, Jacqueline I., and Mariko Namba Walter. *Death and the Afterlife in Japanese Buddhism*. Honolulu: University of Hawaii Press, 2008.

Tamiya, Masashi. "Promotion and Development of Vihara" [Vihara no Teisho to Tenkai]. *Shukutoku University General Welfare Department Study Library* 25 (2007): 5.

Taniyama, Yozo, "What Is *Vihara?*" [Vihara-to-wa Nanika?]. *Journal of Pali and Buddhist Studies* 19 (2005): 39–40.

Tomatsu, Yoshiharu. "Funeral Buddhism as Engaged Buddhism: Problems and Challenges in Redefining the Role of the Buddhist Priest in Contemporary Japan." Lecture presented at the Twelfth Biennial Conference of the International Association of Shin Buddhist Studies, Musashino University, Tokyo, September 9, 2005.

————. "The Secularization of Japanese Buddhism: The Priest as Profane Practitioner of the Sacred." Paper, American Academy of Religion, Philadelphia, November 16, 1995.

Van Lommel, Pim, et al. "Near-Death Experience in Survivors of Cardiac Arrest." *The Lancet* 358 (2001): 2039–45.

Walker, Trent. "Quaking and Clarity: *Samvega* and *Pasada* in Cambodian Dharma Songs." Honors thesis, Stanford University, 2010. Book forthcoming.

Walshe, Maurice, trans. *The Long Discourses of the Buddha: A Translation of the Digha Nikaya.* Boston: Wisdom Publications, 1995.

Wasner, Maria, et al. "Effects of Spiritual Care Training for Palliative Care Professionals." *Palliative Medicine* 19 (2005): 99–104.

Watts, Jonathan S., ed. *Rethinking Karma: The Dharma of Social Justice.* Seattle: University of Washington Press, 2010.

Watts, Jonathan S. and Masazumi Okano. "Reconstructing Priestly Identity and Roles and the Development of Socially Enaged Buddhism in Contemporary Japan." In *Handbook for Contemporary Japanese Religions,* edited by John Nelson. Netherlands: Koninklijke Brill, 2012.

Watts, Jonathan, and Yoshiharu Tomatsu. *Never Die Alone: Death as Birth in Pure Land Buddhism.* Tokyo: Jodo Shu Press, 2008.

Yao, Chien-An. "Spiritual Care in Palliative Care Team." Lecture presented at the 24th General Conference of the World Fellowship of Buddhists, Tokyo, Japan, November 15, 2008.

Index

About the Authors

Carl B. Becker received his M.A. (1973) and Ph.D. (1981) from the East-West Center of the University of Hawaii. He has lived for the past thirty years in Japan, the latter half as a professor at the Kyoto University Graduate School of Human and Environmental Studies and the Kyoto University *Kokoro* (Heart-Mind) Research Center. During this time, he has participated in projects for Japan's Ministry of Science and Technology and Ministry of Education, and cofounded the Japanese English Forensics Association, the International Association for Near-Death Studies, and Society for Mind-Body Science. He also counsels suicidal clients, terminal patients, and bereaved students, and conducts workshops on improving medical communication and preventing nurse burnout. He is author of *Breaking the Circle: Death and the Afterlife in Buddhism*, *Paranormal Experience and Survival of Death*, and *Time for Healing: Integrating Traditional Therapies with Scientific Medical Practice*.

Rev. Caroline Prasada Brazier received her B.A. from Manchester University in 1976 and her postgraduate Certificate of Education in 1978 from Manchester Metropolitan University. She also holds diplomas in counseling and group work from Eigenwelt Institute, Keele University, and College of York St. John. She is a leader of the Amida Psychotherapy Training Program and a Buddhist teacher with Tariki Trust. She has an interest in hospital chaplaincy and has been involved in its development in the United Kingdom for a number of years. She is author of six books on Buddhism and psychotherapy, most notably *Buddhist Psychology*, *The Other Buddhism: Amida Comes West*, and *Other-Centred Therapy: Buddhist Psychology in Action*.

Rev. Beth Kanji Goldring received her B.A. from Carnegie-Mellon University (1966), M.A. from the University of Chicago (1969), and did Ph.D. work in the Committee on Social Thought at the University of Chicago (ABD in 1973). She has taught humanities at the University of Chicago, Prairie State University (Illinois), Southwest College (Chicago), Marist College (Poughkeepsie), and St. Scholastica's College (Manila). In 1982, she became involved in human rights work, living in the Occupied Palestinian Territories from 1986 to 1993. She produced several books and many papers on human rights documentation. She also cofounded Sanabel Press Services, founded the Palestinian Women's Human Rights Organization, and worked with the pre-Oslo Agreement Palestinian negotiating teams as a specialist in residence rights and keeping families together. She returned to the US in 1993 as a Fellow at the Harvard/Radcliffe Mary Ingraham Bunting Institute. In 1995, after ordaining as a Zen priest, she moved to Thailand to work with the International Network of Engaged Buddhists (INEB) and then moved to Cambodia in 1996. She conceived Brahmavihara/Cambodia AIDS Project in 1999 and founded it in 2000. Among awards Beth has received, in 2008 she was one of twenty women named Outstanding Women in Buddhism. In 2009 she received the Karuna Award from the Insight Meditation Center in Redwood City and was given an award by Her Royal Highness Dr. Princess Chulabhorn Walailak at the inauguration of Avalokitesvara's Great Compassionate Stupa of 10,000 Buddhas under the direction of Most Venerable Master Shi Kuang Seng.

Rev. Joan Jiko Halifax is a Zen Buddhist teacher, anthropologist, author, and pioneer in end-of-life care. She is abbot and head teacher of Upaya Zen Center and Institute in Santa Fe, New Mexico; founder of the Project on Being with Dying, the Upaya Prison Project, and the Ojai Foundation; cofounder of the Zen Peacemaker Order; and author of nine books, including *Being with Dying: Cultivating Compassion and Fearlessness in the Presence of Death.* She is an honorary Research Fellow at Harvard University and Kluge Fellow and Distinguished Invited Scholar at the Library of Congress.

Rev. Julie Chijo Hanada completed research-level work in Buddhism at Chuo Bukkyo Gakuin in Kyoto in 1990 and received her master's in Buddhist studies at the Institute of Buddhist Studies in Berkeley in 1986. She received ordination as a minister of the Nishi Honganji (Honpa Hongwanji) branch of the Jodo Shin Pure Land denomination in 1988 and served as a temple priest for twelve years, including assignments at the Los Angeles Honpa Hongwanji and the Oregon Buddhist Temple. In 2008 she received full certification as an ACPE (Association for Clinical Pastoral Education) supervisor. She has been the director of the department of spiritual care at the Harborview Medical Center since 2007.

Moichiro Hayashi, M.D., graduated from Tokyo Medical University in 1972, specializing in obstetrics and gynecology. He then spent three years in residency at Kosei General Hospital, affiliated with the Rissho Kosei-kai Buddhist denomination, in Tokyo. From 1975 to 1982, he worked at Tokai University Hospital and then rejoined Kosei Hospital where he has worked since. In 2004, he became the founding director of the department of palliative care and vihara ward, and in 2007 became director of the entire Kosei Hospital.

Ven. Phaisan Visalo is the chief abbot of Sukato forest monastery in Chaiyapume, Thailand. He ordained as a monk in 1983, after graduating from Thammasat University in Bangkok and founding the Coordinating Group for Religion and Society. He has worked extensively in the environmental and alternative development movement, in conflict resolution (as a member of the National Reconciliation Commission of Thailand), and in monastic reform within the Thai Sangha. More recently, he has led the Buddhika Network for Buddhism and Society in developing a network of religious and medical professionals working for more integrated spiritual and physical care for the dying. He is the author of numerous books in his native Thai language.

Rev. Mari Sengoku ordained as a minister of the Nishi Honganji (Honpa Hongwanji) branch of the Jodo Shin Pure Land denomination in 1989. She was dispatched to Hawaii in 1994 as the first Japanese female minister of the Honpa Hongwanji Mission, serving in this manner for thirteen years. She served as a chaplain at the Queen's Medical Center and Hospice Hawaii in Honolulu from 2002 to 2004. She served as a chaplain at the Asoka Vihara Clinic in Kyoto from 2008 to 2009. She received an M.A. from the University of Hawaii in education in 2000 and from the University of Phoenix in counseling in 2002. She obtained her Ph.D. in medical sciences at Tottori University in 2010. She now works as a researcher at the Kyoto University *Kokoro* (Heart-Mind) Research Center and is a part-time faculty member of the International Center at Osaka Gakuin University, teaching Naikan and Morita psychotherapies and Buddhism to international students.

Rev. Yozo Taniyama received his B.A. in 1994 and his Ph.D. in 2000 from Tohoku University. He was ordained as a minister of the Higashi Honganji (Otani) branch of the Jodo Shin Pure Land denomination in 1981. He worked as a chaplain in the vihara palliative care ward of Nagaoka Nishi Hospital from 2000 to 2003. He helped established in 2005 and then acted as secretary for the Professional Association for Spiritual Care and Health (PASCH). From 2009 to 2010, he acted as an instructor at the Grief Care Institute located in Sophia University. At present, he is a research fellow at the Jodo Shin affiliated Otani University in Kyoto.

Rev. Yoshiharu Tomatsu is a senior research fellow at the Jodo Shu Research Institute and director of the International Relations Section. He received his B.A. from Keio University in Tokyo (1976), a master's in divinity and full Ph.D. credits in Buddhist studies at Taisho University in Tokyo (1984), and a master's in theological studies from the Harvard Divinity School (1991). Since 2005, Rev. Tomatsu has also been teaching bioethics to doctoral candidates at the Keio University School of Medicine in Tokyo. He served as the secretary general of the All Japan Buddhist Federation from 2010 to 2012. His publications include *Honen's Senchakushu* (senior editor), *Traversing the Pure Land Path: A Lifetime of Encounters with Honen Shonin* (coeditor with Jonathan Watts), and *Never Die Alone: Birth as Death in Pure Land Buddhism*.

Jonathan S. Watts graduated with a B.A. in religious studies from Princeton University in 1989 and a M.A. in human sciences from the Saybrook Institute in 2002. He has been a researcher at the Jodo Shu Research Institute in Tokyo since 1999 and the International Buddhist Exchange Center since 2005. He has also been an associate professor of Buddhist studies at Keio University, Tokyo, and has been on the executive board of the International Network of Engaged Buddhists (INEB) since 2003. He has coauthored and edited *Never Die Alone: Birth as Death in Pure Land Buddhism* and *Rethinking Karma: The Dharma of Social Justice*.

About Wisdom Publications

Wisdom Publications is dedicated to offering works relating to and inspired by Buddhist traditions.

To learn more about us or to explore our other books, please visit our website at www.wisdompubs.org.

You can subscribe to our e-newsletter or request our print catalog online, or by writing to:

Wisdom Publications
199 Elm Street
Somerville, Massachusetts 02144 USA

You can also contact us at 617-776-7416,
or info@wisdompubs.org.

Wisdom is a nonprofit, charitable 501(c)(3) organization, and donations in support of our mission are tax deductible.

Wisdom Publications is affiliated with the Foundation for the Preservation of the Mahayana Tradition (FPMT).